MW01063431

Emerging from the Vineyard: Essays by Lay Ecclesial Ministers

Maureen R. O'Brien and Susan Yanos

EDITORS

A FORTUITY PRESS PUBLICATION

The opinions expressed in the essays published in *Emerging from the Vineyard: Essays by Lay Ecclesial Ministers* are those of the authors and are not necessarily the opinions of the editors or the publisher.

Cover design by Steven Hamilton
Cover photographs licensed to Fortuity Press LLC by Dreamstime.com
http://www.dreamstime.com/subbotina_info
http://www.dreamstime.com/irochka_info

ISBN 978-0-9850031-3-5

Fortuity Press LLC
Astor, Florida USA

Contents

Preface

The Emerging from the Vineyard Project:

In 2010, Duquesne University of the Holy Spirit in Pittsburgh, Pennsylvania, awarded a grant for this project. The funding supported a two-year process of theological reflection and writing by a group of lay ecclesial ministers through online journaling and dialogue. Building on this work, ten lay ecclesial ministers gathered for two weekends in 2011 and 2012, and collaboratively developed the essays that form the present collection. The book is appropriate for ministry education and formation, in contexts such as academic courses, diocesan and parish programs.

We offer this work as a gift to other lay ecclesial ministers who labor in the Lord's vineyard, and as an invitation to share their own stories. We also hope that the essays help all those in church ministry to grow in mutual understanding, commitment to collaboration, and faithfulness to the Lord of the vineyard.

Foreword

by

Zeni Fox

Stories. In so many ways, the composing and telling of stories creates and communicates the history of the world, of individual communities within it, of families. The great epics of Eastern and Western culture (such as the *Gilgamesh* and the *Iliad*), the accounts of the great figures of Judeo-Christian history (Abraham and Sarah, Paul and Prisca, Francis and Clare and so many more) as well as family lore shared with the next generation (the adventuresome grandfather, flamboyant uncle, saintly mother)--all of these are shapers of identity, communal and personal. Stories arise from experience, but it is experience which has been probed and pondered, drawing on earlier stories to expand understanding, then shaped to communicate meaning. Sometimes meaning is distilled from stories, creating doctrines--historical, religious, familial--a process which sharpens the clarity of meaning, but loses some of the dynamism of the concrete stories themselves. In this volume, experience is pondered in this way, stories are integrated with aspects of our tradition, implications are probed, pondered, meaning is created and sometimes distilled, identity is strengthened. The result is this rich compendium of the individual stories of these ten writers, and a gift to other lay ecclesial ministers (LEMs) seeking to deepen their own identities as Church leaders and disciples of the Lord.

Because there are multiple writers of these essays, there are varied perspectives--the viewpoints provided by different ministries, diverse ages (including, significantly, a young adult), ethnicities, genders, states of life, and differing experiences of the gifts and challenges of lay ministry--almost like a kaleidoscope presenting an ever-changing picture. And of course their experiences lead these men and women to draw on widely different aspects of our tradition, including Scripture, systematic and practical theology, Church history and spiritual writing, Church documents, insights from another religious tradition, many sources ancient and modern.

Symbol is often the vehicle for sharing the understandings that emerged for them as they engaged with our tradition, with each other and with those lay ecclesial ministers who shared their journal entries with the authors--symbols such as leaven, iron shaping iron, the desert, local farmers' markets, to name a few. Similarly, the great symbolic themes of Christian life are pondered--Baptism, the Kingdom (also rendered as kin-dom), the paschal mystery. Symbols are always multivalent, so even as each author shares the truth he/she has glimpsed, by sharing that truth through his/her story drawing on symbols, each reader is invited to enter into a similar process of meaning-making. Pondering their work in the vineyard yields food for the journey, their own and those of their readers.

Readers seeking to learn about, or to deepen, the identity of lay ecclesial ministers will find many models, many lay persons from our history to focus on--Mary Magdala, Prisca and Aquila, Justin Martyr, Thecla, Origen, the desert fathers and mothers, even Lazarus unbound, and more. The image that comes to mind is the great procession of the saints of our Church (named and unnamed) celebrated in the tapestries of the Cathedral of Our Lady of the Angels, in Los Angeles, a great company with whom we walk even now. As one writer observed, the community of faith mediates the presence of Christ in our world today, and we journey together.

Throughout, practical suggestions for augmenting ministry are included, ideas for empowering congregations for social justice, developing preaching teams to assist in the preparation of homilies, inviting to a missionary consciousness, seeking ways to sustain the difficulties and frustrations of ministry so that they are transforming and not embittering experiences.

Some of the essays focus on growth points for lay ecclesial ministry as a community of ministers in the Church, including a call for more preparation and education of lay ecclesial ministers (LEMs), and all lay ministers; for a fuller development of standards and certification procedures; for a wider use of authorization processes which emphasize the role of the diocese and the bishop. Some name problems such as insufficient compensation, the lack of security of lay ecclesial ministry positions due to changes of a bishop or a pastor, conflicts with other lay ecclesial ministers or parish members--all realistic considerations. However, again and again the authors come back to the centrality of the need to focus on personal spiritual transformation, authenticity, uniting with Christ, not allowing oneself to be a victim, or a hireling, but rather a faithful disciple. One thinks of the journey of the Israelites in the desert, a journey that forged them into a community of faith and strengthened each individually in commitment to YHWH, which is what the journey of these men and women in ministry and in the community "emerging from the vineyard" has done.

Some of the ambivalences experienced by lay ecclesial ministers today are considered. While seeking clearer definition of their place in the Church community, they want to avoid elitism, and to honor the commitments of all the laity who together continue the mission of Jesus. While recognizing the value of oversight of ministry, and therefore of standards and certification and role descriptions and directives, they also want to affirm the call of each to particular forms and styles of service. While emphasizing the importance of discernment of gifts by themselves and the communities in which they serve, they also think that education and formation are essential for effective ministry. Our bishops and theologians have been pondering such issues; here the voices of those most intimately involved are heard, their credibility and whole hearted engagement in seeking ways to sustain the inherent tensions adding new clarity to the issues.

The authors frequently probe collegiality, as an ideal, a gift, a challenge. Frequently, various of the teachings of the United States bishops from *Co-Workers in the Vineyard of the Lord* are cited. Discipleship to Jesus (who, one author reminds, was a lay man) is consistently seen as central. The twin goals of broadening the horizons of the possible and growing in holiness are each stressed. They present these themes as both comfort and challenge, affirmation and on-going invitation. The purpose of the authors is to recount their experiences, yes, but also through the testimony of their growth to invite other lay ecclesial ministers to engage in deep dialogue between their life experiences and our tradition. Their purpose in sharing their stories of joy in ministry, and of struggle, of fruitful, fulfilling ministry and of challenges and obstacles (as one author named this endeavor) is also to invite the Church community, lay and ordained, to come to a fuller understanding of these ministers in our midst.

Having watched the evolution of lay ecclesial ministry from the time before it had a name, and having listened to many lay ecclesial ministers share their joys and sorrows in ministry, I see in *these* stories evidence of a maturing that is happening. Yes, this is evident in the lives of these individual ministers as they grow in holiness (but that was always so), but here even more so a maturing of lay ecclesial ministry as an emerging order in the Church. Lay ecclesial ministers, those who educate and form them, the pastors and bishops who have responsibility for oversight of ministry, and the theologians who ponder the meaning of this development will find the stories of these ten men and women a wonderful gift, and their testimony to the power of grace an inspiration.

Introduction

Maureen R. O'Brien

The metaphor of working in the "vineyard" or for the "harvest" has long been resonant for those who seek to minister in response to Jesus' call--as it is for the lay ecclesial ministers who came together to develop this essay collection. Many have taken inspiration from Jesus' words to the disciples, "The harvest is abundant but the laborers are few; so ask the master of the harvest to send out laborers for his harvest" (Matt 9:37-38).[1] In recent years, the metaphor has gained new meaning through its use by the United States Conference of Catholic Bishops to title their 2005 document, *Co-Workers in the Vineyard of the Lord.* They have identified Catholic lay ecclesial ministers as co-workers with clergy, laboring together in the vineyard of the world for the Lord's harvest. They have enlivened and encouraged that ministry by linking it directly to God's activity: "Lay ecclesial ministry has emerged and taken shape in our country through the working of the Holy Spirit."[2]

Yet at the beginning of Part One in *Co-Workers,* the bishops quote Matthew 20:4: "You too go into my vineyard." Here they bring to mind a parable from Matthew's Gospel (20:1-16) of those who were invited by the master of a vineyard to labor in it, all working in a common endeavor despite arriving at various times. Let us attend to the words of a lay ecclesial minister as she reflected on that parable:

> *The story of the landowner seeking and finding workers for his vineyard throughout the day (Matt 20: 1-16) is pregnant with meaning for the Lay Ecclesial Minister in today's United States Church. The parable tells the story of those called at daybreak, at intervals throughout the day and finally at the very end of the day to work in the master's vineyard. I understand that*

---

[1] Unless otherwise noted, all Scripture citations in this book are from the New American Bible (NAB) translation.

[2] United States Conference of Catholic Bishops, *Co-Workers in the Vineyard of the Lord: A Resource for Guiding the Development of Lay Ecclesial Ministry* (Washington, DC: United States Conference of Catholic Bishops, 2005), 14.

> *the original intent of the verses was to demonstrate that the Jewish people, named and gathered by God from of old, were not the only ones called into relationship with the Divine and were not the only beloved of God. The point of the parable is that the mercy and generosity of the Master will be shared not only with the Chosen People but also with others chosen later in the history of salvation. Can't we also learn something similar from the parable about ministry in the Catholic Church in this present age? Surely there are parallels in the parable with regard to Lay Ecclesial Ministry—both the individual lay person's call to serve as a dedicated Lay Ecclesial Minister and also the communal call to Lay Ecclesial Ministers to impact, bless, and help transform the Church and the world.*[3]

Inspired by *Co-Workers,* this minister glimpsed potential identification for lay ecclesial ministers with those laborers brought in toward the end of the working day, who nevertheless are paid the same "wages" as those who began in the morning. But, as she also recognized, the working day goes on and the harvest is not yet completed:

> *When I get to the end of the parable, I'm brought up short. "Take what is yours and go. What if I wish to give this last one the same as you? (Or) am I not free to do as I wish with my own money? Are you envious because I am generous?' Thus, the last will be first, and the first will be last." At first, I think – Wow. LEMs [lay ecclesial ministers] are definitely "the last" – so we're being pushed to the front of the line. Great! . . . Then I remember that the history of the Church is still being written. It's likely we're not at the last chapter. What I then hear is, "Be ready for what the Holy Spirit is going to do in the Church. Be ready to receive the future with gratitude and graciousness. Learn from the present moment. Even more pointedly, in the present moment,*

---

[3] Throughout, quotes from journal entries of lay ecclesial ministers involved in the "Emerging from the Vineyard" project will be integrated into the text. These quotes will be indicated by *use of italics*.

> *be part of paving the way for a glorious future. LEMs are called to impact, bless and transform the Church."*
>
> *How can we do that in this present vineyard?*

The essays in this collection offer some responses to this question, some "fruits" from vineyard work, through the voices of lay ecclesial ministers. They already are living their response by ongoing, faithful labor. They have, indeed, borne the heat of the late-afternoon sun. They have reaped nourishing food. They have co-labored with those who came "before" them. They have come forth with their own stories to tell, their own insights to offer on effective and faithful vineyard work. Thus, answering the question involves the *praxis* of both action and reflection, both doing and dwelling with what is being done. Most fundamentally, it entails considering how this *praxis* is part of the larger endeavor of the Church as it labors to transform the world—the "vineyard"—in which it journeys, seeking ever to be faithful to the saving mission of the Lord who calls it into being.

Therefore, this collection highlights the active verb, *emerging,* to characterize these lay ecclesial ministers' movements relative to the vineyard. As its authors know, there are layers of meaning and possible ambiguity in this term. At least two senses of "emerging" are represented in what follows:

- Emerging *in*: lay ecclesial ministers are hard at work in the "vineyard" of the world where the Church also lives. Through their sustained witness and recognition by ecclesial leaders, theologians, and the whole community of baptized Christians, their contributions are manifest in ever-clearer ways. They find that their "emergence in" is being acknowledged and, in some cases, authorized, and they are keenly aware that their "day" of labor shows no sign of ending soon. [4]

---

[4] *Co-Workers* is the most significant evidence of this "emergence" to date. Alongside it, professional associations of lay ecclesial ministers as well as initiatives based in institutions of higher education have contributed to the development of lay ecclesial ministry. See Julie Billmeier's essay in the present collection for further description of these.

- Emerging *from:* yet, while the work goes on, ministers need time to come forth from the heat of the vineyard for rest, renewal, and articulation of the meaning of their labors. They seek venues for sharing their practical wisdom with others in prayerful, Spirit-inspired conversation.

In this book, we offer readers some gifts from the interweaving of ministry and reflective dialogue on ministry. Titling it "Emerging *from* the Vineyard" does not suggest that the labor is concluded, or its significance fully understood. Rather, it highlights how the writers—and, they hope, the readers—can benefit from continuous theological reflection on the attempts by all to harvest for the sake of the Kingdom of God. By "emerging from," they intend to strengthen ministry that continues to "emerge in" the vineyard—at any time of the day.

Origins and Dimensions of the Project

Lay ecclesial ministers are invited into the vineyard by Christ, in the loving communion of the Trinity, as part of the baptized faithful universally called to holiness. At the same time, they have a distinctive relationship with the ordained ministers (bishops, priests, and deacons) with whom they co-labor, as well as the other laity with whom they share a particular call to the transformation of the world. As *Co-Workers* puts it, "Ministry in the Church continues the ministry of Jesus through the ages and throughout the world. Continually, the Spirit calls forth new ministries and new ministers to serve evolving needs, as the history of the Church shows."[5] Laypeople who experience this calling into ecclesial collaboration with the ordained and receive sustained, appropriate formation and commissioning for it are given the title, "lay ecclesial ministers." Still being refined, this term nevertheless connotes real people in real ministries throughout the United States. It is a living and growing reality.

I have served as a lay ecclesial minister, immersed in faith communities and challenged to grow in my capacities for service. I have also been privileged over many years to teach, and to learn from, Catholic lay ecclesial ministers in classrooms, on retreats, and amid the swirling activity of the ministry itself. I have seen

[5] United States Conference of Catholic Bishops, *Co-Workers,* 26.

and heard of both life-giving and life-draining settings where they serve. Cognizant of these experiences, I designed the "Emerging from the Vineyard" project to provide a unique forum for a group of these ministers to raise their own voices, to share their own perspectives on the meaning of their ministry. The present book, *Emerging from the Vineyard: Essays by Lay Ecclesial Ministers,* represents part of the rich and ongoing harvest from this effort.

In 2010, Duquesne University awarded a grant from its Faculty Development Fund for the "Emerging from the Vineyard" research project. In applying for the project, I emphasized that while the phenomenon of lay ecclesial ministry in the US Catholic Church has received much attention over the past few decades, most of the writing about it has been done by leaders in the Church and academy. Lay ecclesial ministers have been studied sociologically; their position within the communion and hierarchy of the Church has been articulated; their contribution has been celebrated; standards for their formation and certification have been formalized.[6] They certainly have contributed actively to all these efforts, yet their own, theologically informed reflection on their experience has been less prominent in publications.

The project sought to address this gap through sponsoring a two-year process of reflection, writing, and dialogue among a selected group of lay ecclesial ministers. I solicited applications from around the United States from those who were seasoned in

---

[6]The most recent of the major sociological studies of United States lay ecclesial ministers is David DeLambo's *Lay Parish Ministers. A Study of Emerging Leadership* (New York: National Pastoral Life Center, 2005). The Center for Applied Research in the Apostolate at Georgetown University (CARA) has included statistics on lay ministry formation programs in the US since 1994 in its *CARA Catholic Ministry Formation Directory.* Statistical summaries from this directory are published online (CARA Publications, "Catholic Ministry Formation Directory," http://cara.georgetown.edu/Publications/mfd.html [accessed June 2, 2014]). Several lay ecclesial ministers' professional organizations have recently joined to establish common certification standards, published in *National Certification Standards for Lay Ecclesial Ministers* (2006), and have formed an alliance to maintain these standards and to offer national certification to such ministers. See Alliance for the Certification of Lay Ecclesial Ministers, "National Certification Standards for Lay Ecclesial Ministers (Standards)," http://www.lemcertification.org/standards.htm (accessed June 2, 2014).

ministry, possessed an advanced theological degree, and showed writing passion and expertise. A group of ten agreed to meet for two weekends to pray, converse, and collaboratively write and review essays for the collection, focusing on topics they deemed central to their ministry and relevant for other lay ecclesial ministers. With thirteen other "distance" members, they also posted and commented anonymously through individual, online journal entries during the two years.

A cooperative style was built into the project at all phases. A prominent theme of *Co-Workers in the Vineyard*, and indeed a paradigm habitually pursued by lay ecclesial ministers, is collaboration—to "*co*-labor" in the ministerial fields. "In our time lay ecclesial ministers have emerged, men and women working in collaboration with bishops, priests, deacons, and other laity, each responding to the charisms bestowed by the Spirit."[7] This style is characteristically embraced by lay ecclesial ministers as they have "emerged in" the vineyard. Furthermore, they recognize its importance when they "emerge from" their service to reflect on and learn from ministerial experience. Practices of theological reflection for ministry in formational settings typically involve participants in conversational models and methods that bring together their real-life experiences with faith as expressed in Scripture and tradition, yielding transformed insights and actions for the future.[8] Thus, they engage in formation and education programs in deeply shared ways, with multiple dialogue partners.

Could the authors of this collection do otherwise? Recognizing the need for integrity in "practicing what they preach" already through collaborative ministry, they committed themselves to model collaboration in "Emerging from the Vineyard." Thus, they intend the present book to accomplish four

---

[7] United States Conference of Catholic Bishops, *Co-Workers,* 26.

[8] Many such models and methods have been published and developed locally in the formation of lay ecclesial ministers. Some widely used resources for this are James D. Whitehead and Evelyn Eaton Whitehead's *Method in Ministry* (Kansas City: Sheed and Ward, 1995); Robert L. Kinast's *Let Ministry Teach: A Guide to Theological Reflection* (Collegeville, MN: Liturgical Press, 1999); Patricia O'Connell Killen and John de Beer's *The Art of Theological Reflection* (New York: Crossroad, 2000); and Ann Garrido's *A Concise Guide to Supervising a Ministry Student* (Notre Dame, IN: Ave Maria Press, 2008).

collective goals as identified and refined together by the writers. First, it serves as a voice of hope and possibility for the Church by expanding the boundaries of the notion of ministry; exploring diverse experiences within ministry; and helping laity, religious, and clergy appreciate one another's vocations. Second, it offers a collective perspective on incarnating lay ecclesial ministry by affirming the minister's inner authority; reflecting on key topics such as collaboration, ecclesiology, and servant leadership; and offering the perspective of the "wounded healer" for those struggling in ministry. Third, it engages the readers with material written in an accessible style, including both expository and artistic expressions. Finally, it explores liminal spaces in the life of ministry while remaining grounded in Church teaching.

The ten essayists have written this collection for a primary audience of fellow lay ecclesial ministers. [9] They have sought to craft a work to inspire and encourage these ministers, and especially to spark readers' own reflection and discussion on how they experience collaboration, growth, and support in ministry. Further, they have attempted to honor the insights contributed by the thirteen anonymous "distance" participants, including these voices in several of the essays. They also have worked to offer writing valuable for other audiences with a stake in the development of lay ecclesial ministry—bishops, ministry formators in dioceses and higher education, clergy, and the baptized faithful as a whole—to deepen their understanding of this important set of "co-workers" in the Lord's vineyard.

Prominent Themes and Understandings

In their use of the term *lay ecclesial ministry*, essayists were cognizant of the way that it is characterized in *Co-Workers* as well as previous Church documents.[10] The term is considered to be

---

[9] Subsequent publications will bring in-depth exploration and analysis of the online journaling for research purposes.

[10] The US bishops have been utilizing variations on the term "lay ecclesial ministry" since their 1980 document, *Called and Gifted: The American Catholic Laity* (Washington, DC: United States Catholic Conference). Important interim publications on the way to the delineations of *Co-Workers* include National Conference of Catholic Bishops Subcommittee on Lay Ministry, *Together in God's Service: Toward a Theology of Ecclesial Lay Ministry* (Collegeville, MN:

"generic," not specifying a particular Church position; the role is "lay" because its sacramental basis is in baptism, confirmation and Eucharist rather than holy orders; "ecclesial" through being situated within the Church's structure and subject to hierarchical oversight; and "ministerial" in its participation in the priestly, prophetic, and kingly mission of Christ.[11]

As seasoned practitioners of such ministry, however, the writers never treated the term abstractly. Their own rich and diverse experiences were refracted through the prism of "lay ecclesial ministry" to bring forth a rainbow of colors, with (to change the metaphor), continual interplay of light and shadows. Thus, some writing showed an embrace of the term, while other pieces questioned its value as well as its theoretical underpinnings. In particular, as some essays in the collection indicate, cautions may be raised about undue separation—or elevation—of lay ecclesial ministers from other laity in a way that diminishes the universal calling of all those baptized in Christ to be his disciples.[12]

A second term, "the vineyard," while a central metaphor for the project, likewise lends itself to a variety of interpretations based upon diverse experiences. As participants pointed out, the use of Matthew 20:4's "You too go into my vineyard" by the US Bishops in *Co-Workers* is evocative rather than fully articulated. This allowed some writers, such as the one quoted at the beginning of this introduction, to "play" creatively with the unfolding narrative of the vineyard parable and the respective identities of the vineyard owner, the earlier and later workers, and the vineyard itself. Readers may wish to "play along" with the parable as they reflect on the essays. To encourage further insights, each writer also offers reflection questions particular to his or her work.

This collection is, we hope, a valuable fruit, nurtured, harvested, and brought forth from the vineyard. Where the writers lament stumbling blocks and adversity, they do so precisely in order to build up the Church that they love, and to

---

Liturgical Press, 2004), and *Lay Ecclesial Ministry: The State of the Questions* (Collegeville, MN: Liturgical Press, 2004).

[11] United States Conference of Catholic Bishops, *Co-Workers,* 11.

[12] See especially the essays by Jerid Miller and Susan Yanos on these points.

enhance its ministry through ongoing reconciliation and healing. They ask that their work be read and discussed in light of this foundational intention.

The Essays

The ten essays reflect a blending of ten individual commitments, within the common commitment of the group of writers, to explore key theological dimensions of their own ministry, for the sake of all lay ecclesial ministers and those who foster their service. In Part One, "Foundations for Ministerial Identity," Clare Poupard and Jerid Miller locate the wellsprings for this ministry in Scripture and the labors of Jesus as he proclaims and inaugurates the Reign of God. Poupard draws upon the Matthean laborers-in-the-vineyard parable to suggest how lay ecclesial ministers serve God's Reign amid the dissonant "wilderness" of everyday struggles. Miller, unlike most other authors, sets aside the term "lay ecclesial ministry" in order to lift up the holy vocation of *all* the lay faithful as ministers, following in the path of Jesus and those whom he called forth.

Part Two, "Ministry of Word and Works," also is inspired by love for Scripture and appreciation for its power as heard and enacted through lay ecclesial ministers. Kimberly Lymore prophetically calls them to reach beyond insular, intra-Church preoccupations to bring those with whom they minister into active, prophetic engagement in social justice endeavors. Linda Lee Ritzer argues for an expanded notion of "preaching" as not restricted to breaking open the Word of God in liturgical settings, but rather as the responsibility of all lay ecclesial ministers, called to collaborate in spreading the good news. Then, Rodney Bluml's work takes a different tack in advancing a case for liturgical preaching by laypeople, outlining theological and canonical warrants for doing so and describing vibrant examples of such preaching.

In Part Three, "Transformation through Ministry," powerful possibilities for spiritual deepening and conversion amid one's service are highlighted. This section also includes the most extensive use of excerpts from participants' online journal material to illuminate the theological themes. Dan Frachey writes of how adversities in ministry can also be grace-filled occasions for transformation when a minister figuratively stands in the baptismal waters of the Jordan, like Jesus, and looks around to discover that, indeed, his or her co-workers are also standing there. Virginia Stillwell weaves the dynamic movements of eucharistic celebration into a life-giving spirituality for lay ecclesial ministers. Finally, Vivian Clausing symbolically centers the various "deaths" of ministry within the paschal mystery so as to affirm, through Christ's resurrection, how we are raised from death into new life and new ministerial possibilities.

In Part Four, two essays offer differing visions of how laity may experience "Communal Call and Authorization for Ministry." Julie Billmeier outlines the process by which local lay ecclesial ministry has "gone national" through recent initiatives to establish standards for competency, formation, and authorization in the larger national "market," without losing vital grounding in the soil of ministers' local settings. To conclude the collection, Susan Yanos draws on the writings of the desert fathers and mothers, along with practices of the Society of Friends, to warn us of the potential dangers inherent in preoccupation with ministerial titles, wages, and status.

Acknowledgements

This project would not have been possible without money from Duquesne University's Faculty Development Fund, which financed the two weekend colloquia, as well as supplying readings and other important project materials. The authors wish to express their deep thanks for this support.

We also are grateful to Susan Yanos as editor of this collection. While a project participant, Susan also assisted each essayist in shaping her or his work. Drawing upon years of teaching ministers and other students to write, she helped all to clarify ideas and their expression for a wider audience, as well as crafting the initial book proposal and seeing the project through to completion. She has been a gifted and dedicated servant-leader.

Finally and most especially, the essayists and I wish to thank the other project participants who contributed their journal material to the project through cyberspace. Though they must remain anonymous, their narratives of ministry as laypeople in the twenty-first century Church provided a treasure trove of material that inspired and drove us forward. Their voices will continue to be heard in future publications and, we are sure, their service will continue to transform many sections of the Lord's vineyard.

Section One:

Foundations for Ministerial Identity

Lay Ecclesial Ministry and the Mystery of the Kingdom of God

Clare Z. Poupard

Wilderness Time . . .

God's chosen people spent forty years, a biblical generation, in the desert after their enslavement in Egypt. God saw that the sons of Abraham had forgotten the covenant which made them God's own people. So the Creator's wisdom led the twelve tribes of Israel into the desert. There they could relearn their heritage. They could remember that they weren't slaves worshipping foreign gods and foreign customs. Once a new generation understood their relationship with their loving God, and reformed themselves into a cohesive, faithful people, they were led to the Promised Land, and built the kingdom of Israel. This kingdom provided riches in fertile farmland, grazing land, potable water and existing cities that could be inhabited by the heirs of the redeemed slaves from Egypt.

Sacred Scripture resonates with the motif of God's covenantal promise of abundance for the chosen people. Time after time throughout their history, the people of Israel needed to be reminded what this promise meant. In God's ultimate act of relationship and redemption, God became human in the form of Jesus. Jesus proclaimed a new covenant of love and salvation. Jesus also taught that his presence was a signal of the presence of the Kingdom of God. God's people still struggle to understand and live the Kingdom values Jesus preached to the Jewish people. The Catholic Church and its people have sometimes mirrored the Israelite nation's cycle of losing their core identity, worshipping false precepts of different sorts and ultimately, re-establishing right relationship with God. In past times the Church persecuted scientists whose discoveries did not correspond with the Church's scientific understanding. In more recent times slavery was considered acceptable and women who left abusive marriages were unable to remarry in the Church. Most recently the Church has struggled to change its understanding of the treatment of pedophilia. The Church continues to struggle to find God's truth as Church leaders learn more about the cosmos and the human person.

In a span of years comparable to the time spent in the desert by Jesus' ancestors, lay Catholics have struggled to understand their responsibility to live lives of full, active participation in their Church, a clear directive from the Second Vatican Council. Some lay men and women have felt a call to minister in the Church without entering a religious order or dedicating themselves to a religious vocation. These lay ecclesial ministers are a relatively new form of pastoral minister in the modern Church. The nature of the role is still in formation. Catholics live with the reality of a Church that is organized with a hierarchical model of leadership, steep declines in the numbers of ordained and religious vocations, increases in the numbers of those preparing for lay ministry, painful struggles for both priests and laity about the lack of transparency in instances of Church wrongdoing, and a marked decline in the number of people who attend our weekly communal gatherings at Eucharist. Many wonder where the Spirit is leading us as a Church, in both our sinfulness and sanctity. It feels to many people as if we are once again in the desert, searching for our true identity.

Amidst this wilderness experience, where can the lay ecclesial minister find a home? How are we to shape ourselves into a people of the new covenant in our time and place? As we struggle, we need to listen for the voice of our God, just as Moses, Aaron, and Miriam did. The wisdom of the Council at Vatican II tells us that all we do should be centered on Christ, God made human. As lay ministers, what does this mean in regard to our fledgling ministerial presence? One of our "homelands" can surely be the place to which Christ called all of his followers. This place is not an earthly promised land, flowing with milk and honey, or an institution with a clearly defined power structure. This place, as named by Christ in his teaching, is the Kingdom of God. The Church is still struggling to understand its call to live in the modern world, as Vatican II instructed. But the Kingdom of God, which exists outside of time or place, has always been the desired destination for faith-filled followers.

The Church's Invitation

In Scripture, desert experiences change one. A person enters the desert as one type of person, and leaves transformed into a new self. The shaping is done by God, with the assent of the person God is forming for some task. This is true of our Church's transformative experiences since Vatican II, the most recent, and still normative, Church council. Both the hierarchy and the laity are working to understand how the laity is called to care pastorally for its membership. In 2005, approximately forty years after the publication of Church documents on the role of the Church in the modern world, the United States Conference of Catholic Bishops published a document that labels itself "a resource . . . for guiding the development of lay ecclesial ministry in the United States."[1] The USCCB's document, *Co-Workers in the Vineyard of the Lord,* uses kingdom language in its very title (Luke 10:2). Jesus tells his disciples that the vineyard is ready to be harvested, but the workers are few. Using this metaphor, the bishops invite the laity into ministry. The bishops begin by affirming the reality of the lay ecclesial minister's call and proficiency. They write: "their [the lay ecclesial ministers'] roles often require academic preparation, certification, credentialing, and a formation that integrates personal, spiritual, intellectual, and pastoral dimensions. These lay ecclesial ministers often express a sense of being called."[2] And the conclusion of this section, titled "Understanding the Realities in Light of Theology and Church Teaching," states: "Ministry in the Church continues the ministry of Jesus through the ages and throughout the world. Continually, the Spirit calls forth new ministries and new ministers to serve evolving needs, as the history of the Church shows. In our time, lay ecclesial ministers have emerged, men and women working in collaboration with bishops, priests, deacons and other laity, each responding to the charisms bestowed by the Spirit."[3]

---

[1] United States Conference of Catholic Bishops, *Co-Workers in the Vineyard of the Lord, A Resource for Guiding in the Development of Lay Ecclesial Ministry* (Washington, DC: United States Conference of Catholic Bishops, 2005), 5.
[2] Ibid., 12.
[3] Ibid., 26.

However, this list is nuanced. In following sections of the document, it is made clear that the lay minister serves as directed by the bishops, pastors, priests, and deacons. The document clearly states that those changed in substance, by ordination, are the leaders of ministry. Lay ministers are to serve the needs of the people, as directed by the ordained. For example: Those who are ordained to the priesthood continue to live out their Baptism; moreover, they receive in the Sacrament of Orders, a participation in the priesthood of Christ that is different—not simply in degree but in essence—from the participation given to all the faithful through Baptism and Confirmation. While they differ essentially, the ordained priesthood and the common priesthood of the faithful are ordered to one another and thus are intimately related. Lay ecclesial ministers, especially those serving in parishes, look to their priests for leadership in developing collaboration that is mutually life-giving and respectful.[4]

Bishops and deacons are similarly named as essentially different from the laity. Although the document calls for collaboration, which implies some form of equality, it is made clear that lay ministers are to serve the needs of the people, as directed by the ordained. This limits the lay minister who may have a genuine gift for preaching, comforting and anointing the sick, or administering a parish. The ordained also face a marginalization of their most effective gifts, when the volume of work that is required to minister to a parish or other institution—both sacramentally and administratively—inhibits the use of their other important pastoral gifts. These twin realities of the restricted use of spiritual gifts (whether due to necessity or regulation) do not call into question the value of ordination. But they exemplify how the institutional church is struggling at the intersection of the lay vocational call and the ordained vocational call.

Christ's instruction to his disciples, which forms the title of the bishops' document,[5] is simply to find workers to reap a bountiful harvest. While reaping is an interdependent action (as will be discussed later), lay ministry is clearly articulated by the

[4] Ibid., 24.
[5] Ibid., 7.

Church to be a supporting role: "The ordained ministry is uniquely constitutive of the Church in a given place. All other ministries function in relation to it."[6]

For many lay ministers, it is clear that this hierarchical model leads to an internal dissonance for the lay ministers who have received graduate level training in theological areas, who are perceived as "go to" people in the parishes which they serve, whose supportive pastors assign them to lead areas of ministry which priests often handled in past times. Today's lay ecclesial ministers may be involved in marriage preparation, funeral planning, leading Rite of Christian Initiation of Adults (RCIA) programs or baptismal preparation: areas which are enriched by the lay ministers' own experiences of marriage, childbirth, passing on the faith to their families, or the death of a beloved parent or spouse. These ministers feel within themselves a call from the Holy Spirit, who bestows Wisdom, to serve in the ministry of the Catholic Church.

However, the imagery of the Kingdom of God embraces dissonance. The Kingdom of God is a place where the lowly are made powerful, justice flourishes, the lion lies down with the lamb. It is an ongoing time and place whose existence is acknowledged by our Catholic faith. Surrounded by mystery, as it is, it is the home ground for lay ministers, who often feel dispossessed or powerless. It is the home ground for lay ministers who share their sense of sacramentality—God infusing our world with Divine Presence—with others and yet do not preside at sacraments. It is the home ground of lay ministers who are often the Church's touchstone for those who are marginalized by the Church herself: homosexuals, divorced and remarried Catholics, children whose Catholic experience may have been one of violation rather than love. These marginalized Catholics may find a lay minister more approachable because of the lay person's lived experience, as they struggle on the edges of their own Church.

Teaching about the Kingdom

The word "kingdom" implies an earthly locale with a power structure in place. However, the *basileia* mentioned by Jesus in

---

[6] Ibid., 21.

the Gospels was not a geographic place, but a statement about God's divine rule. While "kingdom" is the usual translation for *basileia*, the phrase "Reign of God" is also an accurate and more nuanced translation. The phrase "Reign of God" is more descriptive of mystery, timelessness, and lack of specificity than the word "kingdom." In the words of Arthur Zannoni, the universally stated characteristics of this Kingdom /Reign include, "Jesus' healing and liberating practices, the inclusive table-sharing of his followers and their domination-free relationships."[7] The Kingdom as preached by Jesus was everything that the Jewish people were not expecting. In their messianic tradition, the Jews were expecting an earthly king whose power would allow the Israelite nation to overthrow Roman rule and dominate their geographic region.

The Catholic Church teaches that it is God's Kingdom made incarnate. But the Church also struggles with how to live this Kingdom mystery. The parables that Jesus tells his disciples make it clear the Reign of God is found outside of institutional or societal norms. These teachings make no reference to the Jewish faith or specific religious practices. Organized religion is not mentioned, either in the Jewish tradition, or as a new faith that is in formation. So, how do Catholic Scripture scholars make sense of Jesus' Kingdom teaching? Scholarship tells the lay ecclesial minister that not only is God's Reign found on the borders of the culture, among the poor and dispossessed, but also that the borderlands are the ripest place for our ministry.[8]

The Jerome Biblical Commentary tells us that a definitive explanation of Jesus' Kingdom imagery is impossible because it is a "tensive symbol" that resonates with many meanings. Jesus isn't describing a spatial territory, but is describing a call to the people to follow God's teaching about, and examples of, love,

---

[7] Zannoni, Arthur, *Tell Me Your Story: The Parables of Jesus* (Chicago, IL: Liturgy Training Publications, 2002), 29.

[8] United States Conference of Catholic Bishops, *Economic Justice for All* (Washington, DC: United States Conference of Catholic Bishops, 2005), 16, 188, 196; United States Conference of Catholic Bishops, *Seven Themes of Catholic Social Teaching: Option for the Poor and Vulnerable* (Washington DC: United States Conference of Catholic Bishops, 2005); Pope Benedict XVI, *Deus Caritas Est,* (Rome: Libreria Editrice Vaticana, 2005), 22.

forgiveness and charity. Domination and subjugation are not part of God's Reign.[9]

Putting it in other words, Richard McBrien writes: "Because there is no limit to the presence of God, the Kingdom of God has no boundaries. The Kingdom may exist in the individual human heart, in groups, in institutions, in nature and in the cosmos as a whole. The Kingdom of God is as broad and as overarching as the presence of God which renews and transforms and recreates everything touched by it."[10]

As these scholarly quotations attest, the Kingdom is in our hearts, in the places in the world where God is named, and it can be found in the presence of our all-loving God. But beyond that, it is an indefinable mystery. To the extent that the Catholic Church herself recognizes these principles, it is a part of the Reign of God.

The Reign of God as Proclaimed by Jesus

Because the Reign of God proclaimed by Jesus is partially a mystery, Jesus had to use stories to explain its depth and elusive nature. Many of Jesus' parables attempt to explain this mystery of the now and not yet, of a time when justice and mercy predominate, where the mighty are brought low and the outcast are raised up. Included in these parables are the story of a treasure so great that a man sells everything he possesses to obtain it (Matt 13:44-46), a story of an infinitesimally small seed that grows large enough to house an ecosystem (Matt 13:31-32; Mark 4:30 -32; Luke 13:18-19), a story of a dinner party hosted by a powerful man that was attended only by slaves (Matt 22:1-14; Luke 14:15-24), a story of a slave punished for not sharing the same generosity he had been shown by his master (Matt 18:21-35). All of these parables reach out to us, just as they did to Jesus' listeners. They are challenging, sometimes confusing, and always true to the vision of a world in which goodness is operative. Three Kingdom parables in particular help to illuminate ways in which the lay ecclesial minister both works for the coming of the

---

[9] Raymond E. Brown et al., *The New Jerome Biblical Commentary* (Englewood Cliffs, NJ: Prentice Hall, 1990), 1320.

[10] Richard P. McBrien, *What is the Kingdom of God?* (*Catholic Update*, September, 1980).

Kingdom and also inhabits the Kingdom, which is always at the outskirts of any social order, including a church's. The mystery and reality of God's Reign, its future hopes and present joys, are our homeland.

Luke writes about Jesus comparing the Kingdom of God to a woman adding leaven to bread dough: "And again he said, 'To what shall I compare the kingdom of God? It is like yeast that a woman took and mixed [in] with three measures of wheat flour until the whole batch of dough was leavened" (13:20-21). What can this parable about the Reign of God tell lay ecclesial ministers about their work? First, the central character is a woman. This woman, making bread, is said by Jesus to be the Kingdom in action. In Jesus' time women were considered ritually impure. The monthly bleeding associated with the menstrual cycle required regular acts of purification before women could touch items that were either sacred or used communally. However, in the land of Kingdom values, female ritual leadership imagery is appropriate. Biological realities, created by God, do not make one unclean.

Second, Jesus uses the image of leaven as an animating, positive force. In Jewish culture, yeast—the product of fermentation, therefore a corruption of a natural substance—was considered unclean. While the use of unleavened bread originated with the first Passover meal in Egypt, facilitating the Israelites' hurried flight from slavery, by Jesus' time it had become the practice for women to empty their homes of anything containing yeast prior to the celebration of Passover. Corners were swept and food discarded from the home. Cleansing was required before ritual action could occur. Thus, the Jews used unleavened bread for ritual actions. The woman in this Kingdom parable is further linked with ritual action when she takes a huge amount of flour. Three measures of flour, an *ephah,* was the amount of flour used to prepare temple offerings, not family meals.[11] This correlation would have been known by faithful Jews who listened to Jesus. The woman then hides a bit of yeast in its midst. What had been considered impure is re-

[11] Brown et al., *New Jerome Biblical Commentary,* 705.

imaged into an animating force. This action of leavening the flour leads to growth, a multiplication of what had been before.[12]

Lay ecclesial ministers know what it is to act as leaven. We serve in areas where need is often overwhelming or where the existing church cannot address a particular need. Like bread dough, we are part of that which we help to animate, granules amidst other grains. We try to make holy that which we touch, just as a woman preparing a ritual offering of bread does. Even in small bits, leaven constitutively changes that which it touches. It increases the available sustenance. Perhaps when the Reign of God arrives, people will be able to see the sacramental nature of transforming heavy, lifeless dough into something lighter, something that provides sustenance in abundance. Perhaps when the Reign of God arrives, the gender of the person who presides at a sacramental moment will not matter. The parable of the leaven teaches us that all humanity can make God's presence real and substantive.

A second Kingdom parable that resonates with lay ecclesial ministers who occupy an amorphous place in both church and the Reign of God is the story of the laborers in the vineyard:

> The kingdom of heaven is like a landowner who went out at dawn to hire workers for his vineyard. After agreeing with them for the usual daily wage, he sent them out into his vineyard. Going out about nine o'clock, he saw other workers standing idle in the marketplace, and he said to them, "You, too, go into my vineyard, and I will give you what is just." So they went off. (And) he went out again around noon, and around three o'clock and did likewise. Going out about five o'clock, he found others standing around and said to them, "Why do you stand here idle all day?" They answered, "Because no one has hired us." He said to them, "You, too, go into my vineyard."
>
> When it was evening the owner of the vineyard said to his foreman, "Summon the laborers and give them their pay, beginning with the last and ending with the first." When those who had started about five o'clock came, each

[12] Ibid.

> received the usual daily wage. So, when the first came, they thought they would receive more, but each of them also got the usual wage. And on receiving it they grumbled against the landowner, saying, "These last ones worked only one hour and you have made them equal to us, who bore the day's burden and the heat."
>
> He said to them in reply, "My friend, I am not cheating you. Did you not agree with me for the usual daily wage? Take what is yours and go. What if I wish to give this last one the same as you? Am I not free to do as I wish with my own money? Are you envious because I am generous? Thus, the last will be first, and the first will be last." (Matt 20:1-16)

While the parable about leaven tells a Kingdom tale of ritual or sacramental practice, this parable tells us something about the "organizational structure" that will be operative in the Reign of God. It can be most instructive for lay ministers whose job description and job security are as fluid as the pastor or church institution they serve. It tells everyone about the relative unimportance of rank or seniority in God's eyes.

In the Kingdom, the owner of the vineyard hires workers to spend a day in the vineyard. The workers appear to be glad for the day's work and its pay. In Jesus' time, the owner of a vineyard would have left such work to a foreman. The owner's social position would preclude his engaging in the hiring and directing of day laborers. Jesus' listeners would have understood this as they listened to his story. Exegesis on this parable recognizes that the owner of the vineyard is God.[13] God walks among the workers in the marketplace, deciding whom to hire. There is no intermediary in this process. And God continues to be present in the marketplace throughout the day. Workers are hired up until the last hour. There is nothing in the parable that would indicate that these final workers were unnecessary. All those hired found that there was work for them to do as harvesters.

To reap a harvest requires skill so that the fruit is not harmed. Therefore, one must recognize ripeness. The overseer

---

[13] Ibid., 663.

may direct the field workers to begin harvesting, and monitor their progress throughout the harvest time. But the worker in the field chooses which fruit to pick and which must be left on the vine to ripen. No one stands beside the field workers telling them what they may and may not touch. The field workers, as a group, tend to the plants and know when the time is right for reaping. They work together to harvest the bounty. It is a part of who they are.

Reading this parable, lay ecclesial ministers learn that we can rely on the generosity of the owner, who hires the workers himself, to reward their work with "what is right." We learn that all are treated equally in the matter of payment; seniority carries no additional wage. We also learn, in this topsy-turvy Kingdom, that the workers who received their agreed upon wage are dissatisfied. They have no reason to expect or demand more, and yet they feel entitled to do so, based on how they see other workers being treated. The landowner chastises these workers with the words, "the last will be first, and the first will be last" (Matt 20:16). This is a difficult truth for those who cannot see the world that Jesus describes because it means that worldly status does not matter. Temporal power does not matter. Authority conferred by institutions does not matter. What matters is being called to work by the landowner and honoring the work one is given until the final hour of the day. We are promised that we will receive generosity from the landowner, even if we do not work in the same mode or manner as those around us.

While it is natural for lay ecclesial ministers to want to know where they "fit" in the hierarchy of the Church, this parable makes it clear that our notion of fitting into a hierarchy is meaningless in the Reign of God. While it may be natural for church leaders to want to differentiate the status or role of lay and ordained ministries, this parable teaches us that no one has the right to claim more than their just wage, or to receive extra status (financial or otherwise, given the landowner's final words) for any work done. The workers who come at different hours do more or different work, but all are treated in exactly the same fashion by the landowner. And the payment and treatment of the workers, no matter the work, is equal. In fact, the landowner's concern is clearly the work that needs to be done, not the compensation he pays.

In a third set of linked parables, also from Matthew, Jesus describes his vision of membership in God's Kingdom: "The kingdom of heaven is like treasure buried in a field, which a person finds and hides again, and out of joy goes and sells all that he has and buys that field. Again, the kingdom of heaven is like a merchant searching for fine pearls. When he finds a pearl of great price, he goes and sells all that he has and buys it." (Matt 13:44-46)

In Jesus' time, wealth was often hidden for protection. If a landowner died without disclosing the location of his treasure, it went unclaimed. Whoever subsequently bought the field, owned whatever treasure had been left. So, somehow the Reign of God can appear, randomly located within daily life. If we dare to claim it, we must sell everything—our comfortable existence and its trappings—to claim the treasure. We must have faith the treasure will be ours if we trust enough to pay the price. Recognizing the Kingdom also requires a discerning eye. The pearl merchant is able to recognize the treasured pearl among all the other jewels. Again, he risks all that he has acquired in order to attain his prize. Something in this merchant's training or life experience has taught him to see what others have not. In the midst of an abundance of pearls, the merchant finds the greatest one.

These parables resonate with lay ecclesial ministers on several levels. Often, when one discerns a call to ministry in the Catholic Church, it requires leaving behind a former career, a former (more comfortable) self, a former standard of living. But the sense of God's Reign at work in one's life is strong enough that the choice is made: I will sell everything to buy this field; I will sell everything to obtain this pearl.

The parables don't describe the characteristics of the central figures. They could be any persons engaged in life's work. The stories certainly don't name the protagonists as recognizable religious authorities. Yet they are people of faith, acting on the mystery that touches their lives. They act with complete faith that the outcome of their decision will be good.

These parables also describe the mystery at the heart of the Reign of God. This Reign can begin at any moment, be found by anyone, appear as if from nowhere, and require total dedication for attainment. How like the life of a lay ecclesial minister these truths seem. Some people don't know why they feel compelled to acquire theological competencies, and yet they do. Some people are not sure how to serve, and then God opens a path for them that is bigger than they would have dreamed for themselves. Some people are hurt by the institutional Church by being dismissed without cause, refused a just wage or given overly burdensome workloads. Yet those who have suffered still speak with love for the people they serve and the truths that they teach. They know there is a treasure chest, even when it appears closed to them. They have faith that giving up all that they have will lead to the receipt of something transformative and enriching.

Called to Suffer for the Kingdom

The metaphoric image of working to bring about the Reign of God is hopeful. Many of the parables tell gentle stories of fields planted, treasures found, abusive leaders losing their status. But if one truly enters into these stories as the followers of Jesus would have, one would understand that the coming of the Reign of God will mean an upsetting of all that is. Social structures will be changed so that all are seen as full and equal members of the Kingdom. Status will not be based on wealth, power, or achievement. Those who truly believe in the necessity of the coming of the Kingdom either implicitly or explicitly assent to an association with the outcast, and the reality of living on the edges of what the world sees as important places.

Lay ecclesial ministers understand this because of their simultaneously peripheral and central role in the ministry of the Catholic Church. In terms of temporal Catholic power and status, many lay ecclesial ministers are outcasts. Ecclesial leaders often define the minister's role by the negative: what they may not do. Those who teach and model the reality of the sacramental life may not preside at sacraments. Those with the knowledge to write theological, homiletic, and scriptural texts may not preach at Mass. Those who have given birth to new life, and ministered to those entering new life through death, are not permitted to anoint foreheads as a sign of our belonging to God. Effective lay ministers are often invited into people's lives at these important moments. While both host and guest are aware of the limitations put on the lay minister's service, their clear ability to help name and form the Body of Christ makes them welcome in people's spiritual lives. Lay ministers who have visited hospice patients may be asked to bless the patients before their death, although this is not an "official" sacramental anointing. Lay ministers who have helped prepare parents for their child's baptism may be asked to be actively present at the baptism, although they cannot baptize the child. This, too, is a part of the mystery of the Kingdom of God. People see God's active presence, which is a sacramental act, in the person of many lay ministers. That is what makes us Kingdom people, hoping in the now and faithfully waiting for the not yet. This can cause tension and grief. It is difficult to accept the role of a marginalized or dispossessed person. But that is the road that leads to the Kingdom of God. Not all can follow it.

Conclusion

The history of the Catholic Church is a long one. Vatican II's invitation for the laity to assume full and active participation in their faith is one generation old. Lay ecclesial ministry that is necessary and effective for our time is still taking shape. Lay ecclesial ministers claim no ontological change in their being, other than that wrought by baptism. Baptism by water and the Holy Spirit were the membership requirements named by Peter at Pentecost, as he guided the early Church. Peter responded to those who were frightened and confused by the Pentecost experience, "Repent and be baptized, every one of you, in the name of Jesus Christ for the forgiveness of your sins; and you will receive the gift of the holy Spirit. For the promise is made to you and to your children and to all those far off, whomever the Lord our God will call" (Acts 2:38-39).

The early Church was also guided by the core teachings of Jesus, including their often-voiced hope for the coming of the Reign of God in their lifetime. Now believers understand that the Reign of God is *always* in the state of becoming. Lay ministers understand that their role is *presently* in the state of becoming. As lay ecclesial ministers and the Catholic Church face this present form of ministry, Jesus' Kingdom parables give us hope, solace, and guidance. If we are true to Christ's words, we can hope for a time when gender is not operative in determining sacramental office, when power is not a constitutive element of church, when the treasure of God's presence is truly obtained with our whole being and life's work. We can find solace in Christ's promises that the Kingdom is a place where justice and fairness will ultimately prevail. And, as our Church instructs us, we can learn how to serve the Kingdom by serving the marginalized of all types, while understanding that at this time and place, we are also among the marginalized. In the Reign of God, the borderlands are holy ground.

Questions for Reflection:

1. Do you agree with the author's message that authentic ministry is meant for the margins of society? Why or why not?

2. How do you balance the needs of working or volunteering within an institution with the need to follow Jesus' teaching about the Reign of God?

3. What other parables describing the Reign of God resonate with you? How so?

With Jesus and His Companions: At the Genesis of Lay Ministry

Jerid Miller

Every spring, here in the Midwest, after months of aching darkness and sterility the earth gradually begins to awaken. Crocuses, the harbingers of an unruly profusion of green, suddenly emerge from the cold soil. What was once a seemingly stark and quiescent landscape bursts forth into a holy mess of grasses, weeds and leaves, inhabited by the insects and creatures that make homes in such environs. Observing this untrained growth the seasoned gardener knows she has a choice to make. Either she can give her land her full attention so that it can become a source of life, a home for many creatures, a wellspring of sustenance abundant in fruits and vegetables that will sustain her through the winter, or she can let it course toward its apogee fruitlessly. The gardener who chooses the latter is no gardener at all. The wise gardener knows that in order for her landscape to flourish it will require a great deal of attention, nourishment and support.

Like the observant gardener, the Roman Catholic Church stands at the dawn of a new spring. As a Church we have a choice; we can seek life in abundance, or we can cling to what is fruitless. At times we seem to be attempting both, and at other times we seem to be doing neither. The re-emergence of lay ministry is a real source of abundant life, but at present it seems to evoke several reactions--fear and paralysis or hope and enthusiasm and all variations in between.

I will argue that many of the questions about the contemporary manifestation of lay ministry known as "lay ecclesial ministry" ignore a fundamental reality--that lay ministry and lay ministers go back to the very source of our identity as Christians, to Jesus himself. Not simply in a "Jesus ministered then--we minister today" type of understanding, but more fundamentally: Jesus was a "lay minister" who instituted "lay ministry" which has endured to our own day. What we are observing today in this contemporary manifestation of lay ministry is simply the budding of a branch on an ancient tree.

Contemporary lay ministry is not an offshoot of this ancient tree; it is not a grafted branch; it is one of the main branches connected to the very trunk of the tree and to the *radix Jesse*.[1] The psalmist wrote of it when he penned the words,

> The righteous bloom like a date-palm;
> they thrive like a cedar in Lebanon;
> planted in the house of the Lord,
> they flourish in the courts of our God.
> In old age they still produce fruit;
> they are full of sap and freshness,
> attesting that the Lord is upright,
> my rock in whom there is no wrong (Psalm 92).[2]

Though dormant and seemingly dead, lay ministry is emerging from a long dark winter and so the words of the poet are apt, "O Root of Jesse, who stand as a sign for the peoples, whom kings will meet with silence, whom nations will entreat with prayer: come to set us free, delay no longer."[3]

Though the United States Conference of Catholic Bishops' document on lay ministry, *Co-Workers in the Vineyard*, provides a great deal of insight into the current manifestation of lay ministry we call "lay ecclesial ministry," it does not explicitly advocate for an understanding of lay ministry that is rooted in Christ Jesus. Further it does not recognize the great affinity between the ministry of Jesus and his companions and lay ministers yesterday and today. In *Co-Workers in the Vineyard* we read, "Like Jesus

---

[1] *Radix Jesse* is translated as "Root of Jesse" and comes from Isaiah 11:1,10: "a shoot shall sprout from the stump of Jesse,/ and from his roots a bud shall blossom"; "On that day,/ The root of Jesse,/ set up as a signal for the nations,/ The Gentiles shall seek out,/ for his dwelling shall be glorious." The "Root of Jesse" is a symbol of the house of David, which many Christians interpret as a pre-figuration of Christ and the Church. I employ it here as a symbol of Jesus' pedigree and by extension the pedigree of lay ministers.

[2] Adele Berlin, Marc Zvi Brettler, and Michael Fishbane, editors, *The Jewish Study Bible*: *Featuring The Jewish Publication Society TANAKH Translation* (Oxford University Press, 2004), 1387.

[3] *Saint Meinrad Liturgical Music: O Antiphons* (Saint Meinrad, IN: Saint Meinrad Archabbey, 2009).

they are called to serve and not to be served."[4] In essence we are called to imitate Jesus' humility and orientation to service, but there is no emphasis or reflection on Jesus' status as a lay minister and his relationship to contemporary lay ecclesial ministry. Another sentence in the conclusion of the document is telling, "The same God who called Prisca and Aquila to work with Paul in the first century calls thousands of men and women to minister in our Church in the twenty-first century."[5] It is interesting that Prisca and Aquila are evoked and noted for their work *with* Paul, the implication being that lay ministers are akin to Prisca and Aquila and they assist and co-operate with Paul who seems to have a status other than lay. While Prisca and Aquila are certainly worthy examples of lay ministry in the first century, why not associate lay ministers with the very work of Jesus, Paul, or the "twelve"? They were all lay people, too. Lay ministers are not like Jesus simply in that we serve; we are like Jesus in our very status as laypersons, in our very orientation to our ministry and the world.

Admittedly, some of what follows will appear to some as historical revisionism. However, I believe that the value in reflecting on the relationship between Jesus and his companions, and lay ministers today outweighs the risks of revisionism. One of the goals of this essay is to provide a parallel narrative, based in contemporary Scripture scholarship, to the fanciful and often a-historical narratives that have dominated understandings of discipleship and ministry. As a lay minister in the Roman Catholic Church, I feel this reappraisal is necessary. The ministry of lay people has dwelled too long in the shadow cast by an anachronistic narrative. The arc of this narrative is formed by several elements: namely, Jesus was a priest; his immediate followers were the first priests and bishops; and we have been a Church of ordained and lay since Jesus' time. Using contemporary scholarship to support my thesis, I hope to advance an understanding of lay ministry that moves it from the shadow of an anachronism to the light of day. In doing so I hope that space is created for reflection and honest dialogue about what it means

[4] United States Conference of Catholic Bishops, *Co-Workers in the Vineyard of the Lord* (Washington, DC: United States Conference of Catholic Bishops, 2005), 26.
[5] Ibid., 66.

to identify with Jesus, his companions, and their ministries, and how that relates to the lives of lay ministers today.

It seems to me that lay ministers and lay people in general have long suffered from an inferiority complex (often encouraged and spiritualized) that places them at a distance from Jesus and his companions. This mindset is informed by a vision of the Church that sees some people as holy and intimately connected to Jesus and the apostles, and the rest as mere recipients of a mediated apostolicity that is the sole possession or domain of a few. This view is reinforced (often unintentionally) when lay ministry is characterized as a new phenomenon, as if prior to Vatican II lay ministry did not exist. Others define lay ministry in ways that imply contemporary lay ministers have something to prove, as if lay people have only recently begun to do ministry in official and recognizable capacities, and we will have to wait and see what it means and determine how to define it.

While this essay has implications for our understanding of priesthood, it is not an attempt to define an understanding of lay ministry over and against the Roman Catholic hierarchy and priesthood. Rather, the primary intent is to define an understanding of lay ministry that is rooted in Christ Jesus. In order to accomplish that objective a discussion about the nature of discipleship in the early *ekklesia*[6] will be necessary, and that may require asking some hard questions about long held conceptions of priestly ministry in that setting. But again, this reflection on early *ekklesial* discipleship is only for the purpose of getting to a less anachronistic view of the early *ekklesia* so that we can reach greater understanding of lay ministry today.

The validity and origins of the Roman Catholic priesthood and development of our sacramental theology with regard to holy orders are beyond question. As a Church we are right to trace the origins of our priesthood and all ministries to the ministry of Jesus and his companions. In doing so, we see that the discipleship instituted by Jesus and exemplified by his companions was

[6] For this essay I will use the word *ekklesia* to reference the early Jewish and Gentile Jesus communities. I do this to avoid any confusion about the nature of these nascent communities of believers and what later came to be known as the Roman Catholic Church.

foundational for the priesthood of all believers and the ordained priesthood that developed from it in the centuries following.[7]

Indeed, Christ truly instituted the sacrament of holy orders and all sacramental signs of his grace, and over centuries those means of grace were recognized by the Church, ritualized and codified. Similarly the sacrament of penance took centuries to develop into a ritual norm and yet we recognize the fundamental reconciling component of the sacrament as present in the ministry of Jesus. This reconciling component of his ministry was passed on to his disciples and all the baptized. The particular ritualized form that the sacrament of penance took in the course of its concomitant development with the ordained priesthood over the centuries still has its ground in the reconciling ministry of Jesus. This is only to say that simply because sacramental instincts and realities were present in the early *ekklesia,* we cannot use that as an excuse to retroject post-apostolic understandings of ordained priesthood onto the Christian communities in the first, second, and third centuries. As is well established, the use of many of the sacramental signs of God's grace (some of which we would later define as sacraments) in the discipleship of early Christians was not severely restricted or identified solely with any one manifestation of discipleship and appear to have been rather fluid at different times and places.[8] As Kenan Osborne notes:

> The naming of Christian leadership, from the years 30 to 500 C.E., was at first very diverse and not at all uniform. The terms *episkopos* and *presbyteros* were included in these diverse names, but they were neither dominant throughout all Christian communities nor did they describe the same role and ministry in a uniform way. From the year 215 to roughly 315, the Greek terms *episkopos* and *presbyteros* gradually became dominant;

---

[7] When referring to those who followed Jesus and ministered with him, I will try to use the word "companions" throughout this text instead of employing the titles "apostles" or "disciples." The reason for avoiding those titles is that they have become so calcified that one can hardly use them and avoid misrepresenting the nature of the ministerial activity that was initiated by Jesus and his followers.

[8] Cf. footnotes 23-26 for examples of the fluidity around the use of sacraments (e.g., baptism and eucharist) and discipleship roles.

> however, the role and ministry of the *episkopos* and *presbyteros* were different from what bishops and priests do today.[9]

These examples about the fluidity of the different roles, functions and identities of early Christian leadership only serve as a caution against a narrative that sees any group of ministers as the sole or privileged heirs to the ministerial legacy of Jesus and his companions. In the centuries following Jesus' earthly ministry, the Church was moved, through the prompting of the Holy Spirit, to recognize in its leadership a certain affinity with Christ; our theology of holy orders is what emerged. The fact that our theology of holy orders and its narrative of apostolicity became dominant does not mean a theology and narrative about lay ministry cannot make unique and equally valid claims to that legacy as well.

A Sin of Omission?

Of all the appellations bestowed on Jesus in the last two millennia, one has scarcely received any attention: Jesus' status as a "layperson." This is a curious phenomenon given the bedrock character the incarnation has in our theological tradition. We have found value and meaning in virtually every aspect of Jesus' humanity that we know about, and yet we have not found a meaningful way to reflect on his status as a layperson. We find value and dignity in Jesus' birth, his trade, his countenance, his maleness, his birthplace, his parentage, his garments, his acquaintances, his suffering, his death, and his resurrection. Virtually all aspects of Jesus' humanity inform our spirituality and theological traditions, yet there is little corresponding emphasis or theological development built around his status as a Jewish lay minister.[10]

---

[9]Kenan Osborne, OFM, *Orders and Ministry: Leadership in the World Church*. (New York: Maryknoll, 2006), 71.

[10] It is worth noting that we have not only mined Jesus' life and ministry for theological meaning, but we have also done the same thing with the "Twelve": we have reflected on their occupations, their calling by Jesus, their gender, and their marital status without giving sustained reflection to the reality that they were lay ministers.

If we consider all the titles bestowed on Jesus, both ancient and new, it becomes clear that his status as a lay minister has yet to be recognized. This is not a minor oversight as it has real implications for how we understand ourselves as Church. How might the character of our ecclesiology change if in addition to the nuanced titles "prince of peace," "king of the Jews," "king of kings," "high priest," we added "Jesus--lay minister"? While all of those titles and dozens more certainly reveal theological truths about his life and ministry and offer insight into what it means to relate to Christ, "lay minister" is not found among the litany of commendatory appellations. This neglect, around a central aspect of Jesus' humanity, amounts to what we might call a sin of omission. As the fathers of the Second Vatican Council remind us in *Gaudium et Spes*, "For, by his incarnation, he, the Son of God, has in a certain way united himself with each individual. He worked with human hands, he thought with a human mind. He acted with a human will, and with a human heart he loved. Born of the Virgin Mary, he has truly been made one of us, like to us in all things except sin."[11]

We are instructed by the council fathers to recognize Jesus in the totality of his humanness, yet there is a hesitancy to recognize him as a layperson doing lay ministry. If we fail to maintain awareness, at the conscious level, of Jesus' historical status as a layperson, we deprive ourselves of a rich part of his humanity. To the degree that we ignore or obfuscate aspects of his humanity, we undermine our understanding of his divinity, as his two natures work in tandem. Conversely, the more we explore the various dimensions of his personhood, the more fully we illuminate the miracle of the incarnation. We know Jesus' divinity through his humanity and as a human he was a layperson doing ministry--he was a lay minister. It is a curious reality that the supposed wood of the cross he was crucified on and the nails that held him there and the shroud he was supposedly buried in have a place of honor in the Church and the spirituality of many. Yet there is little corresponding interest in honoring the reality of Jesus' identity and orientation as a lay minister.

---

[11] Austin Flannery, *Vatican Council II: The Basic Sixteen Documents* (Northport: Costello Publishing Co, 1996), 185.

Apostles, Disciples, the Twelve, Priests, Bishops, Deacons, Prophets. Lay Ministers?

There is no evidence from any of the New Testament writings that Jesus self-identified with any of the sects that colored the first century Jewish political landscape. Further, it does not appear that Jesus identified himself as a member of the religious or political apparatus that governed religious and secular life in the first century.[12] It is true that Jesus is called "rabbi" in some of the New Testament passages but this is not an indication of ordination, or formal schooling as some assume; rather it is simply an honorific.[13] As Benedict Viviano notes, "Rabbi (lit., 'my great one') had only recently come into use (AD 60-80) as a technical term for an authorized Jewish teacher-sage."[14] As Raymond Brown affirms, "the historical Jesus was emphatically a layman, critical to some degree of Temple procedure and treated with hostility by the Temple priesthood."[15] To speak of Jesus of Nazareth in the New Testament as a priest, in the Catholic sense, is an anachronism. Neither Jesus, Paul, the "Twelve,"[16] nor their immediate followers were priests nor regarded themselves as such; rather they were all Jewish lay ministers. As Joseph Martos notes, "Among all these named ministries (presbyteros, episkopos and diakonoi) . . . there was no specifically priestly

---

[12] "Jesus was considered a layman during his earthly life (true in a Christian as well as a Jewish view of him; see Heb 8:4). This helps account for his slighting reference to both priest and Levite in the parable of the Good Samaritan . . . The mortal struggle between Jesus and his opponents has elements not only of Galilean versus Judean, of the poor versus the rich, of the charismatic versus the institutional, of the eschatological versus the this-worldly, but also of the laity versus the priests." Raymond E. Brown, Joseph A. Fitzmyer, and Roland E. Murphy, *The New Jerome Biblical Commentary* (New Jersey: Prentice Hall, 1990), 1319.

[13]Ibid.

[14] Ibid., 666.

[15] Raymond E. Brown, *An Introduction to the New Testament* (New York: Doubleday, 1997), 701.

[16] "The 'twelve' and 'apostles' in the New Testament, according to the best scriptural studies, are not coextensive, for there are more New Testament apostles than simply the twelve. Consequently, the task or role of the twelve is not coextensive or identical to the role and task of the apostles." Kenan Osborne, OFM, *Ministry, Lay Ministry in the Roman Catholic Church: Its History and Theology*. (Eugene, OR: Wipf and Stock Publishers, 2003), 15.

ministry, no priesthood in the later Catholic sense. One reason for this is that priesthood at this time was identified with the ritual offering of animal and other sacrifices to God, and there was no one in the community designated to do this. Another reason is that the first generation of Christians, who were almost all Jews, accepted the legitimacy of the Jewish priesthood, and showed this by continuing to worship at the temple."[17]

While the high priesthood of Jesus is a major theme in some early Christian writings--most notably the Letter to the Hebrews--this emphasis on Jesus' priestly activity comes from early Jewish-Christian reflection on his sacrificial self-offering and intercession on the cross and in heaven. The reflection on his "priestly" role, however, does not speak to his ministerial activity in first century Palestine. As we read of Jesus in the *Catechism of the Catholic Church*, "This human soul that the Son of God assumed is endowed with a true human knowledge. As such, this knowledge could not in itself be unlimited: it was exercised in the historical conditions of his existence in space and time."[18] The apparent, yet neglected, reality of Jesus' life and ministry is that he was born a layman, spent the last part of his life as a Jewish lay minister and was put to death, at least partly, because as a Jewish lay minister he assumed a prophetic stance against the Roman and Jewish establishments. When we discuss the ministry of Jesus and his companions, we are talking about a Jewish lay ministry that after his resurrection became a Jewish and Gentile lay ministry and then finally a Christian lay ministry. To be a part of the Jesus movement in the first century and beyond was to be part of a lay ministry movement.

Theology via Anachronism

Some would argue that Jesus cannot be described as a "lay minister" as the term was not used in reference to Jesus in the first century. In this way of thinking, to speak of Jesus as a layperson doing lay ministry is anachronistic and not a valid

---

[17] Joseph Martos, *Doors to the Sacred: A Historical Introduction to Sacraments in the Catholic Church* (New York: Doubleday, 1997), 407.
[18] *Catechism of the Catholic Church*, 2nd ed. (Washington, DC: United States Catholic Conference, 2000), 472.

description of him or his ministry.[19] However, our use of the term "Trinity" provides an excellent parallel to this situation. Should we not use "Trinity" to describe God's presence and action in the New Testament writing simply because the word does not appear in the texts? There is near universal consensus among Christians that the word Trinity is an apt description of the New Testament reality of God's presence and action and therefore its use is beyond question, though anachronistic. Similarly "lay minister" and "lay ministry" are apt descriptions of the ministry of Jesus and his companions. If not a "lay ministry," then how should we describe their ministry?

Scripture scholars attest that Jesus was not part of a hierarchy. He was not a Jewish priest nor were his followers. We cannot speak of any of Jesus' followers in the New Testament as ordained because no *ordo* existed.[20] As Osborne notes:

> To presuppose that the twelve, the apostles, the *episkopoi* or even others *had to be ordained* is a dogmatic presupposition, which neither historical data nor scriptural data support. To maintain an ordination of the twelve, the apostles, the *episkopoi*, etc., is possible only on the basis of a presupposed dogmatic stance, a stance which a later theology would find ordinary, but which a scriptural theology would find alien. One cannot even maintain in an undisputed way that the twelve and the apostles are coterminous, nor that either the apostles or the twelve were *episkopoi*.[21]

---

[19]Kenan Osborne, OFM, *Ministry, Lay Ministry in the Roman Catholic Church: Its History and Theology*. (Eugene, OR: Wipf and Stock Publishers, 2003), 33, 559.
[20]Osborne notes, "it is only with Hippolytus' *Apostolic Tradition* that we have the first extant and clear indication of ordination in the Christian community. This occurs at the end of the second century and the beginning of the third century. Dupuy's comment on this situation is very apropos: 'How someone in the early church is called to ecclesial ministry is not described in the New Testament, so that the theories relative to ordination have in part a hypothetical quality about them.' The dogmatic presupposition on ordination which has almost created an ontological situation for the ordained is clearly one of those 'theories' which has in part a hypothetical quality about it." Ibid., 29.
[21] Ibid., 26.

If we cannot say that Jesus was a lay minister, then we certainly cannot say that he was a priest in the later Catholic sense, nor can we say this of his immediate followers. However these observations from Catholic Scripture scholars and theologians have not stopped the continued promulgation of a narrative about Jesus and his followers that see him and the apostles as the first priests and bishops.

We read in a popular Catholic catechetical program for the RCIA: "But there can be no doubt that the apostles served the Church as the first priests and bishops...At the Last Supper when our Lord instructed the apostles to, 'do this in memory of me,' he was giving them the power to preside at the Eucharist."[22] There is no question that Christ instituted the Eucharist and we clearly see that he instructed those gathered with him to, "do this in memory of me"; however it is worth noting that Jesus, the layman, was instructing his chosen group of lay followers (the apostles) to continue this practice. As the practice developed, the apostles' and their successors' manifestations of apostolicity became identified with certain roles in the Christian communities. After several centuries apostolic succession came to be clearly associated with the office of bishop, though it clearly originated with Jesus' companions, lay people.[23]

We are an apostolic Church and apostolic succession is conveyed through the episcopacy, but why the insistence that the apostles had to be ordained, or some status other than lay for our apostolic narrative to have validity? Could not a lay Jesus entrust lay apostles with so sacred a task as establishing and perpetuating his Church? The narratives characterizing apostles

---

[22] Thomas Artz, Oscar Lukefahr, and Steve Palmer, *"The Sacrament of Holy Orders," Journey of Faith* (Liguori, MO: Liguori Publications, 2005), C8.

[23] Osborne notes the following in reference to the *Didache*: "In this early work (about 90 to 110), there is no mention of presbyters. Only *episkopoi* and *diakonoi* are mentioned. Johannes Quasten notes: 'There are no indications whatever in the *Didache* which would warrant the assumption of a monarchical episcopate.' H. M. Legrand concludes from his analysis of the *Didache* that the prophets celebrated the eucharist along with the apostles as also the *episkopoi*. In the *Didache*, he notes, *episkopoi* are not seen as successors of the apostles; rather the itinerant prophets are the successors to the apostles. Itinerant prophets were not the ones whom, in the standard view, Jesus had selected, but in the *Didache* they are ministers of the eucharist." *Orders and Ministry*, 127.

and disciples as ordained priests and bishops reveal centuries worth of bias towards the laity, namely that the laity are not worthy of the sacred task of embodying apostolicity in the world as disciples. Of course this has changed somewhat with Vatican II but this bias is still revealed in our core narratives.

Portrayals of Jesus and his earliest followers as priests and bishops beg the question: what is to be gained by clinging to an a-historical narrative? Who benefits? Certainly not the laity, but neither does the priesthood benefit from these claims. The priesthood can make an array of claims to legitimacy. Does it need to buttress its position with an a-historical narrative that comes at the expense of marginalizing the historical origins and validity of lay ministers and lay people more generally? If we accept as valid an anachronistic view of the ministry of Jesus and his companions and we hold that they were the first priests and bishops, are we then free to assert with equal force and validity an equivalent anachronism that re-casts Jesus and his companions as Roman Catholic lay ecclesial ministers? There is much to recommend an understanding of Jesus and his companions as lay ministers. The anachronistic view would be to say that they were Roman Catholic lay ecclesial ministers.

Can we instead acknowledge that: 1. Jesus was a lay person, 2. who called other lay people, 3. whose leadership functions became more solidified and ordered until the time when, through the prompting of the Holy Spirit, and the will of the Body of Christ, holy orders were created? At that point, lay ministry became limited to an anonymous host of men and women who responded to the call of discipleship in their time and place, lived as disciples of Christ, died in his grace and are known only to God. It is the men and women unknown to us in the silence of history who carried on lay ministry.

A final example raises a different question: when Vatican documents refer to "apostles" do they mean the "Twelve"? Or are they using the word "apostle" to mean apostolicity in the Pauline sense? To whom exactly is apostolicity being handed on? Chapter two of the *Dogmatic Constitution on Divine Revelation,* (*Dei Verbum*, hereafter identified as DV), begins:

> God graciously arranged that what he had once revealed for the salvation of all peoples should last forever in its

> entirety and be transmitted to all generations. Therefore, Christ the Lord, in whom the entire revelation of the most high God is summed up (see 2 Cor 1:20; 3:16-4:6), having fulfilled in his own person and promulgated with his own lips the Gospel promised by the prophets, commanded the apostles to preach it to everyone as the source of all saving truth and moral law, communicating God's gifts to them. This was faithfully done: it was done by the apostles who handed on, by oral preaching, by their example, by their dispositions, what they themselves had received – whether from the lips of Christ, from his way of life and his works, or by coming to know it through the prompting of the holy Spirit; it was done by those apostles and others associated with them who, under the inspiration of the same holy Spirit, committed the message of salvation to writing.
>
> In order that the full and living Gospel might always be preserved in the Church the apostles left bishops as their successors. They gave them, "their own position of teaching authority." (DV 7)

Since the call to read Holy Scripture within its historical and cultural context comes from this document, we should apply what we learn from a contextual reading of Holy Scripture to scriptural terms and references as we encounter them in this document (and all Church documents). For example, if we were to learn through modern biblical scholarship that the word "apostle" does not necessarily refer to one of the "Twelve," nor does it refer to a bishop or priest, and instead refers to what might be more accurately described as a "layperson," perhaps even a "lay minister," are we then closer to an authentic reading of both Scripture and Church documents? Wherever we encounter the word "Apostle," in Scripture or a Church document, would it be more accurate to insert the term "lay minister"? As the council fathers write in *Dei Verbum*, "Sacred theology relies on the written word of God, taken together with sacred tradition, as its permanent foundation. By this word it is powerfully strengthened and rejuvenated, as it searches out, under the light of faith, all the truth stored up in the mystery of Christ. The sacred scriptures contain the word of God, and, because they are inspired, they are truly the word of God; therefore, the study of the sacred page should be the very soul of sacred theology." (DV 24)

As the council fathers remind us, sacred theology rests on the written Word of God, and it is "most powerfully strengthened and constantly rejuvenated by that word." In order to have a strong and rejuvenated theology it seems that we need to reappraise our understanding of the term "apostle"[24] and our understanding of apostolicity via contemporary New Testament scholarship. As many biblical scholars have demonstrated, apostolicity was not restricted to "the Twelve."[25] Moreover there is little to recommend an understanding of "the Twelve" as anything more than lay ministers chosen by Christ to continue his mission. "The Twelve" were not ordained; rather they experienced the same grace and presence of the Trinity that we

---

[24] "It was especially true of the Pauline churches that they contained no developed institutional functions. In this context one cannot speak of "offices." The recognizable diversified functions are rather to be understood as "roles" in the context of charismatic groups: apostles, prophets, teachers (1 Cor. 12:28); episcopoi (functionaries for administration of community and perhaps financial affairs) and deacons (Phil 1:1)." Ekkehard W. Steggemann and Wolfgang Stegemann, *The Jesus Movement: A Social History of its First Century* (Minneapolis: Fortress Press, 1999), 279-280.

[25] "Although many are called "apostles" in the NT, we have detailed knowledge of only three. If we begin with the Twelve, most are no more than names. If one excludes Judas Iscariot, the first four alone stand out, namely, the two sets of brothers: Peter and Andrew, James and John. Although in the gospels those four are portrayed as frequently in the company of Jesus, in the NT story of the early church Andrew disappears; James is martyred in the early 40s (Acts 12:2); and John is mentioned only as a shadow companion of Peter in a few scenes (3:1; 4:13; 8:14; Gal 2:9). . . . In fact, then, *Peter* is the only member of the Twelve of whose ecclesiastical career we are substantially informed . . . Outside the Twelve we know a great deal about *Paul* the Apostle, . . . *James*, 'the brother of the Lord,' was probably an apostle, even though not one of the Twelve. . . . by the year A.D. 67, the three apostles about whom we have detailed NT knowledge had disappeared from the scene. . . . the Twelve were not residential clergy; and Jesus never lived in a structured church. Similarly to be queried is the idea that the requirements imposed by the Pastorals are eternally valid." Raymond E. Brown, *The Churches the Apostles Left Behind* (New York: Paulist Press, 1984), 14-15, 36.

experience in the sacraments of initiation.[26] If we are to remain faithful to the principles of exegesis outlined in *Dei Verbum*, then it would seem that we have an obligation to examine the notion that the "apostles" Holy Scripture speaks of and that *Dei Verbum* references were in reality lay ministers who acted under the inspiration of the Holy Spirit and "left bishops as their successors." They gave them, "their own position of teaching authority." (DV 7).

Even with a critical reassessment of the origins of lay ministry and the priesthood, we should not hesitate to say that as a Church we trace the origins of all ministries to the ministry of Jesus and his companions. The priesthood of all believers was instituted by the Body of Christ; his followers entered into it through baptism and Eucharist; and it continues to our day. After more than a century of the *ekklesia* being led by members of the priesthood of all believers, the ordained priesthood emerged and grew into another branch on the ancient tree that has Christ as its source. In the centuries that followed, other branches on the Christ tree would grow, bud and blossom, some dying off, others going dormant, but all finding their source in Christ and manifesting discipleship in unique ways. Lay ministry and ordained ministry are two branches on that tree of many branches.

Neither lay ministry nor the ordained priesthood needs to be compromised or de-legitimated for the other to gain or retain legitimacy. From the perspective of not a few lay ministers, theologians, and other observers, it seems that some cannot conceive of a legitimate ordained priesthood existing in the same space as a fully legitimated lay ministry, but this is unwarranted as both are of equal value and both find their source in Christ.[27]

---

[26] "There is nothing in the Pastorals to suggest that presbyter-bishops dealt with eucharist or baptism. Nor do we know how presbyter-bishops were appointed, although by the time of Acts was written (the 80s or 90s) Barnabas and Paul could be pictured as having appointed presbyters in every church (14:25). That the picture is oversimplified is indicated by Titus 1:5 where it is clear that there are towns of Pauline mission without presbyters. According to the Didache 15:1 (ca. 100?) Christians were invited to appoint for themselves bishops and deacons." Ibid., 33-34.

[27] Osborne, *Ministry, Lay Ministry in the Roman Catholic Church: Its History and Theology*, 527-595.

These ministries are two branches of the same tree. Because one branch on a tree grows before another does not mean the other branches are in any way less a part of the tree. Here, Paul's words to the Corinthians are apt, "Therefore, neither the one who plants nor the one who waters is anything, but only God, who causes the growth. The one who plants and the one who waters are equal, and each will receive wages in proportion to his labor. For we are God's co-workers; you are God's field, God's building" (1 Corinthians 3:7-9).

A Silent Succession

In the Gospel of Mark, the author writes, "While he was at table in his house, many tax collectors and sinners sat with Jesus and his disciples; for there were many who followed him" (Mark 2:15). The last line of the verse is of particular interest: "for there were many who followed him." There is another verse like it in the Gospel of Luke where we are told, "And he came down with them and stood on a stretch of level ground. A great crowd of his disciples and a large number of the people from all Judea and Jerusalem and the coastal region of Tyre and Sidon came to hear him. . ." (Luke 6:17). In this verse the author reports that Jesus stood "with a great crowd of his disciples." In these instances and others, we find Jesus gathering with the un-named, un-defined, the "many." We know that they were his followers; in other instances we are told they are "disciples," but beyond that they have no status, no rank, no identity other than their proximity to Jesus. In fact if we consider the scriptural evidence, it is hard to pin down who exactly is a "disciple," and as Brown notes, even among the "Twelve" most are just names, apocryphal biographies notwithstanding.[28]

Perhaps that is how we should understand lay ministry in our day—as a silent witness, visible and distinguishable only to the degree that it identifies with the discipleship of Jesus and makes that discipleship manifest in the Church and the world. After all, that is the only criterion we are evaluated with in every age. It is not our titles, our rank, or our proximity to power that defines us and legitimates us; it is discipleship alone. We are legitimate ministers and members of a legitimate institution only to the degree that we practice discipleship as outlined in the Gospel.

[28] Cf. footnote 25 .

One can only assume that in the course of twenty centuries, millions of people heard the call to discipleship and set about to seek after the Kingdom of God, and at the end of their earthly ministry, they went to their eternal reward unknown to us. Those men and women were in effect the silent successors of apostolic discipleship and lay ministry. Though their status as lay people is rarely reflected upon, a few names are known outside of the New Testament.

Justin Martyr, a lay minister, and six of his companions were put to death in the middle of the second century. Osborne notes of him, "That Justin, through his academic role both in Rome and elsewhere, was certainly involved in Christian ministry can hardly be denied."[29] At the end of the same century, Apollonius the Apologist, another lay minister, presented his apologia at Rome and was put to death. Not long after we read of Thecla (a lay woman), who compelled by her Christian faith, was sentenced to death because of the public renunciation of her position as a woman in society.[30] Origen for much of his life was not ordained, and in an account that sounds eerily contemporary, we learn that, "on one occasion (c. 216) when he preached before a gathered community at the invitation of the *episkopoi* of Caesarea and of Jerusalem, the *episkopos* of Alexandria, Demetrios, was incensed that a non-ordained gave a homily in the presence of *episkopoi*."[31] Here and there a few references to lay ministers can be found in the patristic period. We find a notable figure in Didymus the Blind (313-398), who "was one of the foremost teachers at the catechetical school in Alexandria. He was the teacher of Jerome and Rufinius… he was consulted by both Anthony the Hermit and Palladius."[32] A few more names could be added, but for the most part there is silence.

What does it mean that there is such great concern around defining the current manifestation of lay ministry as "lay ecclesial ministry"? Cynics may assert that the struggle to define lay ministry is really about one thing: power. Viewed from different

[29]Osborne, *Ministry, Lay Ministry in the Roman Catholic Church: Its History and Theology*, 128.
[30] Ibid., 155.
[31] Ibid., 137.
[32] Ibid., 193.

perspectives, it can seem that it is about retaining power and authority for some, and for others it is about getting power, authority, and recognition. Viewed from another perspective, it seems to be about establishing dignity and justice for lay ministers serving in official capacities in the Church. However we choose to view lay ministry, it is abundantly clear that in spite of several decades of renewed focus and reflection on the nature of lay ministry, especially in its current manifestation, it has yet to gain legitimacy and recognition in significant ways. Until we can recognize lay ministry's rootedness in the ministry of Jesus and his companions, and affirm its apostolic origins and ancient pedigree, it will remain a post-Vatican II phenomenon, an ecclesial trend, a post-modern development, and by-product of the "priesthood shortage." While efforts to professionalize lay ministry and establish national standards for certifying "lay ecclesial ministers" are certainly warranted and much needed, they will prove insufficient when it comes to legitimizing lay ministry. By affirming the origins of lay ministry and allowing a narrative of apostolic lay ministry to exist alongside the apostolicity of the priesthood, we affirm what is good and true about both manifestations of ministerial discipleship. This approach also allows each form of ministry to share a real affinity with the ministry of Jesus without delegitimizing the other.

With Jesus and His Companions

Coming to an appreciation and acknowledgement of the real affinity between Jesus' historical ministry as a lay person and his companions and lay ministers today does not mean that we need to return to some perceived golden age of the Church when all ministries were lay. Nor does it necessitate a devaluation or deconstruction of our theology of holy orders and the existence of an institutional hierarchy. It simply means that we need to develop a sustained recognition at a conscious and practical level that lay ministry is as old as the Church. It is not new. It does not have to prove itself and it is as legitimate as any other form of ministry in the Church by virtue of its connection to the ministry of Jesus and his companions.

In the eyes of some, lay ministry and its hierarchically sanctioned manifestation "lay ecclesial ministry" represent a problem to be solved, but they are, in reality, a branch of an ancient tree that has its source in the ministry of Jesus and his companions. The mission and identity that those first-century companions of Jesus handed on to their successors has been handed on to us through the movement of the Holy Spirit. Our identity and mission as lay ministers is only a question for those who have yet to see our indelible connection to our brothers and sisters in lay ministry, Jesus and his companions.

Questions for Reflection

1. Based on what we know of the ministry of Jesus and his companions, do you think it is valid to describe them as the first lay ministers? Does this characterization challenge the dominant narrative (i.e. Jesus and the apostles were the first priests and bishops) about Jesus and his companions, or can both narratives exist together, even if in tension?

2. In the essay, the author suggests that lay ministers and lay people in general have long suffered from an inferiority complex that has at times been encouraged and spiritualized. Does a narrative emphasizing the affinity between Jesus and his followers and lay ministers begin to address that issue and lend legitimacy to lay ministers and lay people?

3. Some have argued that the early *ekklesia* was neither lay nor cleric and neither was Jesus. Is this neutral view of the status of Jesus, his companions, and the early *ekklesia* the best way to approach questions of ministerial identity and roles?

Section Two:

Ministry of Word and Works

Lay Ecclesial Ministers: Agents of Social Change

Kimberly M. Lymore

Introduction

A sign hangs prominently from the balcony of my church, visible to all as they leave the sanctuary and step out into the larger world: "Discipleship Will Cost! Are You Willing?" Living out and promoting such discipleship is at the heart of the vocation of lay ecclesial ministers.

According to Kathleen Cahalan in *Introducing the Practice of Ministry*, all ministers are called to promote discipleship through six core practices: teaching, preaching, worship and prayer, pastoral care, social justice, and administration.[1] In their description of lay ecclesial ministry in *Co-Workers in the Vineyard*, the bishops explain that lay ecclesial ministry "is *ministry* because it is a participation in the threefold ministry of Christ, who is priest, prophet, and king."[2] This essay will focus specifically on the ministerial practice of social justice as a reflection and practice of the prophetic ministry of Jesus. As *Co-Workers in the Vineyard* explains, "All of the baptized are called to work toward the transformation of the world. . . . [S]ome do this by working in the Church and focusing on the building of ecclesial communion, which has among its purposes the transformation of the world."[3] I will first review theological grounding for this critical role in lay ecclesial ministry. Then I will share reflections of my own experience in ministry to illustrate how a prophetic social justice focus responds to the vocation of the lay ecclesial minister and advances the mission of the Church for the transformation of the world.

---

[1] Kathleen Cahalan, *Introducing the Practice of Ministry* (Collegeville, MN: Liturgical Press, 2010), 70.

[2] United States Conference of Catholic Bishops, *Co-Workers in the Vineyard of the Lord* (Washington, DC: United States Conference of Catholic Bishops, 2005), 11.

[3] Ibid., 8.

Theological Context of Worship and Justice

In both the Old and New Testaments, social justice is a central concern. According to Cain Hope Felder, "The Old Testament is expansive in delineating normative standards for 'doing justice.'"[4] James Cone states that when you look at God's deliverance of Israel from the oppression under the Egyptians, the consistent theme in Israelite prophecy is "Yahweh's concern for the lack of social, economic, and political justice for those who are poor and unwanted in the society."[5] Gustavo Gutierrez, one of the primary founders of liberation theology and a Dominican priest, provides the same reading of the Exodus narrative.[6]

Furthermore, in the New Testament Jesus' ministry was an example of doing justice and the great commission to go out and heal the sick, clothe the naked, and visit those in prisons is foundational to the lay ecclesial ministry of justice (Matt 25: 35-40). In this estimation, Jesus is the lived manifestation of God's justice.[7] Jesus revealed the inherent connection between love of neighbor and love of God. After Jesus' death and resurrection, the liberating power of God and the mantle of doing justice on earth were taken up in the daily lives and practices of Christian people. Therefore, any Christian witness must emulate the power of God's justice by lifting up the lowly and bringing down those social structures that keep people oppressed.

In our relationship with God, we must recognize and acknowledge that God is the source of social justice and, in the words of Searle, the "work of justice—the work of liberation, development, and reconciliation—is the work of God."[8] In doing so, we must acknowledge the cross of Jesus Christ as the standard for social justice. The cross' redemptive mission was to

---

[4] Cain Hope Felder, *Troubling Biblical Waters: Race, Class & Family* (Maryknoll, NY: Orbis, 1989), 54.
[5] James H. Cone, *A Black Theology of Liberation* (Philadelphia: J. P. Lippencott, 1970), 19.
[6] Gustavo Gutierrez, *A Theology of Liberation* (Maryknoll, NY: Orbis Books, 1988).
[7] Mark Searle, "Serving the Lord with Justice," in *Liturgy and Social Justice*, ed. Mark Searle (Collegeville, MN: Liturgical Press, 1980), 17: "In his [Jesus'] life he modeled the radically different social justice which is that of the Kingdom of God."
[8] Ibid., 23.

restore our vertical relationship with God. Flowing out of that vertical relationship with God is an understanding of how to handle our horizontal relationships with one another. The cross is an essential part of our faith. In Luke, it states that in order to be a disciple of Jesus Christ, we must deny our self and pick up our cross to follow Jesus (Luke 9: 23). The practice of worship, focusing on God and not self, puts an individual in a right vertical relationship with God and the praxis of social justice, focusing on others through a sacrificial emptying of self, places an individual in the right horizontal relationship with one another.

In this way, worship and social justice are both actions that point to God. Cornel West states, "justice is what love looks like in public."[9] Worship is showing our love for God and justice is putting that love into action. The coupling of worship and action is what makes it possible for humans to live out the justice that was realized in Jesus Christ.

Catholic Social Teaching

There is a West African wisdom symbol, Sankofa,[10] which means return and get it. Sankofa is a bird whose head is in the opposite direction of its body, symbolizing the importance of learning from the past in order to move forward in the future. Sankofa is taking a look at what is good from the past and using that to inform the future. As a Masters of Divinity student at Catholic Theological Union, I first became familiar with Catholic social teaching. I was surprised at how prophetic the Church had been in the development of these teachings. Unfortunately, the Church today has too often been remiss in its study of the past and its faithfulness towards its own teachings and traditions about social justice. Rarely do you hear about Catholic social teachings from the pulpit and their importance to our being called as disciples of Jesus Christ. In fact, it is frequently said that Catholic social teachings are the best kept secret of the Catholic Church.[11] The last century has seen a development in the Church's social teachings that, according to Thomas Massaro,

---

[9] Cornel West, *Hope on a Tightrope* (New York: Smiley Books, 2008), 181.

[10] W. Bruce Willis, *The Adinka Dictionary* (Washington, D.C.: Pyramid Complex, 1998), 188.

[11] Thomas Massaro, SJ, *Catholic Social Teaching in Action: Living Justice* (New York: Rowman & Littlefield, 2008), 8.

have "grown increasingly insightful, challenging, and sophisticated in helping to shape the personal and collective responses of people of faith to social concerns such as poverty, violence and injustice."[12] Documents such as *Gaudium et Spes, Quadragesimo Anno, Rerum Novarum, Pacem in Terrris* and the *Compendium of the Social Doctrine of the Church* have focused on nine major themes:[13]

1. The Dignity of Every Person and Human Rights. Beginning with the premise that all humans are made in the image and likeness of God, Catholic social teaching insists on the "sanctity and immeasurable value of each human life."[14]

2. Solidarity, Common Good, and Participation. These traits begin "as an inner attitude and, when it has fully taken root within a person, expresses itself through numerous external activities that demonstrate a person's commitment to the well-being of others."[15]

3. Family Life. A society's well-being "absolutely depends upon healthy families, committed marriages, and responsible parenthood." [16]

4. Subsidiarity and the Proper Role of Government. *Subsidiarity,* meaning "assistance," "refers to the way the various levels of society should relate to each other and assist one another in bringing about the best outcomes for all people."[17]

5. Property Ownership in Modern Society: Rights and

---

[12] Ibid., 5.
[13] Massaro, 80, lists the associations of the documents with the Catholic social teaching themes. Although there are many variations on the themes, seven to nine are the most common.
[14] Ibid., 80-81.
[15] Ibid., 84.
[16] Ibid., 87.
[17] Ibid., 89.

Responsibilities. When we ignore the needs of those neighbors who are less fortunate, whether due to our selfish motives or merely from neglect, we "frustrate the very purpose of God in creating the material worlds we share."[18]

6. The Dignity of Work, Rights of Workers, and Support of Labor Unions. Besides other human rights, workers have the right to associate freely, to participate fully in society's economic and political life, and to organize and enter into collective bargaining.[19]

7. Colonialism and Economic Development. Caring deeply about world poverty is a moral obligation for all people who accordingly should "do all they can to address this scourge on our common humanity."

8. Peace and Disarmament. Peace is more than the mere absence of open hostility, for it "calls people to a thorough respect for all their neighbors in relationships that are characterized by an ever-deeper trust and a commitment to providing mutual assistance."[20]

9. Option for the Poor and Vulnerable. As Church, we are more faithful to our identity when we act "on the imperative to meet the urgent needs of the most vulnerable – the ones Jesus Christ so loves."[21]

This is a Sankofa moment when lay ecclesial ministers can look back at Catholic social teachings and then enlarge their ministry by focusing on the areas of social ministries that would then let the Catholic Church be true to the standard it set for itself. Cahalan identified social ministries as: "social services for

---

[18] Ibid., 92.
[19] Ibid., 95.
[20] Ibid., 103.
[21] Ibid., 112-113.

basic human needs such as food, shelter, and clothing; health-care ministries for the sick; prison ministries; orphanages and services for children; justice ministries that address systemic legal and economic issues; relief agencies – all of which operate on local, national and international levels."[22] Lay ecclesial ministers can take the lead in mobilizing their faith communities into service and provide any necessary education, organization and funding that will help the Church achieve its mission of justice.[23]

Laypersons are arguably the Church's greatest resource. Evidence of this is found in the thousands of laypersons who have entered educational programs geared toward preparing them for pastoral positions in the Church. Yet, I would suggest that the Church has not fully taken advantage of this rich, abundant resource. Furthermore, Catholic social teaching can be a tool for lay ecclesial ministers to use to draw the laity into the work of the Church and be a unifying force that rallies people around matters of justice.

Catholic social teachings cover a wide spectrum of areas that concern and have a direct impact on the common good of humankind. When we look at the socio-political problems in the United States, such as poverty, homelessness, healthcare, housing foreclosures, and violence, one cannot help but be struck by how significant an impact lay ecclesial ministers can have. When ministers focus on the things they are told they cannot do, they limit the possibilities to discover and excel in the things that they can do. There is an urgency and need for lay ecclesial ministers to take their rightful place in the leadership of the Church and be the disciples that God has called them to be.

Charity vs. Justice

In the past, charity and justice have been terms that were used interchangeably. However, charity and justice ought to be separated and are two distinct components within Catholic social teaching. Moreover, charity and justice are two ends of a

---

[22] Cahalan, 88.

[23] Ibid.: "The charisms for leading ministries of mercy and justice are the virtue of seeing Christ in each person, knowledge about Christian social teachings and understanding about the contexts and people served, and the capacity to organize and mobilize resources for outreach, service and systematic change."

spectrum for living out our faith. Both embody compassionate caring for "the least of these."[24] Both charity and justice define our call to live out the Gospel of God's love and reconciliation. Charity, or outreach, responds to an immediate need, in that it provides direct services such as food, clothing, or shelter. Most people have a clear sense of when to do charity. Charity is satisfying and generally non-controversial.

However, charity alone is only part of the social mission of the Catholic Church. While charity deals with immediate needs, justice addresses the long-term conditions, promoting social change in institutions, policies, and systems. Social justice is public, political, and oriented to collective action for change. It is based on the concepts of human rights. Social justice directs us toward the causes of social injustice which are many times controversial.

An example of an issue from my own faith community that contains both elements of charity and social justice was the response in 2005 when Hurricane Katrina hit the Gulf Coast. Everyone wanted to help those affected and displaced by the flooding when the levees broke. Seeing all the people who were clustered for days in the New Orleans Superdome without restrooms, food, or water, many found their hearts touched and were moved to do something, anything, to help those in need.

Many of the survivors of Hurricane Katrina had family in Chicago where I minister, so it was only natural that they came here for help. However, when they got to Chicago, they found that their families here could not always accommodate everyone. When many of the survivors arrived in Chicago, it was the Labor Day Weekend and many agencies, like Catholic Charities, were closed. Most of the Katrina survivors left their city with only the clothes on their backs and maybe a few belongings they could carry; their worldly belongings were lost in the flood.

Many people were directed to our faith community because we had a reputation for helping those in need, especially those in the direst of straits. We established partnerships with landlords, other churches, and organizations for donations for housing,

---

[24] Matthew 25:45: He will answer them, 'Amen I say to you, whatever you did not do for one of these least ones, you did not do for me.'

furniture, clothes, and other items. For the next couple of weeks, we cleaned and set up the apartments to be move-in condition and ready to be a safe haven for those survivors. We allowed the children into our school, tuition-free, so that they would not get behind in school due to this situation. We could not let the Katrina survivors experience even more trauma than they had already gone through. We realized that although we do not know what to do at all times, as disciples of Jesus Christ, we cannot be merely hearers of the word. We have to be doers of the word.[25]

The government had failed; the Red Cross had failed. These are the moments when charity turns into a social justice issue, when the Church must fight the systemic effects of racism and classism. It is the Church's responsibility to be the beacon of light in darkness. It is our duty to do whatever we can not only to help those in need but also to be the prophetic voice in the wilderness crying out for justice. The leaders of my faith community constantly raise the congregants' consciousness about social justice through preaching and education. During the Katrina moment, preaching and teaching highlighted the differences in the way in which marginalized people and people of color are often responded to by those in power and with resources to provide assistance. We listened to the stories of the survivors of Katrina in our midst, and through our connection with them as brothers and sisters, we immediately saw the inappropriateness of government references to them as "refugees" rather than American citizens. We wrote press releases, and we spoke with the media. We encouraged Katrina survivors to share their stories in the media. We contacted federal representatives and expressed our dismay at the slow and inadequate response. In all of these activities, the lay ecclesial minister can take a leadership and encouraging role, drawing on the talents and networks of the laity and coordinating the church's messaging and activities. If you are blessed to be in an affluent church, it is important that, as a lay ecclesial minister, you take the lead in moving beyond the four walls of the church and finding opportunities for service and justice. Moving beyond those moments, like Hurricane Katrina, when it is easy to mobilize people in the pews, to a movement,

[25] James 1: 22: But prove yourselves doers of the word, and not merely hearers who delude themselves.

where being a disciple of Jesus Christ and doing justice is a lifestyle.

There are many ways in which lay ecclesial ministers can use their position to be instrumental in training their congregations to live out their roles as disciples of Jesus Christ through the praxis of Catholic social teaching. Below I touch on five: preaching, education, advocacy, protest, and legal and legislative action.

Preaching

Preaching a social justice message is one way for lay ecclesial ministers to make Catholic social teaching tangible and practical for their parishioners and help them become disciples of Jesus Christ. While lay ecclesial ministers do not deliver the Sunday homily, there are other venues where they can preach including adult formation workshops, retreats, conferences, and special services. For example, I presented at the Samuel DeWitt Proctor Conference on how to mobilize congregations to do social justice outreach.

Education

In the church there are usually many opportunities for teaching the catechism to children, yet the adults are left with a dearth of opportunity. Many congregants have a scant knowledge of Catholic social teachings, why social justice is at the center of Christian faith, and their call to be disciples of Jesus Christ. Because many lay ecclesial ministers are involved in teaching and curriculum planning, they are ideally situated to follow the call to be pastoral and theological educators.

Lay ecclesial ministers can facilitate adult Bible studies, discussions, and seminars on discipleship and how our Christian journey is both simultaneously an inward and outward process. We seek to grow in our relationship with God not only for ourselves but in order to be a blessing to others. In the parish where I am a lay ecclesial minister, the pastor states at the end of the service, "Be blessed and go be a blessing to someone." With this, my faith community is saying that God does not bless us so that we can hold onto it. Rather what God has allowed us to reap, God also mandates that we sow. Such an understanding is in lock-step with Catholic social teachings, which propose a set of core values that can guide us in our decision making process. How this process is understood makes for a good starting point in educating our congregants about their responsibility in building the Kingdom of God. As lay ecclesial ministers, it is our responsibility, hopefully in collaboration with clergy, to move congregants from just being believers of Jesus Christ to disciples of Jesus Christ, from a place of inactive belief to active, engaged practice.

As part of my thesis article for my doctorate in ministry, I instituted a teaching component into our adult formation New Believers/New Members classes. I realized that even though our congregation hears social justice messages in the preaching, not everyone was making the connection that what we do during worship on Sundays should move us to go out to make an impact on our community, the city, and the world. Because we are situated in a community, that community should be better because we are there.

These sessions on worship and social justice have increased the congregants' understanding that as Christians it is our responsibility to be the voice for those who are hurting. These sessions also allow them to share with one another their beliefs about the links between worship and social justice activities, as well as other social justice activities that they are involved in outside of what our church is doing.

In recent years, research in adult-based transformative learning theory suggests there are other ways, apart from didactic teaching, by which adults learn better and are more effective in forming moral consciousness. [26] Transformative learning involves the evaluation of one's purpose, feelings, and meanings. Such pedagogy has the goal of helping students to

---

[26] Edward W. Taylor, "Transformative Learning Theory," *New Directions for Adult and Continuing Education*, no. 119 (Fall 2008), 5, accessed November 23, 2008, http://www.interscience.wiley.com: "The transformative process uses frames of reference that are structures of assumptions and expectations that frame an individual's tacit points of view and influence their thinking, beliefs, and actions. It is the revision of a frame of reference in concert with reflection on experience that is addressed by the theory of perspective transformation [producing] a paradigmatic shift. This process leads to a more developed and functional frame of reference that is more (a) inclusive, (b) differentiating, (c) permeable, (d) critically reflective, and (e) integrative of experience."

become active promoters and shapers of their own learning rather than taking on blindly someone else's point of view. When lay ecclesial ministers are involved in the education of the congregation, they can provide safe space, a place without judgment, for adults to share their stories. This process of creating dialogue between external content knowledge and personal lived experience allows adults to potentially reframe their way of thinking. In the context of making the connection between worship and justice, lay ecclesial ministers can intentionally encourage dialogue and reflection around the personal and collective experience of worship and its connection to the external demands of justice, thereby creating new paradigms of understanding.

Advocacy

Advocacy is a third way to engage in social justice praxis. Advocacy is defined as the act of pleading a cause, idea, or policy, or as active support. Earlier I mentioned that charity can turn into social justice because of the underlying issues that caused the need for acts of charity in the first place. In the case of Katrina, racism and classism were at the root of the problem that ensued. Some people think that racism is no longer an issue in this country because we elected an African-American president. However, these people are sadly and tragically mistaken. Furthermore, racism has historically been and continues to be an issue in the Catholic Church. In this way, despite their historically tenuous relationship, the Catholic Church and the United States are intimate bedfellows.

As a cradle-born Black Catholic, I have had to deal with racism within the Church and my country for my whole life. Not being welcomed into Catholic churches and schools because of the color of my skin is one example. When some white priests were sent to predominately black parishes, it was akin to punishing the priests, and they could not wait to be transferred.[27] Unfortunately, not much has changed over the years. For more

[27]*Summoned by the Holy Spirit and Called to New Life*, a document produced for the Black Catholic Convocation that took place on November 3-4, 2000. The Preparatory Document Committee consisted of Chair, Sr. Jamie T. Phelps, Bishop Joseph Perry,Father John Calicott, Fr. Anthony Vader, and Mr. Joseph Spalding.

information on this subject, I suggest you read my colleague Bryan Massingale's book, *Racial Justice and the Catholic Church,*[28] which not only gives an historical perspective on racism in the Church but also examines how Catholic social teaching has been used or not used to combat racism and to promote reconciliation and justice.

The sin of racism within the Catholic Church raises the question of whose problem this is and on whose shoulders ought the righting of the transgression lie. Rev. Dr. Martin Luther King, Jr., states it best in saying, "injustice anywhere is a threat to justice everywhere."[29] As lay ecclesial ministers are involved in the building of the Kingdom of God, we must view issues from a higher perspective. Furthermore, the Bible parable of the lost sheep, found in Luke 15:1-7, is helpful. This parable implies that if one sheep was lost, a good shepherd would leave the ninety-nine to go after the one. Even though the parable is about repentance, this says to me that even if one person is hurting, suffering, and dealing with an injustice, we need to do whatever we can to ease the suffering. Just as God cares for the one, because we are the face of God here on earth, we must care for the one hurting.

In the Chicago archdiocese, the Office of Racial Justice hosts seminars that address the sin of racism and provides participants with tools for combating racism, not only in their parishes but whenever they encounter such situations. I would like to suggest that lay ecclesial ministers must take on racism in the Church. They need to look into the mirror of their own environments to see if there are any issues of racism in their congregations and assist them in any way possible to correct those actions that lead to racism.

During my first year as a lay ecclesial minister, my church , which is located in the predominately African American community of Auburn-Gresham, had to deal with a clear issue of racism. The athletic director wanted the team to join the Chicago Southwest Catholic Conference (SCC) in order to make them eligible for high school football teams and eventually college

---

[28] Bryan Massingale, *Racial Justice and the Catholic Church* (Maryknoll, NY: Orbis Books, 2010).

[29] Dr. Martin Luther King, *Letter from Birmingham Jail, April 16, 1963.* http://www.africa.upenn.edu/Articles_Gen/Letter_Birmingham.html

scholarships. The SCC consisted of twenty-one virtually all-white schools. When the SCC voted on the team joining the league, the team was turned down. The main reason for the rejection was stated as fear that "their children would be unsafe in the Auburn Gresham neighborhood, which admittedly had a higher rate of crime, drug and gang problems than the neighborhoods of the SCC."[30] A few days after this rejection, the story went nationwide with the title, "Black School Can't Join Sports League." There were numerous meetings with the Archbishop, the SCC leadership, and our church.

Our church espouses Dr. King's vision of nonviolence that was born during the civil rights movement. Dr. King had a particular strategy that he used when confronted with evil and apparent standstills from the opponent. While Dr. King enforced his nonnegotiable belief of nonviolence, his strategy or formula created situations of tension where discussions and negotiations were inevitable. Dr. King's strategy involved five action steps: *Education, Negotiation, Self-Purification, Direct Action, and Reconciliation*[31], the latter of which was the ultimate goal. We can learn a lot from his successful strategies.[32] We drew upon these in the SCC case as we worked with the SCC membership and the Archdiocese of Chicago representatives.

Eventually, the children were allowed into the league. The peace was short-lived and only lasted a year before a racial incident happened. Our pastor then decided to pull out of the league. However, the lessons that were taught to the children centered around self-respect and how to stand up for their rights. The entire story is chronicled in Robert McClory's book, *The Radical Disciple.*[33] If you are interested in learning more about how a parish can impact a community through social advocacy, this book is a must read.

Protest

[30] Robert McClory, *The Radical Disciple* (Chicago: Lawrence Hill Books, 2010), 110.
[31] http://www.thekingcenter.org/king-philosophy
[32] To learn more on Dr. King's philosophy, a good place to start is with his *Letter from a Birmingham Jail.*
[33] Robert McClory, *The Radical Disciple: Father Pfleger, St. Sabina Church, and the Fight for Social Justice* (Chicago: Lawrence Hill Books, 2010).

Protest is a fourth way lay ecclesial ministers can engage their congregations in social justice. Protest is a form of justice that many shy away from because it can be controversial, yet it is an effective way to mobilize people to confront an issue. Sometimes clergy hesitate to make waves, in part because protest can lead to bad publicity or, sometimes, even going to jail. However, there has to be someone with a passion for justice in order to lead a people in a successful protest. Many priests and nuns were involved in the marches of the Civil Rights Movement.[34] Even before then, in the 1930s, Dorothy Day, a devout Catholic, helped establish the Catholic Worker movement that uses nonviolent direct action on behalf of the poor and homeless.

As I write this, Chicago is in a state of emergency with the gun violence that has been occurring. It has been reported that there have been more deaths by violence in Chicago than there have been of U.S. troops in Afghanistan.[35] Most of the deaths are young people under twenty years old. On the last day of school each year, our church coordinates an end-of-school year march for the safety of the children during the summer. It is a collaboration of many organizations throughout the city of Chicago. Over 1000 people participated in this year's rally/march.

All summer we walked through the neighborhood every Friday night, talking to residents, reassuring them that there are people who care about what is happening in the streets and letting residents in the area know the activities and support services our church offers. Just our presence on the streets has had a positive impact on the community. However, the violence does still exist so our work is not complete.

[34] Amy Koehlinger, *The New Nuns: Racial Justice and Religious Reform in the 1960's* (Cambridge, MA: Harvard University Press, 2007).

[35] http://www.huffingtonpost.com/2012/06/16/chicago-homicide-rate-wor_n_1602692.html

Legal and Legislative Action

In addition to the marches, our church has worked with state representatives to introduce legislation that will require guns to be titled like cars, and other common sense gun laws. Another legislative issue we worked on was banning alcohol and cigarette billboards from being placed within close proximity of schools. This legislation took fourteen years of effort before becoming a law. Martin Luther King, Jr., once said, "The wheels of social justice turn slow." In other words, when it comes to righting social injustices, it can take a long time. We have to continue to stay on the battlefield and do what God has called us to do in this world.

The successes that we have experienced have not happened in a vacuum. They have taken many years of advocacy, protest marches, and rallies. There have been many alliances established with other like-minded churches of all denominations and organizations. It also takes listening to God in order to discern which battles to fight. Then we can step out on faith and know that God is with us and stand until the victory comes.

Conclusion

Many people do not understand that to be a disciple of Jesus Christ is not only to go to church on Sunday but to fight those things that threaten building up the Kingdom of God. All but one of Jesus' apostles died a violent death. I believe in these dark days of economic recession, violence in our streets, and systemic racism, there need to be some radical disciples willing to step out on faith and wave the banner of a prophetic love of God and neighbor over their community, their city, and their country.

It is only this banner that can confront the apathy that has invaded the pews of the Church. The Church needs lay ecclesial ministers to be the mouthpieces that restore its credibility in the works of promoting the Kingdom of God. There is a lot of work ahead of us, and it sometimes can get very overwhelming and discouraging. But we don't have to look too far back in order to see progress.

Many movements have been born out of Catholic social teaching whether implicitly or explicitly. According to Massaro, "Social reform movements arise spontaneously, in ways that are impossible to explain in terms of historical precedents . . . people of conscience who are confronted with injustice draw a substantial inspiration from established traditions of thought or academic study to which they have been exposed."[36] Lay ecclesial ministers can be the conduits that expose congregants to Catholic social teachings that will propel them to a greater commitment to live out courageously their beliefs about social justice.

Lay ecclesial ministers make up the parts of the body by working in tandem with the ordained. As Massaro writes, "Some will play the role of the tongue, teaching and preaching about the themes of Catholic social teaching. Others will be the hands of this faith-based justice, lifted up to God in prayer or thrust down into the earth, grinding soil under the fingernails as our collective social involvement grows deeper. Others may be the eyes, gathering new information about this fragile world and contributing to projects of social analysis that will illuminate the footsteps of all on the paths of justice."[37] Whether you are the tongue, the hands, or the eyes proclaiming justice, we are called into ministry, as Esther was told by Mordecai, for such a time as this.[38]

My question to lay ecclesial ministers is: will you go out to be the doers of God's word? The God of justice is roaming the earth looking for people who will be the voice for the voiceless, looking to create the Kingdom of God here on earth, engaging in efforts to bring justice for all people. This is why lay ecclesial ministers ought to act and know that God is with them. In this effort, Catholic social teaching offers us an extremely helpful intellectual tradition about why and how to practice justice in following Jesus' call to care for the least among the human community. By virtue of the vocation and calling of lay ecclesial ministers and their witness as disciples of Jesus Christ, if they don't step up and be

---

[36] Massaro, 171-172.
[37] Ibid., 176.
[38] Esther 4: 14: "Even if you now remain silent, relief and deliverance will come to the Jews from another source; but you and your father's house will perish. Who knows but that it was for a time like this that you obtained the royal dignity?"

the credible witness for the Church, then who will? Let us say, like Isaiah, "here I am Lord, send me!"[39]

I have outlined five ways in which lay ecclesial ministers can engage in social justice in their current environment: preaching, education, advocacy, protest, and legal and legislative action. These are ways in which I, a lay ecclesial minister, have been involved in my church context. I believe that this is the time for lay ecclesial ministers, as co-laborers in the vineyard, to be the agents of social change that the Catholic Church needs. The tasks of doing social justice are daunting. If you are in an affluent parish, begin to look beyond your walls of ministry to see who in a neighboring community might need assistance. Then as the old Nike slogan stated, “just do it.”

Questions for Reflection

1. Identify a pressing social need in your community or beyond. Discuss both possible charitable and social justice responses to this need.

2. Identify an issue that you believe could be addressed by a Catholic social teaching theme. Is this an area where you can make impact either through preaching, education, advocacy, protest, or legal and legislative action?

3. Using the method you have chosen, outline a plan of action.

---

[39] Isaiah 6: 8: Then I heard the voice of the Lord, saying, “Whom shall I send? Who will go for Us?” “Here am I,” I said; “Send me!”

The Preaching *Habitus*: A Way of Life

Linda Lee Ritzer

Proclaim the Word

The mandate of Jesus, "Go into the whole world and proclaim the gospel to every creature" (Mark 16:15) reminds us what the preacher must do: announce the Gospel to everyone. The preacher is called to unfold the blanket of God's holy Word, giving life to the hearts of those on whom it is laid. In every place, among every people, we are called to speak of God's love, of Jesus' dying and rising, and the power of the Holy Spirit.

In this essay, the term "preaching" is not limited to liturgical preaching, which is commonly understood to be the homily, and references to "preacher" are not limited to clergy. My understanding of preaching is derived from the Church's broader mission, which is to proclaim the Gospel to every creature. Lay people and lay ecclesial ministers of the Roman Catholic tradition are primarily non-liturgical preachers. However, lay preaching should not be construed as restricted simply because it is not proclaimed from the liturgical pulpit. The liturgical pulpit, which is the most essential and indispensable setting for the preaching of the ordained, is not the only pulpit. There are many other pulpits outside of the sanctuary in which lay preachers are called to render the Word. The laity in general, and lay ecclesial ministers through more specific and professional responsibility, are commissioned to bear the Word to the faithful and the world.

Current trends reveal that fewer and fewer Catholics are attending Sunday Mass. According to a 2011 CARA (Center for Applied Research in the Apostolate) statistical report, only 22% of the 65.4 million U.S. Catholics say they attend Mass every week.[1] The result is less exposure to preaching in liturgy. Even so, we know that

---

[1] "Frequently Requested Church Statistics," http://cara.georgetown.edu/CARAServices/requestedchurchstats.html (accessed September 2, 2012).

people outside the conventional places of sacred worship are longing to hear, know, and find God.

Like Mary of Magdala who was transformed by the life, death, and resurrection of Christ, we too are sent to witness and preach the Gospel we embrace. We act by giving our voices to what we believe. Our faith in the Gospel, coupled with our close proximity to those longing to be inspired, calls us to proclaim the sacred Word and announce meaning for contemporary believers and non-believers. It is clear that for some people their only exposure to the Good News will come from the proclamation of lay ecclesial ministers. This is a privileged occasion. It is imperative that we are dedicated to the task of proclaiming the Gospel with confident voices that advance the Gospel.

As a guideline, and particularly for the purpose of this essay, I offer the following definition: Preaching is an integral component of the ministry of the Word in which hearers are exposed, through spoken words, to the saving work of Jesus Christ who is the incarnate Word of God. Preaching announces the Good News of the life, death and resurrection of Jesus leading to a personal experience with the Divine. It creates a symbolic face-to-face encounter with the God of hope by proclaiming promise, calling for repentance and eliciting response. Preaching is a cooperative responsibility between the ordained and laity. It is a vast enterprise announcing the Gospel in life's various locations including secular, familial, catechetical, and liturgical settings.

Undoubtedly lay ecclesial ministers, at parent meetings, care centers, funeral homes, hospitals, ecumenical gatherings, and even occasionally in the liturgical setting, will be called upon to preach. My essay is not an exposé on where one preaches. For a survey of those situations I refer you to my colleague, Rodney Bluml, whose essay describes in detail such settings. Rather I write to encourage lay ecclesial ministers to be ready to accomplish the task of sacred preaching with excellence. To this end I will present two main points: 1) lay ecclesial ministers possess the genuine right to preach, and 2) by making fuller use of established liturgical preaching practices, lay ecclesial ministers will strengthen their ability to proclaim God's Word.

The Baptized/Confirmed

Catholics believe that baptism brings into being a share in the messianic mission of Christ. The anointing of baptism affirms that the Christian is made like and belongs to Christ. The holy anointing also grants each Christian gifts of the Holy Spirit, to further the mission of Christ which includes proclaiming the Good News of salvation. The charisms of baptism and confirmation are graces of the Holy Spirit granted for building up the Church on earth. These charisms, in addition to many other virtues, strengthen the faithful to participate with Christ the High Priest in proclaiming Sacred Scripture. St. Paul explains that the Holy Spirit dispenses a variety of gifts but with unity of purpose (1 Cor 12:4-11). St. Peter declares the baptized to be, " a chosen race, a royal priesthood, a holy nation, a people of his own, so that you may announce the praises' of him . . ." (1 Pet 2:9). In section two on the People of God, *Lumen Gentium* states:

> The baptized, by regeneration and the anointing of the holy Spirit, are consecrated to be a spiritual house and a holy priesthood, that through all their christian activities they may offer spiritual sacrifices and proclaim the marvels of him who has called them out of darkness into his wonderful light (See 1Pet 2:4-10).[2]

Endowed with baptismal grace and gifts from the Holy Spirit, the faithful are prepared to "undertake various tasks and offices for the renewal and building up of the church" (LG 12). Christ, who proclaimed the Reign of God by his life and words, continues this work in the baptized/confirmed. "For that very purpose He made them [the baptized/confirmed] His witnesses and gave them understanding of the faith and the grace of speech so that the power of the Gospel might shine forth in their daily social and family life" (LG 34). Announcing Christ through living witness and the spoken word is a vital task that is accomplished by the laity in the ordinary circumstances of the world.

While the Church clearly acknowledges that ministry is a diverse enterprise, with the ordained and laity each possessing unique

---

[2]Austin Flannery, O.P., ed. *Vatican Council II: The Basic Sixteen Documents: Constitutions, Decrees, Declarations* (Northport, NY: Costello Publishing Company, Inc., 1996), *Lumen Gentium* 10.

functions, there is a unity of purpose. Believers, through the sacraments of initiation, are disciples of Christ united in a common vocation. According to *Co-Workers in the Vineyard,* that vocation is "to give glory to God and to continue Christ's work of salvation, which includes redemption from sin, by proclaiming and celebrating the Good News of God's saving presence through word and sacraments."[3] The Word of God requires special agency. By virtue of baptism, confirmation and ministerial role, lay ecclesial ministers are agents of God's Word.

Our tradition regards clergy, almost exclusively, as responsible for the preaching ministry. In liturgy this is absolutely true. However, in situations outside of liturgy it is a ministry that is easily shared. This might cause some to ask, "By what legitimate authority does a lay person preach the Word?" The response is that baptism and confirmation grant authentic gifts for building up the Church, including gifts that advance the Gospel through the ministry of Word. As the *Catechism of the Catholic Church* states, the baptized "share in the priesthood of Christ, in his prophetic and royal mission...Baptism gives a share in the common priesthood of all believers."[4]

Lay Ecclesial Minister – Partners in The Ministry of the Word

Lay ecclesial ministers, by virtue of baptism/confirmation and with delegation from their diocesan bishops and/or pastors, share in the exercise of the ministry of the Word through catechesis and preaching. The *Catechism* states, "Those who with God's help have welcomed Christ's call and freely responded to it are urged on by love of Christ to proclaim the Good News everywhere in the world"[5] . The treasure of Good News announced by Christ and proclaimed by the apostles is a treasure to be shared. By virtue of Christ's call and baptism the laity shares in the commission of proclaiming the saving mysteries through catechesis and preaching. In the following

---

[3] United States Conference of Catholic Bishops, *Co-Workers in the Vineyard of the Lord* (Washington, DC: United States Conference of Catholic Bishops, 2005), 19-20.
[4] *Catechism of the Catholic Church: Revised in Accordance with the Official Latin Text (CCC)* Promulgated by Pope John Paul II, 2nd ed. (Vatican City: Libreria Editrice Vaticana, 1997), 1268.
[5] Ibid.

definition, the *General Directory for Catechesis* explains that catechesis and preaching are equal yet different kinds of the ministry of the Word:

> The important forms of the Ministry of the Word are: the first announcement or missionary preaching, pre and post-baptismal catechesis, the liturgical forms and the theological forms. Then, it often happens, for pastoral reasons, that the important forms of the ministry of the word [sic] must assume more than one function. Catechesis, for example, together with its initiatory forms, has frequently to discharge tasks of mission. The same homily, depending on circumstances, can take on both the functions of convocation and of integral initiation.[6]

Missionary preaching, an example of shared ministry between the laity and ordained, announces the name of Jesus to those who do not know him. A lay ecclesial minister in the United States does not have to travel to a foreign land to engage in missionary preaching. A Catholic school principal told me the following story which illustrates missionary preaching. A kindergarten student had been sent to her office for misbehaving. In the course of her conversation with the student, she took the child upon her lap, pointed to the crucifix on the wall and asked her, "What do you think Jesus would think about that?" The child responded by saying, "Him, I didn't even know him until I came to this school. I just met him in the stories you have been telling me in Morning Prayer." In her school the principal has developed a program of prayer that is based on the proclamation of the Word. She and the faculty preach Good News every day. I say "preach" rather than "catechize" because they rely on the content of Scripture for the daily message. Catechesis, which relies in part on the content of Scripture, also encompasses moral and doctrinal teaching and often employs a didactic method. The lay teachers who are proclaiming God's Word are engaged in a form of preaching. They are announcing the Gospel, interpreting the text, translating the meaning for a particular audience and creating reflections which enable their students to reflect on faith and contemplate God.

---

[6] National Conference of Catholic Bishops, *General Directory for Catechesis* (Washington, DC: United States Catholic Conference, 1998), 52.

Even though the above example demonstrates a form of lay preaching, I know through years of pastoral experience that an imbalance exists in the process of training for lay ministers of the Word. As collaborators in this important work of communicating the message of salvation, I have observed that lay ecclesial ministers are often insufficiently trained in biblical studies and rhetoric. I am not suggesting that they have insufficient education or no formal training in preparation for their professional tasks. Rather, what I have observed is that training for lay ecclesial ministers in biblical theology, biblical criticism, and rhetoric—the very tools that enable one to decipher, interpret, and communicate Sacred Scripture—are surprisingly minimal, and in some cases, negligible.

Priests, on the other hand, step into a pulpit with eight years of seminary training. A considerable portion of their instruction includes critical biblical study and homiletics. Because their primary responsibility as ministers of the Word is to proclaim the Gospel and preach the Good News in the liturgical setting, one can be assured that every Roman Catholic priest has been very well prepared for the preaching task. Admittedly, some clergy possess a special God- given talent for preaching, but regardless of natural ability, all the clergy have been taught how to decipher, interpret, and communicate Sacred Scripture. This instruction comes through formation in the preaching *habitus,*[7] which is invaluable in practicing the ministry of the Word.

It is my sincere hope that lay ecclesial ministers, as partners in the ministry of the Word, will have a greater opportunity not only to deepen their understanding of the preaching ministry but to be formed in the preaching *habitus*. This will further enable them to proclaim the saving mysteries of faith and lead others to encounter God's revelation in Sacred Scripture.

We turn now to examine tools of the preaching trade which are necessary to accomplish a portion of the preaching task. In the following section, I will present a brief outline of four basic preaching

---

[7] By preaching *habitus* I mean the discipline required to accomplish the preaching task. The discipline involves familiarity with specific methods and skills which are acquired through prayer, study, appropriation of setting, and understanding of rhetoric.

practices: *lectio divina*,[8] contextual or situational analysis, biblical criticism, and crafting language. Familiarity with these four practices will enable lay ecclesial ministers to approach the preaching mission with new understanding. The practices provide a framework upon which to build greater skill and capacity for the preaching enterprise.

Preaching Practices

Lectio Divina

In the Book of the prophet Ezekiel, the prophet is told, "Son of man, eat what is before you; eat this scroll, then go, speak to the house of Israel" (3:1). In order to preach a word, one must first "eat" the Word. Consuming the Word initiates an intimate encounter that awakens the heart to Holy God. One who eats the Word becomes one with the Word and is transformed by its substance, thus making a connection with God that effects a total change. This change is beyond temporality and time, for it is a change of heart. One can never pretend or invent the transformational reality of an authentic encounter with the Word. It is only by conscious, meaningful, and receptive contact with the Word that the Word transforms the person.

Lectio divina is an immersion in the Word of God. It is a reflective process aimed at union with the Mystery contained in the Word. Sister Jean-Marie Howe, an expert in the method, says *lectio divina* "is a way of being with the Word, a process that requires a specifically contemplative attitude, a mode of being rather than doing."[9] The prayer invites the individual into the presence of the Word in which one attends to the Divine Other. The process requests that the individual be present and open rather than decisive and dominant. It bids a gentle submission to the Mystery contained within the Word and genuine surrender to indisputable Truth that is perceived and sensed rather than systematically appraised. Howe explains, "*Lectio divina* is an immersion in the Word, day and night. It is not a bridge that must be built. It is a pure *movement into* the

---

[8] *Lectio divina* is Latin for "divine reading." It is prayer that uses Sacred Scripture for meditation and contemplation. See below.

[9] Jean-Marie Howe, OSCO, *La secret du Coeur: l'etre spiritual* (Notre-dame-du-Lac: Abbaye cistercienne, 1999). Translated by Kathleen Waters, OSCO, *Secret of the Heart: Spiritual Being* (Kalamazoo, Michigan: Cistercian Publications, 2005), 47.

Mystery, requiring a simplicity of approach that renounces this temptation to hurdle the abyss by man-made means, whatever they may be."[10]

The practice of *lectio* requires a discipline of simplicity and unrestraint. It is often humbling for the participant because the practice insists on the submission of one's will to the dynamic work of God who, through love, opens the ears and eyes of believers to new conversations and understanding. *Lectio* elevates the art of sacred listening and urges the participant to wait silently with attentive focus for a word. In the holy and patient silence God promises to speak and Divine Presence is encountered.

This process involves four progressive phases or steps that enable and develop a loving relationship with God. The practice is built on a continuum progressing from *lectio* (reading) to *meditatio* (meditation) to *oratio* (prayer) to *contemplatio* (contemplation). *Lectio divina's* role is to advance one's participation in prayer's development and process. Prayer, and thus *lectio divina*, is to give self to God in loving openness. It must be connected to everyday life and will advance meaning by its connection to everyday experiences and relationships. Finally, since the medium is Scripture, the greater one's familiarity with the Word of God, the more plentiful will be this practice of prayer.

Lectio divina is a practice that lay ecclesial ministers are urged to employ because it fosters a personal relationship with God and theological insight. It advances the work of preaching by steeping the minister in prayerful encounter with the sacred Word. This practice assures that the minister is always ready to proclaim. By practicing *lectio,* preachers are quick and nimble to communicate with others what has already been taken deep into one's own heart.

Contextual or Situational Analysis

Lay ecclesial ministers would also benefit from learning methods of analysis that will enable them to proclaim the Good News with relevance in local settings. The tools of this discipline, which are typically applied by a liturgical preacher in a specific

[10] Ibid., 49.

congregation, can be used to illuminate any setting in which the Word is being preached.

The present experience and objective reality of a people is always contextualized and interpreted from a perspective. This is true in worship settings and other settings such as a funeral home, school, or church meeting, where lay ecclesial ministers may be called upon to preach. Preachers should always be evaluating the context in which the Word is being preached.

The historical and cultural situation in which people live constructs the perceived reality in which they live, thus influencing their understanding of God and matters of faith. Excavating the layers of context in which people live, the preacher assesses their world so to see as they see. Recognizing the importance of the situation, the preacher attends faithfully to the needs of the people within a specific setting, thus avoiding the critical mistake of preaching to the needs of oneself.

Contextualized preaching, which is highly adaptive in practice, is the translation of the unchanging Gospel into forms and expressions decipherable for a specific, contemporary local congregation and/or setting. Leonora Tubbs Tisdale says contextualized preaching is preaching "which not only aims toward greater 'faithfulness' to the Gospel of Jesus Christ, but which also aims toward greater 'fittingness' (in content, form and style) for a particular congregational gathering of hearers."[11]

According to Tisdale the three aims of contextualized preaching are: 1) to help preachers remove false stumbling blocks which prevent the hearing of the Gospel in their proclamation; 2) to bridge the powerful Word of God with humanity's capacity to grasp the mystery of revelation; and 3) to give new meaning to Gospel proclamation and occasion a new understanding of it for a particular people.[12]

Paul Tillich in *Theology of Culture* asks the question, "How shall the [Gospel] message be focused for the people of our time...How do

---

[11] Leonora Tubbs Tisdale, *Preaching as Local Theology and Folk Art* (Minneapolis, MN: Augsburg Fortress, 1997), 33.
[12] Ibid., 34-37.

we make the message heard and seen, and then either rejected or accepted?"[13] Tillich's answer to the question instructs preachers and teachers to avoid thinking there is a guaranteed method in communicating the Gospel. Belief in or denial of the Gospel message is not contingent upon the preacher, but upon the Holy Spirit and the hearer. Thus the question for the preacher becomes how to communicate the Gospel without false stumbling blocks.

Before we can answer that, we must distinguish between genuine and false stumbling blocks. As Tisdale says, "Any message that has as its center a crucified messiah, requires its adherents to love their enemies and pronounces it easier for a camel to get through the eye of a needle than for a rich person to enter the realm of heaven is intrinsically offensive."[14] Though such a message may lead to rejection of the Gospel, Tisdale asserts that genuine stumbling blocks may never be removed from proclamation because doing so alters the Gospel itself.

False stumbling blocks are of another sort. They are stumbling blocks created by the preacher or the preaching event. Tisdale cites the following examples as false stumbling blocks: "the use of theological jargon which is empty of meaning for the hearers, the employment of a sermon structure that is too complicated and obtuse for the hearer to follow or the use of images and illustrations that fail to embody the Gospel in a believable way for a particular culture or faith community."[15] False stumbling blocks hinder the bona fide Gospel, creating needless barriers for the hearer. Therefore, the preacher is charged with removing false stumbling blocks—the first aim of contextualized preaching—because only when they are removed is the Gospel authentically proclaimed and the audience led to genuine hearing and the ability to accept or reject God's Word. Removing false stumbling blocks is a call to proclaim in ways that are, according to Tisdale, "simple, direct, authentic and clear."[16] However, that which is simple, direct, authentic, and clear fluctuates from congregation to congregation

---

[13] Paul Tillich, *Theology of Culture,* ed. Robert C. Kimball (New York: Oxford University Press, 1959), 201.
[14] Tisdale, 34.
[15] Ibid., 34-45.
[16] Ibid.

(or setting to setting). Thus, the preacher through methodical analysis must be familiar with the culture of the congregation, setting, or situation to avoid the use of false stumbling blocks.

The second aim of contextualized preaching—bridging between God's Word and humanity's capacity to grasp mystery—does not imply concession of the Gospel message. Rather, as Tisdale says, it reflects "the accommodating way in which God has dealt with humanity in revelation."[17] Accommodation reflects the very nature of God's interaction with humanity from the moment of creation. God condescends to our capacity. Human authors are appointed to express, through the Spirit's assistance, a divine message. The divine message, a revelation of God, is adapted to human ability and capacity for understanding. The divine message is in no way the fullness of God's revelation. It is accommodated for humanity's benefit. The message enables humanity to see something of God which otherwise may not be seen.[18] Scripture is one avenue (sacrament is another) that reveals the Divine in as much as humanity is able to capture the Divine. Preaching, according to Tisdale, must reflect the same accommodating way in which God has dealt with humanity in revelation.

The third aim of contextualized preaching is to give new meaning to Gospel proclamation by causing the Gospel to be heard in a new way for a specific community or situation. It is the act of making a text, even a text previously or frequently known, accessible in new ways. This third aim of contextualized preaching connects an ancient text with the contemporary experience in such a way that something is heard, and more importantly discerned, in a fresh and revitalizing way. New awareness leads to new meaning which is the ultimate goal of contextualized preaching.

Let us take for example a teen retreat in which a lay ecclesial minister has the responsibility to preach about the Cleansing of a Leper from the Gospel of Luke (5:12-16). A preacher who reflects on the average lives of teens in our culture is quick to assess that today's youth have very little understanding about leprosy and the social condition of lepers in the first century of the Common Era. The

[17] Ibid., 35.
[18] CCC, 101-104.

preacher begins by reflecting on the environment in which today's teens live. She must search for a way to relate the depth of exclusion experienced by the leper to something of the teens' own experiences. School is common ground and in their own schools they know the kids who are considered outcasts because of ethnicity, disability, sexuality, or socio-economic background. They all know the kids, albeit themselves or others, who seem to have no place with their peers, walk the halls alone, eat lunch alone, or ride the bus alone. By unpacking for the audience the leper's chiasmic separation from the village of life, the preacher enables a deeper understanding of the impact of Jesus' healing touch.

Contextual analysis is a methodological process the preacher engages to investigate the background, circumstances, and perspectives affecting a particular situation. Fidelity to the process will increase the chances of creating a message that has meaning for a particular people in a particular setting.

Biblical Criticism

The first question a lay ecclesial minister might ask when confronted with the term biblical criticism is, "What actually is biblical criticism?" *Biblical criticism* is a broad expression denoting a technical and methodical study of The Bible. It derives from the need to interpret and further discover what God has revealed to inspired authors and what those authors have communicated to humanity through the words of Sacred Scripture. Critical biblical study carefully examines biblical documents observing their historical setting, including geographical conditions and cultural circumstances, and analyzes the people and situation in and from which the documents were produced. Beyond historical study, biblical criticism also surveys the text and its literary forms to discover what the message was saying to its first audience and to make clear its message for today's believer. Thus, employing the term biblical criticism refers to a variety of methods that are engaged for the purpose of gathering and assessing comprehensive data about The Bible.[19]

---

[19] For further reading see *Dei Verbum* in the documents of Vatican II, Joseph A. Fitzmyer, *The Interpretation of Scripture: In Defense of the Historical-Critical Method* (Mahwah, NJ: Paulist Press, 2008) and Raymond E. Brown, *The Critical Meaning of the Bible* (Ramsey, NJ: Paulist Press, 1981).

Exegesis is another process by which a biblical text is systematically interpreted or explained. It raises questions about the text in search of understanding. The process does not begin with the question of meaning for the present time, but rather with the question of meaning within its original context. *Exegesis* investigates historical circumstances regarding authorship and composition so as to better grasp the message and meaning of Scripture. Utilizing resources that provide scholarly commentary of the biblical text will aid lay ecclesial ministers in the exegetical process.[20] Familiarity with the practices of biblical criticism will increase knowledge of Sacred Scripture and strengthen the ability to preach with fidelity the original meaning of the sacred text. By gathering and assessing comprehensive data about the Scriptures, the preacher is doing the hard but necessary work of uncovering the depth of Scripture's meaning. Engaging in critical biblical study, the preacher avoids the mistake of creating a message that is shallow. Dedication to intellectual study, in partnership with prayer and contextual analysis, results in a comprehensive and thorough outcome for the preaching event. However, one last, important practice awaits the preacher.

Crafting Language

Communicating the truth of an ancient text and converting it into meaningful language for contemporary people is a challenging task. It requires diligent study of the ancient text and the ability to craft a message that articulates the Word for present-day listeners. Converting language literally and metaphorically without compromising the original authors' intentions, while also allowing God's holy Word to speak as it will in the present moment, is a learned skill. It necessitates an understanding of basic rhetoric. The following rhetorical techniques are submitted as a means by which the task, at least in part, may be accomplished.

---

[20] An excellent biblical commentary for lay ecclesial ministers is *The Collegeville Biblical Commentary*, published by Liturgical Press. The series is the work of contemporary scholars who write for easy understanding of the biblical text. On-line resources offering biblical overviews and commentaries can be found at www.newadvent.org, www.BibleStudyTools.com, and www.Bible.org.

"The New Homiletic" is a term that describes a paradigmatic shift that occurred in preaching as a result of the changing cultural milieu in the United States during the last four decades of the twentieth century.[21] Christian preachers, of the late 1960s, 1970s, and 1980s, dreaming of new ways to connect with people in a radically changing society, are credited with new proposals that revised long-standing methods of Christian proclamation. The first book advocating The New Homiletic was *As One Without Authority,* by Fred Craddock.[22] Craddock's pioneering contributions to the inductive method of preaching were formally introduced in 1971.

Inductive preaching begins with concrete human realities and experiences and moves to the Gospel message. The power of the Gospel is to shed light upon and give meaning to the human experience. Inductive preaching identifies common and tangible experiences, and then applies Gospel principles to those experiences so that meaning can be established. Conclusions are drawn by allowing the assembly to participate in the process of understanding and to arrive at their own decisions or conclusions.

Inductive preaching espouses a different movement than deductive.[23] The movement is rooted in the experience of the hearer. A particular experience to which the hearer can relate is stated first and the preaching then moves to a general truth. From the general truth the hearer can draw his/her own conclusion, rather than the preacher making the application. I share the following as an example: Last year on a Sunday evening, I experienced the worst toothache I have ever had, and clearly the greatest pain I have ever known. The tooth had cracked so severely that the nerve was overtly exposed. There was a highway of wrenching pain moving between

---

[21] See Richard L. Eslinger, *A New Hearing: Living Options in Homiletical Method* (Nashville, TN: Abingdon Press, 1987) for more information on the founding principles and practitioners of The New Homiletic.
[22] Fred Craddock, *As One Without Authority: Revised and with New Sermons* (St. Louis, MO: Chalice Press, 2001).
[23] In the deductive method the main point is stated first, meaning that the conclusion precedes the development. There is a downward progression of thought. There is no collaborative exchange between speaker and hearer. It is an authoritarian delivery that has no dialogue with the assembly. Deduction reasons syllogistically from premise to premise to conclusion.

my jaw and the top of my head. Up all night and beyond desperate, I called the dentist's office and left a message saying that I would have to go to the emergency room if they did not call me the very first thing in the morning. I got the call. Come to the office. I walked in the door and was taken directly to the back room. The doctor walked in with a giant needle and told me to open wide. Within minutes the serum began to take effect. I looked directly at the dentist and said, "How do you spell salvation?" Before he could answer I spelled out "Novocain." In that moment I discovered a new way to relate to others what it is like to be freed from pain. I wondered, is this what St. Paul meant when he wrote, "The sting of death is sin, and the power of sin is the law; but thanks be to God, who gives us the victory through our Lord Jesus Christ" (1 Cor 15: 56-57)?

The success of the inductive method lies in the preacher's ability to engage the listener in the movement of thought. It is, as Craddock says, a trip the listener alone must make. The implication is that the journey leads to one's own personal conclusion; a conclusion not superimposed by the preacher. Thus, states Craddock, Christian responsibilities rely on "the intrinsic force of the hearer's own reflection."[24] The inductive method of preaching avoids imperative speech and abandons exhortation. Instead, it uses language that is illustrative and expressive and employs the use of analogy to paint mental pictures and create vivid ideas. The experiences of the gathered assembly are the explicit constituents (elements, ingredients, and ideas) forming the message; they are not postscript.

Explicit constituents include experiences that are common to all people. In the inductive approach the preacher can utilize a specific story that communicates a universal reality. Death, suffering, and love are examples of elements that are common to every people in every age in every place, regardless of the particulars by which one is affected. I use this story of my husband's grandmother as an example: During the last six weeks of her 101 years of life, my husband's grandmother became bedfast. We all began to wonder who of us would be with her when her time came. The Saturday before she died, I was the one sitting at the house. Every ten minutes or so, I would leave the sofa and walk gingerly into her bedroom, checking to see if her frail little frame was still breathing. Each time I

[24] Ibid., 49.

looked in on her, I wondered how much longer it would be. Three days later my sister-in-law called at the break of dawn and said, "Her hour has come." Long did I ponder "the hour" which was neither logical nor sixty minutes. I pondered the symbolic hour that signified the whole purpose of Jesus' life (John 12:23). I thought hard about the appointed time and what it meant for our Lord, for our loved ones, and ultimately for me. How do we live in the minutes of life always anticipating the hour of our real purpose?

The dawning of the New Homiletic brought forth another alternative to traditional deductive preaching. This alternative honed the use of image and imagination. Thomas Troeger in *Imagining a Sermon* suggests that preachers learn to be more imaginative in the art of preaching and offers numerous principles for accomplishing the task. He believes that experience and reflection inspire imagination which opens believers to God's revelation. Imagination requires attentiveness and close observation. It asks the question, "What do you see?" There are no preconceptions, and there is a certain freedom of experience as one begins to trust that common things are sources of revelation. Troeger recommends that preachers begin to ponder images that arise out of the daily world and to engage those images in creating messages of meaning which evoke reflection in listeners.

As preachers we are urged to alert the eye to keener sight, to find the extraordinary in the ordinary. It means to look and observe so that fresh images fill our hearts and vitalize our preaching. It beckons us to ask more questions of the world in which we live and answer them with graphic descriptions so that others can begin to see a picture. A keener eye uses visual detail to create messages of meaning. The question is: How do we help people "see" God? Paying attention to the things around us and the messages we receive enables us to create visual details that engage listeners.[25]

One day a pastor I know shared with me the following minor incident. Minor as it was, I began to sense something extraordinary in the ordinary. He told me that the bottom of his foot was really bothering him and he was going to the doctor to get it checked out. When he came back, he said that a piece of glass had lodged deep

---

[25] See Thomas Troeger, *Imagining a Sermon* (Nashville, TN: Abingdon Press, 1990).

into his skin. I asked him how that might have happened. He explained that a couple of weeks ago he had put some drinking glasses on the floor by his bedroom door to remember to take them to the kitchen in the morning. During the middle of the night, he made a trip to the bathroom and knocked over both glasses breaking them to pieces. He picked up the broken glass, ran the vacuum, and went back to bed. Obviously a piece of the glass was missed in the cleanup and at some point went into the foot, thus his little problem. Through his story I began to "see" ways in which a preacher could connect the things of life: good intentions, shattering silence, stumbling in the dark, a festering wound, and the need for healing, to Scripture (Luke 12:3, Luke 1:1-38, John 12:46, 1 Pet 2:9).

Troeger's method presses the question, how do we as ministers of the Word embrace the use of imagination in creating new ways of communicating the Christian message? Do we understand the world of symbol that influences contemporary youth and young adults? Can we consider new ways of communicating religious meaning to post moderns, generation Xers, and millennials? Embracing our own imaginations to come to new insights requires taking a risk. Conventional biblical images upon which many lay ecclesial ministers have been formed may have to give way to new images that expand our previous notions. By way of example, I offer the image of God as Father. It is true that Jesus used the image to describe God's likeness. The image is used to help us understand something very personal and intimate about God's relationship to Jesus and us. At the same time we recognize that all language of God is analogous; no word can ever fully communicate the totality of who God is. God is not only like a father, God is also like a rock (Ps 18:3), shepherd (Ps 23), mother (Isa 66:13), king (Ps 10:16), and light (Jas 1:17). It is exciting when one begins to think anew theologically. By exploring with people the full medley of biblical images that Scripture offers, a greater panorama is created by which to imagine, contemplate, and relate to God.

George A. Kennedy says, "Rhetoric is that quality in discourse by which a speaker or writer seeks to accomplish his purposes."[26] Crafting language and rhetoric advances preaching's goal which is to

---

[26] George A. Kennedy, *New Testament Interpretation through Rhetorical Criticism* (Chapel Hill: University of North Carolina Press, 1984), 3.

participate in the proclamation of God's dynamic saving Word, enabling the engagement and transformation of human hearts for the sake of Christ and the Reign of God. The art of organizing speech, selecting and arranging words, and creating a metaphorical dialogue in which the listener engages is the focal point of this preaching practice.

There is power in language. In preaching, language usage determines response. Successful preachers understand the importance of keeping words simple, inclusive, and suitable to the context. Meaningful language is used for the purpose of initial and ongoing conversion, transformation, and spiritual growth. Preachers attending to vivid, dramatic, and emotive language strive to unite intellect with spirit in order to accomplish the goal of preaching. Developing both sensitivity and skill in the choice of language is a fundamental preaching practice that should not be taken for granted. Knowledge, dexterity, and strategies of word usage all contribute to the outcome desired.

Shifting from classical forms of rhetoric—which promote logic, reason, clarity of argument, and persuasiveness of claim—to new models of rhetorical approach drive the preacher to the creative imagination. Principles to increase imaginative strategies guide this preaching process, creating forms that garner new responsiveness and perceptions of Scripture often previously unidentified.

Conclusion

The first action in the preaching *habitus* is to know both general themes and particular stories of Sacred Scripture. By daily and exhaustive immersion, we are called to engage the Word. This can be done in private prayer, at daily Mass, with prayer groups, or even through electronic media. The point is, in order to proclaim, teach and/or preach a word, one must first eat the Word. We grow in familiarity with Scripture through daily exposure. Daily exposure that is mixed with the discipline of critical biblical study creates the fermentation necessary for a deeper understanding of the Word of God.

Second, we are to develop the skill to see in the ordinary events of life, the extra-ordinary meaning of revelation. Sacred Scripture reveals all that is necessary for salvation. It is a book of promise. It is also a text that is culturally, religiously, historically, and socially diverse. It was written over centuries in a time very different than our own and yet it is filled with truths about the human condition. In our desire to experience and thus communicate God's love more fully, the preaching *habitus* calls us to be interpreters of the Word by engaging both the ancient world and our own.

Third, in many and varied settings, our task is to communicate, with contemporary image and story, sacred meaning that is often hidden from the understanding and knowledge of others. As lay ecclesial ministers we are less the academicians (though not without education or training) and more the artisans. We are called metaphorically to paint pictures, to compose melodies, to write prose, to dance new steps that reveal the God of love and mercy, who is made known to us most fully in Christ Jesus the Lord. We are craftspeople carving messages of meaning for the sake of salvation.

The preaching *habitus* is a way of life. The daily routine beckons us to eat right, see the ordinary in new ways, work creatively to craft a message, and use our gifts generously in proclaiming the Good News. I conclude with this final reflection which I believe communicates, in part, the responsibility we share as coworkers in the ministry of the Word.

I learned in the birth of my first child that giving birth is serious business. After the labor and delivery of a beautiful baby girl, the nurse assisted me to the restroom. Feeling the physical strain, I noticed that my legs were shaking, actually trembling uncontrollably. Without saying a word, I looked at the nurse who said, knowing the question that was never voiced, "It's the trauma of birth." Many years later during Morning Prayer I had the opportunity to preach at a day of recollection for priests. It was a minor feast day honoring the Blessed Mother. I began by saying, "Giving birth is serious business," and then retold my experience of "trauma." Reflecting with the priests I asked them, "Is it possible that the Mother of Jesus in her time of delivery also experienced the trauma of birth? Did it cause her to tremble? Or was it her honored status as the Mother of God, her unique role in giving birth to the Word that caused the real trembling?" There is no doubting it, giving birth is serious business and I suggested to the holy men gathered before me that they too participate in the serious business of birth every single time they bring forth the Word, preaching and teaching the Good News. I asked them, as I do you, "When was the last time it caused you to tremble?"

Questions for Reflection:

1. In what ways has your understanding of preaching been broadened or challenged?

2. In what ways do you think lay ecclesial preaching benefits the Church?

3. Would a better familiarity with the preaching *habitus* benefit your ministry? How?

Fruit on the Vine: Lay Ecclesial Preachers and Preaching Teams

Rodney Bluml

As we approach this important conversation about ministry of the proclaimed Word, let us keep before us a prayer and a few relevant quotes from recognized Church authorities that give us glimpses of the topic's import: Come Holy Spirit! *Ruach*! Breath of God! Animate us with the power of your divine love. Speak through us and together we will renew the face of the earth. Amen.

John 20:18:

> *Mary of Magdala went and announced to the disciples, "I have seen the Lord," and what [Jesus] told her.*

Canon Law, Code c. 759:

> *The lay members of Christ's faithful, by reason of their baptism and confirmation, are witnesses to the good news of the Gospel, by their words and by the example of their Christian life. They can also be called upon to cooperate with bishops and priests in the exercise of the ministry of the word.*[1]

John Paul II:

> *The images taken from the gospel of salt, light and leaven, although indiscriminately applicable to all Jesus' disciples, are specifically applied to the lay faithful. They are particularly meaningful images because they speak not only of the deep involvement and the full participation of the lay faithful in the affairs of the earth, the world and the human community, but also and above all, they tell of the radical newness and unique character of an*

---

[1] *Code of Canon Law, Codex Juris Canonici* (CIC), c. 759, (Washington, DC: Canon Law Society of America, 1983).

> *involvement and participation which has as its purpose the spreading of the Gospel that brings salvation.*[2]

US Catholic Bishops:

> *...we are pleased to support the ways in which more and more Catholics are celebrating the power of God's Word in evangelistic gatherings, in the catechumenate, and in groups devoted to the study of the Bible and to prayer. We also recognize that for the vast majority of Catholics, the Sunday homily is the normal and frequently the formal way in which they hear the Word of God proclaimed.*[3]
> *. . . and that lay members of Christ's faithful in each community are carefully trained for various liturgical functions, in keeping with the variety of charisms and in keeping with the norm of the law.*[4]

In 1982, when the United States bishops ratified and released the document *Fulfilled In Your Hearing,* "in hope for a renewal of preaching in the church today,"[5] they most likely did not imagine the reality that would emerge in the North American Catholic Church over the next three decades, a reality that now includes regular diaconal presence in parishes of the United States as well as the significant work of well educated lay ecclesial ministers and lay leaders. An example of this changing reality was felt in the 1980s and 1990s when some pastors were lifting up lay voices from the community to participate in the homiletic endeavor. This pastoral preference, which flowed from the spirit of the Vatican II liturgical renewal, gave the faithful additional

---

[2] *Christifideles Laici*, John Paul II on the Vocation and the Mission of the Lay Faithful in the Church and the World, accessed 08/23/2012, http://www.vatican.va/holy_father/john_paul_ii/apost_exhortations/documents/hf_jp-ii_exh_30121988_christifideles-laici_en.html, 15.

[3] Bishops' Committee on Priestly Life and Ministry, *Fulfilled in Your Hearing: the Homily in the Sunday Assembly* (Washington, DC: United States Conference on Catholic Bishops, 1982), 4.

[4] *Redemptionis sacramentum: On certain matters to be observed or to be avoided regarding the Most Holy Eucharist, USCCB publishing, Washington DC, 2004, or,* http://old.usccb.org/liturgy/documents/instruction.pdf, last modified 03/25/2004, accessed 08/18/2012, or http://www.vatican.va/roman_curia/congregations/ccdds/documents/rc_con_ccdds_doc_20040423_redemptionis-sacramentum_en.html, 150.

[5] Bishops' Committee, *Fulfilled in Your Hearing*, 2.

perspectives on the proclaimed Word, similar to shared storytelling during a Christmas meal.

As lay women and men embraced the invitation of Vatican II to become more theologically aware through pursuits in higher education and increased participation in the sacraments and Church polity, they often expressed a hunger for opportunities to hear truth explored by preacher voices that more closely reflected the makeup of the congregation. Often, the priest presider or deacon was exactly the right person to provide the homily. Other times, the priest called forth from another faithful person the *charism* and/or passion to deliver a word that could be effective. I recall several trusted pastors sharing with me during my college years that from their perspective this practice was in keeping with the demands of canon law and served as an act of humility and true apostolic discernment that reminded them of life in biblical Christian communities. In their opinions, this practice also confronted the human tendency to be threatened by another person's ability to manifest Holy Spirit's gift of proclaiming truth.[6] One seasoned priest quipped, "Why wouldn't I invite a woman to break open the experience of childbirth at Christ's nativity or a mother's perspective on the feast of the holy family? I can always expand on the theology if necessary, but I can't tell the story the same way she can." His comment was indicative of the climate that shaped the ecclesial world of my young adult years and enticed me to service in the Church.

Pastors such as these had the happy opportunity to shepherd their people in an ongoing dialogue with the proclaimed Word. However, after talking with some of those same priests in recent years, I would be hesitant to say this describes the prevailing climate of the Roman Catholic Church in the new millennium. Perhaps the new, more restrictive climate has developed because calling upon other community members to break open the Word doesn't ensure "orthodoxy" (understood to be the prevailing magisterial teaching) and actually manifests the Church's deepest concerns about who preaches. But the lack of "heresy" (used loosely to reflect a rigidity or lack of nuanced

---

[6] In this essay, the author's omission of the particular article "the" with "Holy Spirit" is intentional, as it refers to God's name.

thought) is never assured, especially in an eight minute homily. Limiting who can deliver homilies is one way to respond to the fear of misguided preaching, but perhaps our leaders have already opened a different, more inclusive path to addressing these apprehensions.

One of the changing aspects of the Catholic Church over the last twenty years has been the emergence of lay ecclesial ministers, as the bishops chose to refer to us in the *Co-Workers in the Vineyard of the Lord* document.[7] At a meeting of lay ecclesial ministers, I took the opportunity to informally survey the group about the ways they were breaking open the Word with their people. Of course, the responses were as varied as the *charism*s and faces in the room. A couple of people from smaller rural communities with elderly pastors reported giving reflections in the homily time of Sunday Mass, but this was not representative of the group's experiences. In the dialogue, though, I heard some powerful stories about circumstances which led to the calling forth of spiritual gifts in ways that pushed the boundaries of the norms of the Church, and when shared, were celebrated as true encounters with Holy Spirit.

I would like to share a few examples that confirm what the United States bishops lifted up in the introduction to *Fulfilled in Your Hearing:* "Indeed, the proclamation of the Word of God is the responsibility of the entire Christian community by virtue of the sacrament of baptism/confirmation."[8]

1. To Follow the Letter of the Law or Your Pastoral Nose; That Is a Question: The parents contacted the pastor the day after their twenty-seven year old daughter died. She left a grieving husband whose relationship to the Roman Catholic Church was tenuous at best. They were seeking comfort, reaching out for sturdy handholds in their community of faith. "Can Ann, the youth minister, give the homily at Laura's funeral?[9] She knew her so well and was an important part of Laura's high school years,

---

[7]United States Conference of Catholic Bishops, *Co-Workers in the Vineyard of the Lord*: *A Resource for Guiding the Development of Lay Ecclesial Ministry* (Washington, DC: United States Catholic Bishops, 2005), 10.

[8] *Fulfilled in Your Hearing*, 4.

[9] All names and places in the anecdotes have been changed to protect the privacy of the individuals involved.

helping her through some tough times. Laura often referred to her with affection. It would mean a lot to us."

The pastor intently listened then said, "I'll have to get back to you." He went to the office and shared the conundrum with the pastoral associate. The pastor recognized that Ann had a personal relationship with Laura's family and that her Master's degree in pastoral ministry certainly provided her the competency she needed for the task. He wanted to recognize her ability to deliver an inspired and informed message to the grieving family; after all he had witnessed her enthusiasm for the Scriptures and Church tradition in large group confirmation sessions with 150 adults and teens, but he worried that someone in the congregation would get wind of it and complain to the bishop.[10] It had happened once before and led to a quick reprimand from the chancery.

Having already had a funeral on Monday, and a wedding on the docket for the weekend, he was being asked to prepare his fourth major homily for the week, a number which doesn't include daily Mass reflections or the Vigil Service. He revealed that he often grows exhausted, not because the preaching ministry is difficult for him, but because of the sheer time and mental and spiritual energy it demands to craft a homily that inspires while bringing glory to God. He was concerned that because of the number of homilies he was asked to deliver, he was beginning to grow stale. He knew of other priests who rotated through a series of four or five funeral homilies they pulled out of a file after meeting with the family. He wondered if this request wasn't actually an answer to a prayer.

As the conversation continued, the pastoral associate related an experience he had some years earlier when a couple asked if he could preach at their wedding. He had known the couple since high school, and had become friendlier with their families during the wedding preparation. The pastor at the time recognized the existing relationship and because it was a wedding without a Mass, reasoned that it was within preaching norms to have the pastoral associate use his well-known *charism* for speaking and

---

[10] see note 21 below, specifically: "Preaching by the lay faithful may not take place within the Celebration of the Eucharist at the moment reserved for the homily."

teaching, his theological prowess, and his training in Scripture to break open the Word. It was memorable to the pastoral associate because it became a time he felt most fulfilled in his ministry with the flock whom he had served for fifteen years as a married lay man.

The pastor thanked the pastoral associate and decided to investigate the commentary on canons 766 and 767 for some additional insight on preaching. There, he learned that the reservation of the homily to the ordained was not part of the deposit of faith but could be understood as an ecclesiastical preference.[11] The ideals supporting the priest presider's primary preaching role, as expressed in *The Decree on the Life and Ministry of Priests*[12] were set forth to maintain the unity of the two tables: Word and Eucharist. In the person of the priest, the organic connection between story and meal is maintained for the sake of order within the body of the faithful, but that does not mean preaching need be exclusive to the priest presider. While this exclusive preference is clearly stated without explanation in the 1983 *Code of Canon Law*, exceptions already exist, as when a deacon or guest homilist preaches.[13]

After careful reflection, the pastor invited the youth minister to preach following his two minutes of introductory remarks.

---

[11] *New Commentary on the Code of Canon Law*, edited by John P. Beal, James A. Coriden, and Thomas J. Green (Mahwah, NJ: Paulist Press, 2000), 927-930.

[12] *Presbyterorum Ordinis:* Decree on the Ministry and Life of Priests, Pope Paul VI, December 7, 1965, found in *Vatican Council II: the Conciliar and Post Conciliar Documents*, edited by Austin Flannery, O.P., Costello Publishing Co., Northport, NY, 1987: "4. The People of God is formed into one in the first place by the word of the living God which is quite rightly sought from the mouth of priests. For since nobody can be saved who has not first believed and it is the first task of the priest as co-workers of the bishops to preach the Gospel of God to all men. In this way they carry out the Lord's command: "Going therefore into the whole world preach the Gospel to every creature" (Mk 16:15), and thus set up and increase the people of God. For by the saving Word of God faith is aroused in the heart of unbelievers and is nourished in the heart of believers. By this faith then the congregation of the faithful begins and grows, according to the saying of the apostle: Faith comes from what is heard and what is heard comes by the preaching of Christ. (Rom 10:17)."

[13] Code of Canon Law, c. 767, §1(Washington, DC: Canon Law Society of America), 1983, 289.

They agreed to meet before the vigil service to talk through her outline. Pastorally, he felt good about responding to the family's request, mostly because he was confident Ann would not eulogize as much as break open the Scriptures through the deceased woman's life story. Personally, he didn't want to appear as though he was playing a game to get around canon law, but this was the accommodation needed to create the right situation. He would let the pieces fall as they may. As it turned out, there was nothing but gratitude expressed in the aftermath.

2. Calendar Conflicts and Charism; More than One Crisis Here: The priest of the parish where Sharon served as a lay ecclesial minister called her in a panic. He was leaving the country on his vacation a day earlier than expected and a funeral was now scheduled. No other ordained ministers from the area were available to preside. "I have not yet met with them. Would you please minister to this family?"came the request. Because of her training for certification in her diocese (which included a Master's Degree in Theology and several years of ecclesial employment) and her past experience preparing funeral liturgies with bereaved families, she felt adequate for the task.

When Sharon arrived at the funeral home, she sought out the two adult children of the deceased to talk through the service scheduled to begin in sixty minutes. As she attempted to discuss the readings she had selected and some logistics for the *Funeral Liturgy Outside Mass*, the family's alienation from the Church began to emerge through their timid responses. She probed a little and found there had been unresolved hurt feelings from many years earlier when the pastor publicly reprimanded their now deceased mother for chewing gum as she processed into Mass with her first communicant. Sharon listened, reflecting on how fragile some people are while recognizing that an opportunity for healing was opening in front of her. As time melted away, she sensed growing internal panic about being prepared for the funeral service. Her head swam with new details about the deceased person and her heart strained with the desire to reach through the family's alienation.

Just as she finished perusing the ritual Scriptures for a final time, the funeral director approached and asked if she would gather the family for prayer in a side room while he closed the casket. She graciously agreed and upon entering the room was surprised to find herself surrounded by thirty people. She steadied herself and led them in a spontaneous prayer for consolation and comfort. When it came time for the Amen, only a handful responded. She looked around at the heads bent in sorrow. The grief was palpable. The funeral director was not calling them out into the main room, so she grasped the opportunity to engage in story telling about the deceased woman as would have been invited at a funeral vigil, had there been one.

Much to her surprise, the people lit up. For ten minutes, the group regaled her with heart-warming stories of baking, traveling, singing, and Thanksgivings past. The group was now smiling; alive with some new sense of communion. She was able to carry the mood of the group into the prayer service, coaxing them to sing a few verses of "Though the Mountains May Fall." Moved by Holy Spirit, she was able to weave a few of the images the family had shared into the Scripture reflection. She even invited one sister to retell her story of a family Christmas because it brought to life the message Paul was making in Philippians 4: 4-7, "Rejoice in the Lord always! I will say it again, Rejoice!" She told the mourners that Paul was responding to a quarrel between two women leaders in the Christian community at Philippi. He told them that kindness, or patient forbearance when provoked, was to be their first virtue, especially in settling a dispute. She took Paul's message one step further by reminding them that they are called to reconciliation, and this death was an opportunity to allow new, healed life to emerge.

At the graveside, after they had committed their mother and friend to the loving embrace of God, the pastoral associate was embraced by several family members whom she had met a mere two hours earlier; she was held again and again in wordless thanks. Their tear-filled eyes reflected the depth of their encounter with God that day.

Two weeks later, Sharon received from the family a copy of a thank you letter sent to the pastor: "While we understood why you couldn't be with us, we so appreciated having Sharon lead our mother's funeral service. She listened and guided us towards the possibility of returning to the faith. Her sermon in particular touched our hearts. Thank you. We have included a gift."

When she shared this story with colleagues, she began to cry, not out of joy for having been the instrument of God for these people, but because the pastor never acknowledged the letter, the gift, or her willingness to step in when needed. "Why?" she wondered. "Is it because I'm a woman or not ordained or did a good job and that's threatening? Why?" she asked on the verge of a sob. Her colleagues sat with her in stunned silence.

With some encouragement, she asked the pastor about it. She later reported that when she inquired about the letter, the pastor seemed surprised and fumbled through his words. She walked away from the encounter feeling caught in an uncomfortable disconnect, empowered by Holy Spirit to be a vineyard co-worker but disempowered by the one she had assisted in tending the vineyard.

3. Ecumenical Affirmation: Jerry is a lay pastoral associate in his Catholic parish. For ten years, he has been gathering with the local ecumenical group. The Protestant ministers marvel at his depth of faith and even rib him about not being a "real Catholic" because of the breadth of his scriptural knowledge. Last Thanksgiving, the group invited Jerry to give the sermon at the city-wide ecumenical service that usually draws about 250 people including a sizeable number from Jerry's parish. After momentarily wondering aloud if he should defer to his pastor who would be attending, he shook his head, smiled, and gratefully accepted.

Attendees heard Jerry artfully apply Luke 17: 11-19, the healing of the ten lepers, to the event. He began by sharing about his own first Communion. It was the early 1970s, and his mother while under the influence of "flower power," dressed him in a wine-colored outfit. Of course, at church he stuck out like a bruised thumb and felt totally embarrassed for being different than the rest of the "normal group" of boys dressed in polyester grays and greens. He was sick to his stomach through the Liturgy of the Word and desperately wanted to flee the situation, but then his feelings slowly began to change as he knelt, listening to the words of Jesus in the Eucharistic Prayer. When he received Communion, he had an encounter with Christ. No longer did it matter what he was wearing. Christ came to him, just like all the others, and he had a warm sense of being okay.

Jerry talked about the lepers being part of the "out group" and how serious the religious leaders were when determining who was "in or out" based on observable differences like flaky skin or improper clothing. He went on to contrast Jesus' response with the assumptions of those leaders. "When the lepers longingly cried out, what did they expect," Jerry pondered, "to be ignored, to be scowled at, to be silenced?" Jerry continued:

> Much to their surprise, Jesus spoke to them with dignity. He did not see sinners; he saw brothers in pain. He pronounced them not-responsible for their condition; clean. "Go show yourselves." On the way, they realized they were healed. Filled with joy, nine hurried back into the fray of family and village life.
>
> The lone foreigner returned to the place of his encounter with Jesus to say "Thank You." The one who was considered devoid of grace became a symbol for the righteous because in naming the dignity shown him by Jesus as the source of his healing, he could return to wholeness again and again. It was for all ten that Jesus came, but for this one, Jesus became communion.

Jerry scanned the sanctuary, "I wonder which of us will be the first to act as Jesus did: calling out 'Come in!' to the outsider; listening for the voice that asks for mercy or pity; looking for an opportunity to engage in communion. We come together this time of year with the invitation to receive each other as brothers and sisters in Christ. No foreigners, no lepers, no Gerezim or Jerusalem, no one deprived of communion. It is in this gathering that we encounter the healing Christ and it is here that we pause to say 'Thank You, God.'" The congregation responded to his words with sustained applause while Jerry looked down at the section of smiling clergy.

After the service, in between mouthfuls of pie, a Methodist man asked Jerry when he would be preaching again in his home church because he might like to hear him. Jerry had to confess that he was not allowed to preach at Mass and rarely is asked to reflect on the Word in his own community. Another minister standing nearby queried if Jerry would be interested in preaching in his church. Jerry scanned the ceiling as if an answer was etched there, then, with a wry smile on his face, respectfully declined the offer saying, "It would probably be too confusing for my family, Catholic friends, and most likely, my own heart. But let me pray about it, and if the invitation remains open down the road, I may take you up on it."

4. Validation That Invalidates: Stephanie is invited by the pastor to be in a regular preaching rotation at the weekday parish Masses when the Catholic grade school students are in attendance. He sees it as a way to integrate her voice into the preaching ministry while keeping with the exception noted in the *Directives for Masses with Children*: "With the consent of the pastor or rector of the church, one of the adults may speak to the children after the gospel, especially if the priest finds it difficult to adapt himself to the mentality of children."[14] While he feels comfortable speaking with the children, he enjoys sharing this forum in which her storytelling abilities and keen scriptural insights can be lavished upon the children.

One morning, Stephanie was playfully dialoguing with the students about the multiple ways Christ is really present in the Eucharist.[15] Suddenly, a man began shouting from the back of the church. He stood up, slammed his backpack to the ground, and began to spout canon laws concerning who could validly deliver a homily. As his voice grew in volume, he accused her of making the entire Eucharist invalid by violating liturgical law. It appeared he was going to charge down the center aisle, but when the presider stood up, the man abruptly turned on his heel and ran out the door of the church, leaving behind his backpack. Many of the younger children were murmuring in confusion and even crying because of the harsh attack on their friend; an air of chaos enveloped the Mass. Stephanie resolved her reflection with the invitation, "Let us take each other's hands and pray....

---

[14] *Directory on Children's Masses*, Congregation for Divine Worship, Nov. 1, 1973, found in *Vatican Council II: the Conciliar and Post Conciliar Documents*, edited by Austin Flannery, O.P., Costello Publishing Co., Northport, NY, 1987, 24§2.

[15] *Sacrosanctum concilium: Constitution on the Sacred Liturgy*, found in *Vatican Council II: the Conciliar and Post Conciliar Documents*, edited by Austin Flannery, O.P., Costello Publishing Co., Northport, NY, 1987, (Article 7: Congregation, Word, Presider, song/prayer, Bread & Wine).

God, be very close to us right now." She stood still, and slowly, calm replaced the cacophony.

Because the cultural climate involved a heightened sensitivity to the protection of children, the principal and several support staff immediately pursued the man. The gym teacher grabbed the abandoned backpack on his way out. Someone called the police as they locked down the church. The police found the man crouched behind a truck in the parking lot. After briefly talking with the man and sensing he was not a physical threat, the pastor asked the police to remove the handcuffs.

The pastor learned that the man was visiting a parish family affiliated with a movement bent on ridding the Church of abuses. He ranted at the pastor about his "sin" in allowing a woman to preach. To the pastor's credit, he never apologized for the decision and simply rebuked the man for not knowing Church law as well as he claimed. The pastor pointed out that the man's behavior had done more to invalidate the Eucharist than anything the female pastoral associate could have said. The man left in the company of a highly embarrassed host family.

An Opportune Time to Expand the Preaching Ministry

In each of these four episodes, a lay preacher was called upon to break open the Word of God and successfully emerged to honor God by expressing knowledge rooted in his or her relationship with the Word. Even in potentially adverse situations where there was angst about how the voice of a lay preacher would be received, some priests chose to respond to pastoral needs by calling on lay preachers while attempting to respect the spirit of the official guidelines. Regardless of how you feel about the correctness of these pastoral decisions, hopefully the stories about lay ecclesial ministers faithfully proclaiming God's Word within formal liturgical gatherings opened a place in your heart for the idea of a new ecclesial designation: that of the trained but not-ordained Preacher, formed and supported by local preaching teams.

Generally speaking, people respond to authentic preaching; hopefully, the first response is not a negative reaction to the preacher's gender or marital status. A less than positive response to a female or married male preacher these days is somewhat understandable since the official position of the Church on lay preaching is muddled partly due to the lack of uniformity in the practice. However, the anecdotes accentuate a modern reality in which lay preaching is being done, and done well; a type of "historical aha." Perhaps it is time to read canon law concerning liturgical preaching a bit differently for the sake of charismatic lay preachers and hungry Eucharistic bodies who yearn for their voices to be heard, their perspectives to be embraced and their questions to be answered.

As the priest in the "Following Your Pastoral Nose" story noted, reserving the Eucharistic preaching role to the priest presider is not part of the deposit of faith but is an ecclesiastical preference.[16] The designation of who preaches is not codified in a creed or Scripture.

It occurs to me that the Church has experienced tension around the role of legitimate preaching authority virtually from the beginning. In the second chapter of this book, Jerid Miller reminds us that the Church's gospel was first spread by lay preachers such as Mary Magdalene, the Emmaus disciples, the Samaritan woman at the well, and Jesus himself. Further, a brief review of Church history shows us that in response to historical trauma, lay leaders consistently emerged to search creatively for a new "historical aha" or expression of truth.

As the Church expanded throughout the Roman Empire in the first century after Christ, established roles of leadership and structure organically emerged. The empowerment to act or speak in the name of the Church came through laying on of hands and quickly was equated with clerical status. In the Christian Testament, we notice this act being reserved for men almost immediately. We find the first written statements concerning a restricted role for teaching and preaching the Good News by the second century when the *Didascalia Apostolorum* forbade women, even deaconesses, to teach because they were not commissioned to do so by our Lord.[17] While this opinion reflects a stunted reading of the gospels and Acts, the author believed that potential Gentile converts who were used to being taught by

---

[16] see notes 11 & 12 above

[17] *Didascalia Apostolorum* , translated by R. Hugh Connolly, (Oxford: Clarendon Press, 1929), chapter 15.

men would scoff at the gospel being delivered by uneducated women.

By 453 CE, Pope Leo the Great wrote a letter forbidding laypersons to preach, reserving that function only to those of the priestly order. Apparently, this was to ensure the orthodoxy of several newly defined articles of faith adopted at the Ecumenical Council of Chalcedon in 451 as they were taught to the faithful, including the doctrine that Christ was one person with two natures.

Similarly, the Church fathers of the Fourth Lateran Council (1215) sought to eradicate creeping heresy by regulating the quality of preaching and thus required ordination to preach publicly. The exception to this policy came with the rise of the mendicant orders under Francis of Assisi and Dominic of Castile. They were lifted up by Pope Innocent III to replace the self-serving clerics whose spiritual abuses were being highlighted in the street preaching of lay Cathars and Waldensians. These new orders of wandering preachers mostly comprised of lay brothers were officially integrated into the Church and provided personnel for preaching that went beyond the accepted practice of ordained canons or monks.[18] The hierarchy of the Inquisition hoped that the preaching of Dominicans and Franciscans would help increase fidelity to the Word and the Church.

Following the Reformation in which Martin Luther attempted to remove the distinctions between clergy and laity for the sake of the full recognition of the universal priesthood of believers, the prohibition against lay preaching was intensified by the counter-reforming Council of Trent (1545-1563) in order to reinforce the unique role of the cleric. Likewise, it could be reasoned that the 1917 Code of Canon Law, which stated that "all laymen, religious as well, are forbidden to preach in church" (c. 1342 §2) was written to maintain order during the rapid expansion of Catholic missionary efforts in which women and men religious orders were establishing schools and churches throughout the world. This idea is carried into the 1983 Code; however, the necessity for Eucharistic preaching to be done

---

[18] Patricia A. Parachini, A *Guide for Lay Preachers* (Chicago: Liturgy Training Publication, 2000), 14-16.

exclusively by the ordained is being challenged in some circles as we negotiate a modern historical trauma of a different type; one that is not focused on the control of laity but rather on the credibility of the clergy after an actual and perceived sexual abuse scandal.

The Roman Catholic Church presumes the preaching *charism* in the person of the ordained and ratifies it in the faculties granted at ordination. At different times in history, it has been necessary for the Church to protect the ignorant faithful and the mission of the Church by relegating the public preaching role to the ordained that were presumed to be more scripturally educated. The various Codes of Canon Law were written throughout history because it is right and just that the Church helps all her members to grow in the word of God. But as I mentioned above, much has changed since the 1983 Code was passed, and the enforcement of the canons becomes more difficult when respect for authority has eroded. To that end, James Eldon Hayes, STL, points out what might be significant for our day and time: "The *Code of Canon Law* arises from the values of the Church, but those values are explicitly lived in daily experience and in the prayer, or liturgy, of the same People of God. The success of liturgical preaching requires knowledge of God's people, the sacred Scriptures, and the rites of the Church, as well as an appropriate amount of time spent in preparation. The liturgies of the Church seem to recognize the significance of liturgical preaching and the rubrics therein provide some latitude to the 'who' of preaching in order that it might be done effectively."[19]

As we search for another "historical aha" and consider the "who" of preaching, we keep in mind the signs of the times—the significance of people's exposure to the Scriptures through the Eucharistic homily, more highly educated laity, greater amounts of data readily accessible through technology and media, the invitation by the bishops for collaboration in the vineyard of the Lord, and the pastoral relationship lay ecclesial ministers already

---

[19] James E. Hayes, *Ongoing Formation of Preachers within a Diocese: A Collaborative Model*, presented to the faculty of the Aquinas Institute of Theology, Saint Louis, MO, in partial fulfillment of the requirements for the degree Doctor of Ministry in Preaching, 2004, 66.

have with the flock— and we might find ourselves speculating that it is time to move away from an either/or stance on preaching authority to a both/and perspective by considering a new designation or office in the ecclesial structure; that of Preacher.

In her essay in this volume, Linda Lee Ritzer describes the *habitus* needed to form any preacher, inside or outside the ecclesial structure. In this case, a person—female or male, married or single, who is inspired by Holy Spirit or called upon by his or her community—could seek formation in the art of homiletics without a desire for ordination, and after a period of scrutiny by duly appointed authorities, be commissioned or appointed by the bishop to preach in liturgical assemblies in concert with the priest presider. This is not intended to add another clerical layer but would serve to legitimize any person's call and subsequent formation to proclaim a homily. A precedent has been created in that the functions and faculties of the deacon have changed throughout history, from the call to serve at table to the preaching ministry of Philip and Stephen to the presidential and administrative roles of modern deacons. Can we not also recognize this evolution in the liturgical roles of the formed and impassioned lay baptized?

For a fuller development of these ideas, I turn to the excellently constructed and researched exploration of this topic by Hayes. In his thesis project, Hayes made a strong case for a new team approach to preaching that would allow for and even support the role of Preacher. He submitted that collaborative, regional preaching teams or pods, consisting of both lay and ordained preachers raised up from within a cluster or parish, could provide effective, ongoing preacher formation and accountability. At the discretion of appointed preachers, other trusted lay people or preachers from other churches could be invited into a pod. This arrangement becomes possible and even desirable if one reads the US Bishops' *Complementary Legislation for Canon 766* as an empowerment of local clergy to call other people into ministry of the Word based on their sense of community need and competency of potential preachers:

> If necessity requires it in certain circumstances or it seems useful in particular cases, the diocesan bishop can admit

> lay faithful to preach, to offer spiritual conferences or give instructions in churches, oratories or other sacred places within his diocese, when he judges it to be to the spiritual advantage of the faithful.
>
> In order to assist the diocesan bishop in making an appropriate pastoral decision (Interdicasterial Instruction, *Ecclesiae de Mysterio*, Article 2 §3), the following circumstances and cases are illustrative: the absence or shortage of clergy, particular language requirements, or the demonstrated expertise or experience of the lay faithful concerned.
>
> The lay faithful who are to be admitted to preach in a church or oratory must be orthodox in faith, and well-qualified, both by the witness of their lives as Christians and by a preparation for preaching appropriate to the circumstances.[20]

When one looks at the first part of this commentary along with documents like *Christifideles Laici* and *Co-Workers in the Vineyard,* it seems that the bishops have laid the groundwork for a creative response to the current dilemma of diminished clergy numbers by recognizing the authentic call of lay leadership. However, bishops and local clergy are prevented from fully utilizing lay people in preaching teams by the last paragraph of the same commentary which inexplicably reiterates: "In providing for preaching by the lay faithful the diocesan bishop may never dispense from the norm which reserves the homily to the sacred ministers (c. 767, §1; cfr. Pontifical Commission for the Authentic Interpretation of the Code of Canon Law, 26 May 1987, in AAS 79 [1987], 1249). Preaching by the lay faithful may not take place within the Celebration of the Eucharist at the moment reserved for the homily."[21] Based on the bishop's earlier statements, we know that the empowerment of lay preachers is not a concession but an act of justice on behalf of the community; so, why the

---

[20]United States Conference of Catholic Bishops, *Complementary Legislation for Canon 766* (Washington, DC: United States Conference of Catholic Bishops, 2001), accessed August 24, 2012, http://usccb.org/beliefs-and-teachings/what-we-believe/canon-law/complementary-norms/canon-766-lay-preaching.cfm.
[21] Ibid.

continued exclusion of lay preachers from the pulpit in Eucharistic liturgies? Hayes writes: "In the liturgy of the Word, we could make the case that no one is an expert or a novice; all are servants of the Word. In the instance of preaching, the needs of the congregation, the experiences of the preachers themselves, and the work of God's Spirit, active in the pages of Scripture and the lives of all involved also animate the process. After all, the entire community is responsible for the animation of the preached Word."[22] If what Hayes writes is true, what is to prevent the Church from implementing fully inclusive preaching teams?

When I reflect on my many experiences of liturgy planning over the years, I am led to lend my voice in support of preaching pods being made normative for the benefit of the Church's preaching ministry. One of my most positive experiences came when I had been invited to preside and preach at a parish Ash Wednesday Service. In the prior week, I broke open the readings with a group of teenagers, lay adults, and a deacon. The shared insights and suggestions guided me to read Dr. Seuss's *The Sneetches* as a modern parable about the hypocrisy Jesus was addressing in the religious leadership of his day, an effective thought I would not have come to on my own. The experience was so rewarding, I find myself longing to be part of a preaching team today.

More than likely, we can all reference experiences of preaching where the one who has competence/authority does not express a *charism*, and the ones with preaching *charisms* are not given authority. Presided over by the local priest or deacon, the preaching pod could enhance the marriage of *charism* and competence by providing a dignified environment for mutual support and critique between clergy, commissioned lay preachers, and trusted members of the flock. It is a way the professional ministers can empower the baptized to carry out their call to preach and teach in all forums while forming their own *habitus* for effective preaching.

For bishops who see the benefits of supporting this structure, there are a variety of preaching preparation programs throughout the United States in seminaries, permanent diaconate

---

[22] Hayes, *Ongoing Formation*, 109.

programs, and for lay people in some dioceses (e.g., Milwaukee, Saginaw, Minneapolis) to assist with basic theological training. In addition to theological formation, local preaching pods would include regular meetings to view recorded homilies and share feedback statements solicited from parishioners in order to form preachers in previously established competencies.[23]

It can be difficult to know how to communicate effectively these ideas to decision-makers in the Church. Not many of us feel empowered to approach the bishop with what may be perceived as an idea that is radical, or worse yet, disrespectful. Yet knowing that new ideas and programs often take decades to root and flourish, let us commit ourselves to introducing the idea of Preacher and/or preaching teams into conversations when parishioners, peers, or clergy appear open to receiving it. Perhaps over time the ideas will bear fruit.

Conclusion

It is true that lay people are already preaching in a variety of venues, particularly when priests/deacons are not available: funeral vigils, ecumenical services, parent meetings for sacramental preparation, RCIA sessions, mission/fundraiser talks, Children's Liturgy of the Word, Communion Services in nursing homes, etc. Still, the Sunday pulpit is the primary place of encounter between the majority of Catholic worshippers and Scripture. For this reason alone, perhaps it is time for the Catholic Church to join the church universal in recognizing and calling forth the *charisms* that undergird effective proclamation

---

[23] Ibid, 79, 139: Examples of these competencies include: Personal (ability to present self and message to others, intro/conclusion, eye contact, enunciation, pace, use of examples, etc.); Liturgical (ability to speak and act as minister of the liturgy, including rites and seasons); Interpretive (inculturated, ability to correlate and interpret Scripture and human experience, congregational/relational awareness, historical context); Clarifying (ability to speak clearly and insightfully about the Scriptures, theological context, use of commentary); Actualized/Sacramental (ability to facilitate actualization of Scriptures, use of images, story). For further exploration of the PLICA application, see chapter three and following of Stephen DeLeers, *Written Text Becomes Living Word: The Vision and Practice of Sunday Preaching* (Collegeville, MN: Liturgical Press, 2004).

of the homily already present within the wider ecclesial body. The Word is given to build up, and to that end has real authority, regardless of the preacher's gender and/or marital status. Objectively, it appears many lay ecclesial ministers already recognize that faithfulness to the Word is itself empowering and that vitality in a community is the fruit of a competent *charism*. Let that be an equal factor when deciding who is invited by local leadership to break open the word in the Eucharistic assembly.

There are countless stories of lay ecclesial ministers allowing Holy Spirit's power to explode through them, and regardless of the Catholic Church's official stance on the role of lay preachers in the context of Eucharist, the Word of God is faithfully being proclaimed. Since it is everyone's responsibility to foster the *charism* for preaching through study and formation, I would encourage lay ecclesial ministers to engage this task by breaking open the Sunday Scriptures with local groups of interested people. Invite the clergy to join you and begin to form the *habitus* of team scriptural reflection so that wherever and whenever the call to herald the Word is heard, the lay ecclesial minister can faithfully respond.

Questions for Reflection:

1. In what ways did this essay challenge or reinforce your beliefs about preaching? Did any of the four anecdotes resonate with your experience?

2. What could be some personal, professional, and/or ecclesial benefits of participating in a "preaching pod"?

3. How do you identify and nurture the preaching *charism* in yourself and others?

Section Three:

Transformation Through Ministry

Adversity and Identity: Transformed Together in Jordan's Currents

Dan Frachey

Like any other relationship, be it romantic or simply friendly, many enter into ministry impelled by the expectancy that we can join others who are also striving to further the Kingdom of God. As the needs of the community surface, we set about the work at hand with a joyful vigor, poised for action and achievement. In the midst of our ministry, inevitable moments occur when those of us working shoulder to shoulder bump into one another, introducing a moment of friction resulting from such close proximity. That friction has the tendency to reveal the different assumptions and ministerial dispositions that each person brings to that communal work. Tensions often rise, and that original zeal everyone brought wanes a bit. Life on a ministerial team now appears more challenging than we anticipated!

For any minister who tries to stay true to his or her calling, adversity surfaces from time to time. In such situations, the source of adversity may stem from the difficulties of working with one's pastoral team. Though each team member may be a person of integrity and basic goodness, there are times when the differences in temperament and personality might seem substantial enough to become the cause of our undoing and self-removal. Gradually we can come to see how adversity has the power (pleasant or not) to shape positively our identity as one working in parish ministry.

For the laity in the Church, working as a team is especially a struggle in so far as we are attempting to forge an identity as lay ecclesial ministers. Such team work has brought to mind the account of Jesus' disputes with the religious leaders in John 10, where he clashed with some of the Jews about his statement to the people that he was one with his Father in heaven. After some intense sparring about his identity, Jesus returns to the Jordan River; to the place where John baptized others. It is here that Jesus is affirmed by those who recognize his authority and goodness. The adversity in John's story is the result of the conflicted relationship between Jesus and the established religious leaders who have come to hate him. We must work and pray that this fractured relationship John depicts does not prevent today's lay ecclesial ministers from collaborating with our ordained brother priests and bishops as called for in the document *Co-Workers in the Vineyard of the Lord.*[1]

As a lay ecclesial minister I have observed conflict between lay ministers, some ordained ministers and our fellow lay members. Conflict is inevitable for anyone who strives to serve as a minister because entering into the waters of ministry eventually brings one against the currents of the status quo. To be a minister today means becoming a proponent of change and conversion. It is an odd juxtaposition of truths that greets the would-be minister. On one hand the word "religion" has at its root *legare* referring to how the ligaments, bound together, help connect the body's muscle tissue and help it work as a singular force of mobility. Ligaments magnificently keep the body aligned by allowing the flesh to maintain a sufficient tension with the structure of the bones. As this is true for our bodies, it is true for the Church because of how we seem to bear the tension of conflict where people meet the hard institutional structures that keep the Church standing tall. On the other hand, to be religious today is to stand posed in an uneasy tension, rather, in opposition to the dominant culture which seeks to find its own way without ties to most religious traditions. More difficult still is how within the body of Christ, the minister can find him or herself suddenly feeling like an embattled hockey player checking his or her own teammates--the very ones that God has called us to serve *with!*

Given this present and undeniable state of tension that all ministers must reckon with, we will first examine the basis for our ministerial identity and contextualize it within the realities that we face in our attempts to fulfill the calling that brought us into the coursing and foreboding waters of service to the Church. Such a proposition is guaranteed to sweep the hopeful lay ecclesial minister into swift currents and deeper waters that will throw him or her headlong into the path of others who are now, and who have long been, striving to keep the ship of the Church moving on those waters. Second, we will explore how we can

---

[1] United States Conference of Catholic Bishops, *Co-Workers in the Vineyard of the Lord* (Washington, DC: United States Conference of Catholic Bishops, 2005).

utilize adversity--through reflection--to bring about a more authentic collaboration between lay and ordained members of the Church. In my heart of hearts, I recognize this situation as the present churning and rumbling that inevitably must occur before positive, beneficial, sustainable change takes hold within the Church.

Entering the Jordan: The Basis for Ministerial Identity

At the Second Vatican Council, the world's bishops proclaimed and reemphasized the rich theology that allowed the Church to see itself as the Body of Christ which is grounded in the mission to bring the gospel of Jesus Christ to the whole world. From this renewed place of self-understanding, the bishops articulated who we are as a people of mission: "In the church, there is diversity of ministry but unity of mission. To the apostles and their successors, Christ has entrusted the office of teaching, sanctifying and governing in the name and by his power. Lay people too, sharing in the priestly, prophetical and kingly office of Christ, play their part in the mission of the whole people of God in the church and in the world."[2] At the time of the council, such a proclamation about the identity of the people of God, coupled with the revisiting of the realization that it is Jesus Christ who is the one entrusting all with the mission, was cause for celebration. Nonetheless, those words *entrusting* and *play their part* denote an order of primary and secondary status of the baptized within the Church.

If all the baptized truly share in the priestly, prophetic and kingly office, what are we to do when lay people begin to live out that office of Christ in such a way that brings them strangely close to the teaching, sanctifying, and governing of God's people? The attempts by some within both the clergy and the laity to somehow solidify the distinction between these two statuses in order to preserve them seems as ineffectual as the child playing with a beach ball in the pool who feverishly tries to push the ball down and hold it beneath the surface. Eventually the ball, impelled by its very nature to rise, will at some moment slide beyond the child's grasp, burst upwards from the child's hands

---

[2] Austin Flannery, ed., *Vatican Council II, Constitutions, Decrees, Declarations, Apostolicam Actuositatem* (Northport, NY: Costello Publishing Co., 1996), 2.

and *whoosh* its way into the blue sky with much aplomb. How we react to this sudden display of color, unpredictable movement, and unexpected drenching will determine how well this emerging state of collaboration within the Church will succeed or once more be stifled.

As I reflect on this issue, I keep returning to John 10, looking within that story for words which will speak to our situation as lay ministers today. Three themes emerge: recalling by whose authority we minister, returning to our baptismal call to ministry, and re-imaging the mission of lay ministry.

Jesus answered them, "I have shown you many good works from my Father." (John 10:32)

On numerous occasions, I have observed many good works from my fellow lay ecclesial ministers that emerged from hearts and minds fully dedicated to God and God's people. Whether it was in front of a group of parents whose sons or daughters were preparing for the sacrament of confirmation or at a gathering of catechumens and sponsors preparing for their baptism, I've witnessed real competence and commitment as each one presented the faith to others with clarity and joy. I've heard about the transformative moments of healing and holiness that happen during a hospital visit or in the midst of spiritual direction. Recently I've seen lay men and women demonstrate admirable leadership while helping to guide a pastoral plan for our diocese as we struggle with the reality of a severe shortage of priestly vocations.

Just as the presence of Jesus unnerved some of his fellow Jews to the point of great fear which began to foment a violent response, there are still those within the Church who see such examples of teaching, sanctifying, and governing as somehow leading to disorder among the faithful and thus resulting in a weakened Church. Just prior to creating a new opportunity to develop lay ecclesial ministry at the Aquinas Institute of Theology in St. Louis, then President Fr. Charles E. Bouchard, OP, addressed just such fears: "We must stop acting as if the Holy Spirit only allots so much ministry so that if lay people 'get' more of it, priests will get less. It is important for us to recall that ordained and non-ordained ministry is different *in kind.* The development of lay ministry does not diminish priestly ministry. It *enhances* it by providing more support for it and allowing priests to focus on the work that is specific to their charism."[3] This process of summoning forth and utilizing the immense giftedness that is found in the Church is unsettling. Just as Jesus' own authority and identity were called into question by others in his midst, we too as lay ministers will also be challenged by those who object to the particular way in which we manifest our work in the Kingdom of God.

He went back across the Jordan to the place where John first baptized, and there he remained. . . . And many there began to believe in him. (John 10:40,42)

Because the character of the laity is grounded in the sacramental graces of baptism, Eucharist and confirmation, our identity as disciples is located within the person of Jesus Christ. When his very identity was being assailed by those who could not make room in their hearts and minds for the presence of God in their midst, Jesus literally went back to the place that signified the beginning of his mission. This profound act took Jesus back to the place where God confirmed his identity in the presence of others saying, "You are my beloved Son; with you I am well pleased" (Luke 3:22). In his gospel, John substantiates the truth about Jesus through the words spoken by John the Baptist: "Behold, the Lamb of God, who takes away the sin of the world" (John 1:29). In addition to both God and John the Baptist affirming and recognizing Jesus publicly, the gospel writer indicates that many people witnessing his actions also came to believe in him.

As we observe the religious leaders questioning or rather denying Jesus' true identity, we can imagine and feel his anguish. Sensing this deepens our awareness of his humanity and, in the moments when we are rejected, we find that we too can endure the scrutiny that we experience while serving the Church as lay ecclesial ministers. The fact that the place of Jesus' baptism is also the place of his great affirmation from God greatly substantiates the Church's recovery of our rich baptismal theology that grounds our being and Christian character in Jesus

[3] Fr. Charles Bouchard, OP, *A Blessed Adequacy* (St. Louis: Aquinas Institute of Theology, 2005), 2.

Christ. In order for the Church to re-order herself effectively in terms of gifts and charisms, we have to go back to the common source of all gifts and charisms which is baptism. To retreat back to our own interior Jordan as the place that affirms our being, our calling and our utmost rootedness in ministry is more than a beneficial topic for reflection--it is critical for replenishing and refocusing our sense of ministerial identity.

When I first grasped the power of this Scripture passage and imagined myself going back to that place of affirmation, that wondrous place of refuge for the soul, it became important that I saw myself standing in those waters alone with God. However, the truth is more unnerving than that because as I gazed upwards, hearing and feeling the powerful words from our heavenly Father, I began to realize that such a momentous pronouncement must somehow be more than just for my ears alone. When love entered in and began to penetrate the fear and hurt that I held onto in my angst, rejection, and fatigue, something within compelled me to turn my gaze gradually to those within my periphery. Surprised or perhaps even shocked, I was amazed and humbled to discover standing next to me, eyes gazing upwards, arms extended outward, were the very people whom I perceived as the source of my troubles—*hearing the very same words that I heard.*

Through God's mercy and grace, we begin to marvel that the very ones we deemed as obstructions and hurtful are actually standing right next to us in the warm and wondrous waters of our baptismal identity. To realize that God's affirming voice is directed to these as well can take some doing on our part. Eventually we become aware that it is also their task in love to turn their gaze to see us and recognize our common stance in the Jordan. This realization is the fertile ground of real collaboration that the writers of *Co-Workers in the Vineyard of the Lord* could only pray that we'd discover someday and mutually find our way to, with God's grace.

When the council fathers proclaimed that all the baptized had a common or universal call to holiness which invites all the faithful to consider their place within the relationship of service within the church, could they have foreseen the vast number of its laity who really listened? Should it be a surprise that so many would respond with a hearty and hopeful, "Here I am . . . send me!" (Isaiah 6:8). Whenever any group of innovative leaders invites others from its membership into the process of coming to the table to add their voices, change is soon on the way. For example, current research in educational organizational dynamics indicates that there are many stakeholders (parents, teachers, community members, students, and other school staff) whose participation, once ignored, is imperatively necessary to the success of their mission in an educated society. In the Church as more people respond to this universal call to holiness, all the faithful will be challenged to adapt courageously and welcome these changes.

Even if you do not believe me, believe the works . . . (John 10:38)

As Jesus grew in the knowledge of who he was by virtue of his own baptism, he extended that baptismal call to other human beings who, however faulty and fallible, then took the keys of the Kingdom and set about the process of becoming Church. No doubt, this was one of the main reasons for the scorn Jesus received from those in authority. During the Second Vatican Council, when the Church was flush with religious and priestly vocations, the council fathers acted with generosity in like manner and extended a new invitation to the laity to bring their gifts into play in ways the Church had not seen since perhaps the times of the apostles.

Many of the lay faithful did in fact discern and celebrate a vocation to further their work *from within the Church* and began to bring forth their giftedness, infusing it into the Body of Christ in so many places and unique ways. For example, one fellow lay ecclesial minister in a neighboring diocese felt a particular call to serve the Church in a manner which honored and respected her primary vocation as a married woman. Soon after, she accepted an invitation to enter into a graduate program designed for such lay people with budding vocations. When reflecting upon those first instances of an actual calling to serve as a lay ecclesial minister, she wrote, *"My journey toward God began within as I sought to know myself, and then in prayer as I sought to know the Christ who lived within me. Of course my prayer moved me outside of myself as I found myself discovering Christ in community."*[4]

After some intense formation and many masters level theology courses (which built upon her previous graduate work and extensive parish ministry), she began to craft her ministerial identity within a well-established communal structure that included her spouse, pastor, fellow pastoral ministers, fellow students, and a whole host of professors and advisors at her school. Reflecting back on her journey she said, *"By listening to the voices of others continuing to call me, I was able to hear the voice of the Spirit within me. . . . I looked at where I was experiencing the most joy in my life and it was always being with people who were also hungry to learn."* This woman now serves at her parish as a strong and vibrant member of her pastoral team who works with adult faith formation. When her pastor was forced to take a long leave of absence due to an illness, she was well equipped to strengthen and buttress her parish community with all the gifts, skills, and strengths woven into her during her formation.

Mindful of laity's special character rooted in the secular world that the council fathers articulated in the document *Gaudiem et Spes*, the theologian Aurelie Hagstrom speaks of how the laity manifest their service to and within the Church: "They are called in a preeminent way to incarnate the Church in the world. The laity are to bring the Church into the heart of the world while bringing the world into the heart of the Church."[5] While many looked with great hope at the emergence of the laity who found new ways to serve their ecclesial communities, particularly those who were termed *lay ecclesial ministers*, others began to wonder if this new reality was actually compromising the secular character of the lay members themselves.

As one of the contributors to a 1997 Vatican document, *On Certain Questions Regarding the Collaboration of the*

---

[4] Throughout, quotes from journal entries of lay ecclesial ministers involved in the "Emerging from the Vineyard" project will be integrated into the text. These quotes will be indicated by *use of italics.*

[5] Aurelie A. Hagstrom, "The Secular Character of the Vocation and Mission of the Laity," in Susan. K. Wood, ed., *Ordering the Baptismal Priesthood: Theologies of Lay and Ordained Ministry* (Collegeville, MN: Liturgical Press, 2003), 159.

Nonordained Faithful in the Sacred Ministry of Priests, then Cardinal Ratzinger commented on the possible trajectory of a continued lay presence at the heart of Church life: "A member of the lay faithful who, over a long period of time or over a lifetime, actually exercises the pastoral duties proper to a priest, with the exception of celebrating Mass and sacramental confession, is in fact no longer a true lay person and has lost his true identity in the life and mission of the Church."[6] Given such a strong statement, some may very well ask if the present pastoral reality of the Church where lay ecclesial ministers serve in the areas of religious education, sacramental preparation, or pastoral visits to the sick is actually bringing about the dissolution of a character unique to the ordained.

Especially where there are increasingly more lay ministers and religious serving as pastoral associates, it might be helpful to examine whether or not such forays into the ecclesial center of Church ministry are in fact compromising the ability of these lay members to infuse the world into the Church. Is being present with and blessing a sick parishioner in a hospital such a foreign practice for the lay person, whose nature it is to be out serving God in the world? Do those with the charism of preaching who also have a mastery of biblical research really step beyond the boundaries of their identity as lay disciples of Jesus by studying and preaching? If so, how do any of these acts harm or diminish the lay person's role in the Church? With every blessed act of presence, healing, studying, or preaching, *lay people are in fact re-imaging what it means to be a true lay person*. It seems that for the present time, Ratzinger's query will not immediately become an issue because of how strongly those in official Church leadership adhere to and uphold the given jurisdictional placement of all within the Church. The fact remains that such compelling questions are now part of the present conversation by clerics and lay people alike. That spinning beach ball has indeed gushed upwards and has caused many to marvel at such an emergence of gifts within the faithful.

---

[6]Cardinal Joseph Ratzinger, "Reflections on the Instruction Regarding the Collaboration of the Lay Faithful in the Ministry of Priests," *L'Osservatore Romano*, English ed. (29 April 1998): 18.

Jesus dealt with this very question when his disciple John noticed that someone other than one of the twelve disciples was casting out demons using the name of Jesus Christ (Mark 9:38). Perhaps what is more interesting than Jesus's response, "Do not prevent him" (9:39), is the fact that immediately preceding this passage was that embarrassing moment when Jesus caught his disciples arguing about who was the greatest among themselves. Instead of just verbally correcting them, Jesus radically reframes their reality of power by choosing a child who is symbolic of the most marginalized members in their society and then goes on to insist that they receive such little ones in his name and with deference.

The following story illustrates how one particular lay ecclesial minister serving at the parish level began to re-image what it means to become fully a lay person:

> *Our current pastor recognized the relationships I shared with the elderly and sick, and he began asking me to meet with parish families after experiencing a loss. This was not ever something I envisioned myself doing. My pastor saw natural gifts in me that I could share with the community that I did not know I had, and now I typically plan funeral liturgies, select scriptures for the rites based on those memories that the family members share of their loved one. By delegating this responsibility to me, my gifts are better used and the pastor is able to devote his gifts to other areas in service to our community.*

Recovering the awareness that there are abundant charisms operating within a community that caused the early Christian assemblies to flourish and spread, it is imperative that a pastor set about the task of unearthing these charisms in order that they be cultivated and put to good use in the enlivening of a parish community.

As more and more lay members are given the kind of theological training called for in *Co-Workers in the Vineyard*, there is the possibility that a lay ecclesial minister on staff could help develop a process that serves to identify, cultivate, and discern the most advantageous use of those charisms which surface. One particularly challenging reality is when one or more of the lay ecclesial ministers find that they have the charism of leadership--in terms of the financial, human resources, and organizational attributes and requirements that are part of leading a parish--while the pastor may have little affinity for this charism. This is especially challenging when these lay ecclesial ministers are women. In such a case, it takes a wise and savvy pastor to take a more nuanced approach to guiding his team in a manner that benefits the overall parish community. In order for there to be a mutually life-giving and respectful collaboration, the team does well to recognize that all people within the Church desire to hear the Father's words from John's gospel, "you are my beloved son or daughter, with whom I am well pleased!" For example, while attending a workshop a few years ago designed to help pastoral staff grow and develop, I distinctly recall one moment when the issue of leadership within parish teams took a whole new shape. As we shared the results from a personality indicator tool, one parish team's pastor scored very low in the leadership profile while a female pastoral associate was the only one in that group with strong attributes of leadership. Certainly these situations require some thoughtful discussion in order to maximize the service rendered by that team to its parish community. Such realizations as these are a testament to how the lay and ordained members now operate in the more complex and diversely gifted Church that exists today.

By keeping our collective focus on Jesus Christ and his ability to be present to all humanity, and by staying true to our baptismal theology, we will find a way to navigate through any change in a manner that allows the Church to remain vibrant, relevant, and authentic. One particular place where the Church is navigating through this change is at the point of contact between lay and ordained leaders in the midst of parish ministry.

Beyond the Jordan: Moving Towards a True Collaboration

Having considered Jesus's own awareness of his calling and identity in moments of adversity, we more fully understand that as lay ministers our identity is forged and proven when we enter into the crucible of serving others. Unlike Jesus, the conflict that emerges in our ministry need not end in crucifixion. In fact, this adversity can actually become a blessed teacher who has come for some unforeseen benefit. Our next challenge then is to decide whether or not we move towards the adversity in our ministry which could shape us as disciples more fit for service or whether it will drive us away from fulfilling our call to ministry. To help depict this reality, I would like to paraphrase the ancient Proverb 27:17, As iron sharpens iron, so one person sharpens another. On a cursory level, this image might seem pleasing as one envisions some wise old sword-smith preparing a shiny blade for a noble purpose. However, in my own ministerial experience, I've come to know that this often means that sparks are flying as the metal of one person's trait draws across the metal of another's way of being. This action comes complete with all the sharp sounds, oily metallic residue and the occasional cut on the fingers as a result of trying to sharpen or be sharpened. At the same time, the proverb implies that sharpening is a good thing that results in our growth, so our deeper selves call upon us to welcome the would-be teacher of conflict and give him a seat at our table.

But first we need to consider what real engagement looks like when we set about the work of moving forward as a unified pastoral team. This process includes listening to one another, finding mutual understanding, removing obstacles in order to manage or resolve conflict, practicing real collaboration, and finally moving towards a holy synergy where the team takes on a purposeful and spirit-filled leadership for their faith community.

Listening to One Another

Knowing that God is the one who calls all the baptized, the first task for lay and ordained ministers is to listen to one another. It starts with the fundamental recognition of the other person as Christ in our midst. "Can I look at him through the lens of Jesus? What is her story? What animates his desire to serve here? What expectations does she contend with in order to stay as a minister in the Church?" Openly sharing with another person, let alone a pastoral team, is very difficult for some. A pastor who can honestly acknowledge the power differential between clergy and the laity will have a better chance of promoting sharing that is vulnerable and transparent. Everyone on the team has the responsibility of helping to create a ministerial environment that promotes positive regard for the other. Authority that listens with openness is capable of shaping a great future for those who follow and contribute to the well-being of that community.

With this as the basis for open-heartedly hearing others, we can then strive to understand how each person views and articulates his or her present ordering within the relationship of the baptized (Church) and how that ordering or placement serves to guide them in service to God's people. This kind of listening requires an intentional and shared commitment. It also compels us to seek a deeper truth that may challenge or threaten the team beyond their present level of communication. It calls upon the other to ask keen questions such as, "How does your baptismal character call you to live out your role as pastor, director, liturgist, etc.?" Trusting in the grace of the Holy Spirit, the team will need the courage to allow these truths to surface so that the fruits of this sharing might benefit all involved.

Finding Mutual Understanding

Making the choice to ask questions, rather than to deliver statements and pronouncements, helps to determine whether or not we will have a healthy environment for listening. Unlike the pointed discourse found in much of today's political conversation, ministers in the Church need to be proactive in terms of promoting mutual understanding. If we adopt a stance of curiosity and inquiry, we can demonstrate openness while modeling an honoring and willing spirit that strives to understand rather than be understood, as Saint Francis of Assisi once penned in his prayer for his community and the world. Inspired by this prayer, one of my personal goals in life is to use more fluently such phrases as, "Could you help me to understand where you're coming from," or "So if I hear you clearly, you're saying that. . . ."

If members of a pastoral team can achieve a sufficient level of mutual trust to be transparent in their sharing with others on the team, they can foster development of an important aspect of human formation that the US bishops include for lay ecclesial ministers. In *Co-Workers in the Vineyard*, lay ecclesial ministers are reminded that they must be open to the "*[r]ecognition of the traits and abilities one lacks*, leading to the goal of collaborating well with those who have different, complementary gifts."[7]

---

[7] United States Conference of Catholic Bishops, *Co-Workers in the Vineyard*, 37; emphasis in original.

This reality is what the ordained, vowed religious, and lay ecclesial ministers are now engaged in, as pastoral teams take on new forms. For instance, imagine a setting where the pastor is gifted with a keen intellect that operates in the Thomistic tradition that celebrates knowledge as the primary pathway to prayer and holiness. Now add a religious sister whose communal charism celebrates a strong experiential connection to creation as the primary means of relating to God and to all others. Combine these two with the lay ecclesial minister whose experience has been shaped by having worked as the chief human resources officer in the corporate world while finding God in the midst of being married and steeped within a boisterous family life, replete with soccer games and children's homework assignments. Such an arrangement, if not handled well, could result in a lot of discord that threatens our need for harmony and unity. As with the process of iron sharpening iron, the result might be a lot of dinged blades and possibly a heap of scrap metal. On the other hand, this scenario could lead to a pastoral team that enjoys a synergy which allows them to serve the parish in a way that acknowledges and celebrates its diversity while maintaining sufficient unity to truly live out our great Catholic tradition.

Removing Obstacles in Order to Manage and Resolve Conflicts

I suspect that for many pastoral teams the ability to cultivate mutual understanding is much more subdued and fraught with obstacles that prevent them from ever approaching the aforementioned climate of openness that seasoned ministerial teams enjoy. Frankly speaking, there are some team members who are not capable of or at least willing to create a healthy environment that engenders a successful and collaborative pastoral team. To discuss this subject fully would require another essay altogether! For our purposes, I will share a part of my own story. When trying to reveal how I was feeling about a recurring problem with a team member, I eventually came to the realization that I had to first see, listen, understand, and affirm his point of view. This may seem obvious, but feeling so passionate about my position prevented me from putting into practice the prayer of Saint Francis. Giving up the need to be understood truly is dying to self. I realized I wasn't making any progress and so I began to seek the counsel of others in the hopes of finding a new approach in order to achieve a more productive outcome. This prayer began to emerge from my frustration: "Lord, I trust that you are now bringing about the most benevolent outcome for everyone involved. Give me the clarity to see it, the wisdom to understand it and the courage to accept it, even if it appears not to be in my favor." It's very possible that the greatest obstacle to managing conflict is the presence of our hidden wounds that require forgiveness. Because we don't always know that we've done something to offend or hurt another person, this requires a commitment to prayer and self-reflection.

Praying in this manner challenged me to practice effective communication when interacting with others. For example, I began asking clarifying questions, introducing topics for discussion prior to a meeting, and humbly acknowledging my need of the other's assistance in order to proceed. I hoped to achieve in this more open environment what the writers of *Co-Workers in the Vineyard of the Lord* encourage: the "ability to learn from both praise and criticism, receiving and assessing both with honesty and equanimity."[8] Instead of the adversarial relationship like the one that existed between Jesus and the religious leaders who confronted him concerning his identity, real collaboration that manifests itself in an honoring manner has at its root a growing trust in one another. Just as Jesus trusted the words of the Father when recalling the pronouncement heard at the Jordan, there must be occasions when both lay and ordained ministers have the opportunity to reaffirm the trust in one another that began when the team was called together.

Other useful insights have to do with the awareness that our ability to hear and accept criticism may be marred or skewed if we take things too personally. In their *New York Times* best-selling book *Difficult Conversations*, authors Douglas Stone, Bruce Patton, and Sheila Heen highlight the importance of being aware of any "identity issues" that could threaten our concept of self as a competent person who tries to do what is good and worthy of love.[9] When recognition of our particular "growing edges" is brought forward by a team member who has been critical of us in

---

[8] Ibid., 37.

[9] Douglas Stone, Bruce Patton, and Sheila Heen, *Difficult Conversations* (London: Penguin Books, 1999), 112.

the past, we have perhaps a powerful opportunity to effect real and lasting change in the manner in which the team speaks to one another. For me, this means learning to take my lumps when I've botched something. There are times I need to accept quietly such criticism as a form of pruning that will lead to new growth. On the other hand, it serves the team well if I can speak up when I feel that I am being unjustly criticized.

The awareness of how we wield and receive the sharp blade of adversity is truly a powerful tool for individual and collective growth that could prove beneficial. While we cannot always resolve conflicts, we may find that we can sufficiently manage them enough to keep moving forward as a team. I recently delighted in hearing a young priest teach our teens during a retreat that the word reconciliation basically meant "to see together again."

Practicing Real Collaboration

Pastoral leaders who manage to listen to one another, seek mutual understanding, and learn to manage their conflicts are poised to move beyond simple cooperation. They are ready to engage in the type of real collaboration, that authors Loughlan Sofield and Carroll Juliano describe as "the identification, release and union of all the gifts of ministry for the sake of mission."[10] As we envision what this state of collaboration could look like, the US bishops offer us a starting place: "While they differ essentially, the ordained priesthood and the common priesthood of the faithful are ordered to one another and thus are intimately related. Lay ecclesial ministers, especially those serving in parishes, look to their priests for leadership in developing collaboration that is mutually life-giving and respectful."[11] Such a hopeful development begins when a pastor sets the tone by honoring the gifts that lie within a ministerial team that can be a complement to what he hopes to accomplish within a parish community.

The reality for some parishes is that the pastor may not be sufficiently adept at summoning forth the needed gifts for a

---

[10] Loughlan Sofield, and Carroll Juliano, *Collaboration: Uniting Our Gifts in Ministry* (Notre Dame, IN: Ave Maria Press, 2000), 17.

[11] United States Conference of Catholic Bishops, *Co-Workers in The Vineyard*, 24.

thriving parish community. Such a situation is not necessarily problematic so long as others are able and willing to come alongside the pastor and assist in that summoning process that engages others in ministry. Even if those who have been summoned are not welcomed or utilized in one of our given ministerial sites, we can accept the consolation that those gifts that are surfaced are still worthy of being cultivated and nurtured for the sake of the wider community. Because the Church's task is to help enliven and sanctify the world, gifted souls may find themselves serving outside the Church ministries that we care for. The word "release," from Sofield and Juliano's definition, is well chosen because it reminds us that this is the great and mighty work of the Spirit.

Perhaps a good metaphor for the collaborative process that might better suit our focus on the pastoral team at this point is that of a doorway to which God is summoning us. As our pastoral team approaches this doorway, God asks us to muster the courage to go through this darkened passageway into an unseen room. Once inside, we become aware of how tight the space seems and then notice that there are many mirrors hanging on the walls. Finding it dark and sensing that the floors are uneven, we are further unnerved that there are no hand-rails to help steady our walk. We only have one another to hold onto as we progress forward. Gradually we notice that the only light in the room comes from a doorway on the far end of the room. Together we fumble our way towards a strange antechamber, which happens to be very short and narrow. Moving closer, we peer through and discover that it leads to a lovely table set with silver and crystal, indicating that this place is for those who intend to feast at a banquet. Finally we realize that the only way we'll all make it through that door is by embracing and bowing down together.

Moving Towards a Holy Synergy

Beyond the limited metaphors and idealistic language are real examples of what pastoral teams look like when they find themselves operating at heightened levels of collaboration. Some begin to realize a kind of "holy synergy" that allows them to serve the parish in a way that welcomes and celebrates diversity, while remaining united in our great Catholic tradition. A fellow lay minister of faith formation in my diocese was brimming over with gratitude as he told me about three families who recently came into the fullness of communion in the Church during Pentecost. Sharing this gratitude over pizza with the RCIA coordinator and youth minister, he used the imagery of the Venn diagram to depict how the three of them came together and witnessed the joy of how their particular efforts coalesced around these families given their distinctive areas of accountability within the one parish. Leading this motivated pastoral team is a parish priest whose leadership set the stage for this celebration and whose vision sustains the energy within the group.

In an age when vocations to the priesthood remain stifled and those serving presently feel the ill-effects and mistrust that still linger as a result of the child sexual abuse scandal, it is crucial that lay ministers take the initiative to honor their pastors to help foster this collaboration. A timely word of praise in a letter to parents or an article supporting the pastor's vision in the newsletter can help bolster support for the direction they wish to take us. Likewise, a word of blessing given by the pastor helps the community to trust and value the lay ecclesial minister working hard to enliven the parish.

Imagine a Church where all parish ministers validate and celebrate the particularities involved in each other's vocational character! Priests who can affirm the presence of fully-engaged lay men and women infusing their gifts into the Church will likely see volunteerism flourish within their parish. Lay ecclesial ministers who can acknowledge and celebrate the generous and full outpouring of self by their priests will enliven and strengthen their vocations as well. After seeing and feeling the fruits of a harmonious collaboration in their midst, I suspect that the people of God would support *both vocations* with their assent. Furthermore, I believe this will result in parents encouraging their sons and daughters to consider the possibility of entering these great callings.

Shepherding, in the ministerial sense, entails that the bishop and his curial staff have a key role to play by helping to ensure that this process unfolds in a positive, beneficial, and intentional manner for the local church. By bringing all parish ministers together for on-going discussion and training, the bishop has the ability to inspire and equip everyone with the means of maintaining and supporting an open process that fuels mutual respect and appreciation. As part of these gatherings, one important role bishops might play would be to establish policies and organizational processes to foster the growth and communication dynamics. No doubt this would require a serious commitment on everyone's part, but eventually trust would grow after a few positive experiences. Such occasions could allow the bishop to speak a common blessing of appreciation for all ministers that fully acknowledges the beauty of an ordered diversity.

In this age of civil, political and religious strife when disparate voices seem to dominate the discourse of the day, such a flourishing of Church leadership would be a soothing balm to Catholics who have endured so much and whose spirits are weary from discord and strife. If we fail to address the problems that ministerial teams are actually facing right now, local parishes are at risk of losing viability and may even suffer and shrink. To create a word-picture, imagine one of those dusty over-head projectors found in classrooms of the past. To the extent that lay ecclesial ministers and clergy cannot forge a common ministerial identity that is rooted in selfless service, it would be as if we took a picture of Jesus that was etched upon one of those old acetate transparencies and began cutting it into pieces, forcing everyone to behold a distorted picture of our Lord. This strange Piccasoesque version of Jesus is not one that will encourage and teach parishioners about the splendor of God incarnate. However, those pastoral teams who do present a compelling image of Jesus Christ by virtue of how they charitably demonstrate their mutual respect and proven collaboration will encourage and truly bless the members of their parish.

Given the distrust by so many towards those in civil, military and religious authority, there is a great need for a rapprochement between individuals and institutions, particularly between many Catholics and the hierarchical leaders of the Church. With a renewed emphasis on what it means to be a faithful disciple in the Church today, many Catholics long to see a thriving and functioning reality of combined ministry. As men and women of varying backgrounds lead, teach, and shepherd together, these graced moments of collaboration, born from adversity and honed into magnificent and powerful instruments for good, would go a long way to help everyone visualize and celebrate how good life can be in the vineyard of the Lord.

Questions for Reflection:

1. What are some sources of adversity from within your own ministerial site? How much is each person contributing towards those adverse situations and where are the greatest chances for understanding and healing?

2. In reading the essay, what primary issues surfaced for you that today's lay ecclesial ministers need to bring into dialogue with their ordained counterparts?

3. The central issue that writing this essay raised for me was dealing with the confounding reality that God brings disparately tempered individuals together to both build and celebrate communion as ordained and lay members of the Church. How do you see this reality unfolding in your ministerial site?

A Eucharistic Spirituality for Lay Ecclesial Ministry

Virginia Stillwell

Sunday after Sunday and, for some of us, day by day, lay ecclesial ministers in the Catholic Church gather with our faith communities to participate in the Eucharist. We enter our churches and sign ourselves with baptismal water in the name of the Trinity. We listen to the Word of God, seeking meaning for our lives of faith. We pray for the world. We recall in gratitude the saving love of Jesus Christ present to us through the paschal mystery. We offer our gifts, our needs and our ministries to be transformed by the Holy Spirit into something holy and fruitful. We pray as Jesus taught us and offer the peace of Christ to others. We receive the Body and Blood of Christ to unite and nourish us. We are sent forth to glorify the Lord with our lives.

The Eucharist has the power to uphold and guide all ecclesial ministers in the collaborative work of ministry. In the words of the U.S. bishops in *Co-Workers in the Vineyard of the Lord,* "the minister encounters Christ and his grace in the Eucharist, expresses and grows in faith, strengthens the bond with the Church, and receives nourishment to fulfill the mission."[1] Even so, these effects of the Eucharist are not always readily apparent to lay ministers; like all Catholics, they may encounter any number of internal and external obstacles to their spiritual appreciation of the liturgy. Lay ecclesial ministers, however, share a distinct spirituality that offers a doorway into fruitful participation in the Eucharist, which, in turn, can provide spiritual nourishment and formation for their ministries.

This essay will lift up the spirituality at the core of lay ecclesial ministry (LEM), as expressed in the writings of participants in the "Emerging from the Vineyard" project. Their ministerial and liturgical reflections reveal a spirituality of participation, presence, collaboration, dignity, discipleship,

---

[1] United States Conference of Catholic Bishops, *Co-Workers in the Vineyard of the Lord* (Washington, DC: United States Conference of Catholic Bishops, 2005), 39.

paschal mystery, communion, and service. We will see that this spirituality resonates with the Eucharist, which then upholds them in the life of ministry. Supporting documentation will come from liturgical sources and from the guidance of the U.S. bishops on spiritual formation for lay ecclesial ministers.[2] In each area of spirituality, the insights of lay ministers and the Church's liturgical practices will be seen to inform and challenge each other. Concluding remarks will summarize the implications of this exploration into the eucharistic spirituality of lay ecclesial ministry.

A Spirituality of Full Participation

Lay ecclesial ministry can be seen as the fully ripened fruit of a spirituality of participation—in the sacraments, life, and ministries of the Church. Such spirituality finds its roots in the "full, conscious, and active participation" in the liturgy which the Constitution on the Sacred Liturgy *(Sacrosanctum Concilium)* (SC) affirms to be "the primary and indispensable source" of "the true Christian spirit" (SC 14).[3]

Many lay ecclesial ministers name a direct correlation between liturgical participation and their ministries. One minister said participation in the liturgy *"challenge[s] me to a full, active and conscious participation in the life of Christ."*[4] Indeed, many *"find their call to LEM* [5] *in the course of full, active and conscious participation in the liturgy."* And the participation of the assembly in the Eucharist often can support lay ministers in their faith and work: *"When we pray the Our Father and exchange the Sign of*

---

[2] United States Conference of Catholic Bishops, "Part Two: Pastoral Applications; Section B. Formation for Lay Ecclesial Ministry (Spiritual Formation)," in *Co-Workers in the Vineyard of the Lord,* 38-42.

[3] Austin Flannery, ed., *Vatican Council II: Volume 1, The Conciliar and Post Conciliar Documents* (Newport, NY: Costello Publishing, 1996).

[4] Throughout, quotes from journal entries of lay ecclesial ministers involved in the "Emerging from the Vineyard" project will be integrated into the text. These quotes will be indicated by *use of italics.*

[5] The participants in the "Emerging from the Vineyard" project often utilized the abbreviation "LEM" in their journal entries to refer to lay ecclesial ministry or lay ecclesial ministers. That abbreviation will be preserved in quotations where it was used by the author.

Peace, I have the distinct impression I am riding the crest of a wave."

We know that the spiritual participation of the assembly in the Church's liturgies depends largely on their interior dispositions, but participation also relies on many choices that are made in the preparation for and celebration of the liturgy. When assembly singing is diminished to mere traveling music for the presider, scriptures are read perfunctorily, homilies are lacking, sacramental rituals are omitted or celebrated poorly, or consecrated wine is withheld from the laity, the liturgy cannot bestow the true Christian spirit to its fullest potential. If the spirituality of participation at the root of lay ecclesial ministry is directly related to liturgical participation, then practices that diminish the participation of the laity can seriously hinder the development of new vocations and starve the spirits of those currently serving in ministries. This presents an additional reason that "the full and active participation by all the people is the aim to be considered before all else" (SC 14).

How might lay ministers overcome such obstacles to their participation in the Eucharist? What can be done when they find themselves in situations where the liturgy is celebrated in a minimal or clerical manner? How do they quiet their own internal struggles with some public stances and behaviors of clergy long enough to enter deeply into the Sunday liturgy? Lay ministers recognize that essential to the life of discipleship is the commitment to witness their faith to others and give thanks to God every Sunday. But what are they to do when the Sunday liturgy leaves them feeling starved and parched?

Some grasp onto knowledge passed on from previous generations: that the saving work of Christ in sacramental grace flows from the Eucharist *ex opere operato*, without regard to the worthiness of the minister or the celebration, and the spiritual benefits may not be realized until much later. Others say that they find strength in looking at the bigger scope of Church history. There they find disciples who doubted their faith; and those who were silenced, excommunicated, or imprisoned for speaking the truth to Church authority, only later to be canonized as saints. Still others tune in to the faithfulness of the people in the pews, calling to mind the struggles that people go through to keep and pass along the faith. They watch the children and the elders; they listen to the assembly at prayer or in song and discover their own faith buoyed up by the community of disciples. Or they remind themselves that another worshipper may be looking to them for a welcoming presence and a public witness of discipleship during difficult periods in the life of faith.

An Incarnational Spirituality of Presence

"An incarnational spirituality of presence"[6] is foundational for most lay ecclesial ministers, who recognize a call to mediate and model incarnational presence within their communities of faith. One minister captured this perspective in her writing: *"who we are in what we do, both as individual ministers and as a community of believers, far surpasses an end product."*

Ecclesial ministers can, however, be tempted to distance themselves from their ministerial communities. Perhaps they have been told that bonding too closely may cloud judgment, limit the ability to lead, and cause too much pain if they leave the parish. One liturgist resisted forming relationships with parishioners until his mother died suddenly. Despite his previous efforts to maintain distance, members of the community surrounded him with cards, condolences, hugs, and prayer. One Sunday a member told him, "You might not be able to pray right now. Don't worry about it. We'll pray *for* you." This experience drew the liturgist more deeply into the life of the community. Many participants in this project told similar stories of the community of faith mediating the presence of Christ to them.

The Sunday Eucharist, we know, is a key setting for experiencing the presence of Christ in the gathered community (SC 7). It may also be seen as a prime place for lay ministers to exercise their spirituality of presence. When they mediate pastoral presence with members of the community in the gathering for the Eucharist, those encounters can become sacramental "Ah-ha" moments. Parishioners can recognize Christ "really" present in the assembly of God's people.

And yet, many lay ministers choose not to attend weekend liturgies at the parishes they serve. Some have families who are

---

[6] United States Conference of Catholic Bishops., *Co-Workers*, 39.

actively engaged in a different parish. Others *"are bombarded by 'work' questions from people when they attend Mass at the parish in which they are employed."* One person wrote: *"when I make time to worship with another community, I feel a sense of freedom that . . . gives me fresh energy for my ministry"*; and another: *"the diocesan leadership [said that] working where one does not worship was actually healthy."* It is clear that there are good reasons for lay ministers to worship outside their ministerial settings.

On the other hand, there are those who favor being actively present in the worshipping community. One wrote that her ability to lead is strengthened by forming bonds within the community where she ministers. *"I choose to minister from a place of immersion with those I worship and live with . . . a "sign" of one who serves from within this community."* Another embraces interactions with parishioners on weekends as integral to the Sunday liturgical experience. *"While it is true that people hand me registrations, checks, and permission forms I am happy to help them get to where they need to be in relation to the life of the church. By working from this vantage point, I believe that I am helping to model the active role of lay members and demonstrating the kind of vestedness that helps to enliven a community of believers."* And those most in need of pastoral presence may only come to the parish for weekend Masses.

In the end each person has to discern what will best nurture his or her spirituality of presence in ministry: *"Some folks seem to have an innate need for time away in order to re-charge, while others experience a sense of renewal in the midst of everyday service."* The call of ministers to an incarnational spirituality of presence resonates with the Catholic understanding of the presence of Christ in the liturgical assembly. Recognizing that the Sunday gathering can lend a deeper significance to any personal interactions, lay ministers may want to consider worshipping in their ministerial communities when possible and reframing the tasks of ministry not as distractions, but as an essential aspect of mediating the presence of Christ in the Christian community. In turn, by being present at weekend liturgies, they can increase the likelihood that they themselves might experience the presence of Christ in and through the communities they serve.

A Spirituality of Genuine Collaboration

Participation in ecclesial ministry, as in the Eucharist, is a collaborative venture that cannot be undertaken alone. Those ministers involved in this project seem to *"be keenly aware of the urgent need to develop (or continue) a relational model for ministry. This is the only way we, as ministers will be nourished, and in turn, be nourishment for the people of God."* In two recent documents the US bishops urge lay and ordained ministers to ground their identities and ministries in a spirituality that reflects genuine collaboration. In *Co-Workers in the Vineyard of the Lord* they expressed their "strong desire for the fruitful collaboration of ordained and lay ministers."[7] In an earlier document the bishops stated: "To speak of a genuine collaboration of ordained ministers and lay ecclesial ministers diminishes neither the sacramental character of ordination nor the properly secular character of the laity, but rather enriches both."[8]

A spirituality of collaboration in ministry may, in fact, be a natural repercussion of the collaboration that plays out in the liturgy, where all members of the assembly have specific functions to carry out under the ordering of, and in collaboration with, the priest.[9] One can envision the presider at Eucharist, not playing a solo, but at the center of an orchestra conducting all who are gathered in unity and harmony. Each instrumental section plays a musical line that is necessary to the whole, and a skilled musician sits in the first chair of each section to lead and provide an example of how to play their part. This vision becomes a reality on Sunday mornings as various liturgical ministers collaborate to support members of the assembly in fulfilling different functions throughout the liturgy. Oftentimes, *"lay*

---

[7] Ibid., 6.

[8] United States Conference of Catholic Bishops, *Lay Ecclesial Ministry: The State of the Questions* (Washington, DC: United States Conference of Catholic Bishops, 1999), 18.

[9] The *General Instruction of the Roman Missal* states: "The celebration of the Eucharist is the action of Christ and of the Church, namely, of the holy people united and ordered under the Bishop. . . . All, therefore, whether ordained ministers or lay Christian faithful, in fulfilling their function or their duty, should carry out solely but totally that which pertains to them." GIRM, trans. International Commission on English in the Liturgy (New York: Catholic Book Publishing, 2011), 91.

ministers literally set the tone and carry it in liturgy." Just as members of the orchestra tune their instruments to the oboist, members of the assembly attune their voices and hearts to lay leaders in their midst.

One participant wrote that the many ministries that work together to make good liturgy *"lead me to dig more deeply in the hopes of finding what real and true collaboration might look like in a ministerial setting with a diverse team."* Thus, collaboration within the liturgical assembly can function as a sacramental symbol, both manifesting and increasing collaboration among lay and ordained ministers and the holy people of God.

Yet, a spirituality of collaboration has yet to permeate fully either Catholic liturgy or ecclesial ministry. Institutional and interpersonal hurdles remain. As one person summarized: *"We struggle to understand the points of view of our co-workers. Laity and clergy are socialized so differently from one another, and yet it is crucial that we communicate well."* The spirit of collaboration in ministry can be sabotaged by a variety of negative spirits – a spirit of misunderstanding, fear, overwork, anger, competition, suspicion, abuse of power are a few of those mentioned by participants in this project. Such difficulties often go hand in hand with a lack of liturgical collaboration—a music minister who cannot compromise, or a priest who rushes into the sacristy at the last minute and dismisses careful liturgical planning. If, as Catholics believe, sacraments act both as signs and instruments of spiritual realities, then a spirituality of genuine collaboration in either ministry or liturgy will re-echo in the other area and reverberate throughout the Christian community as a whole.

A Spirituality of Baptismal Dignity

Recent scholarship and bishops' statements have pointed to baptism as the spiritual source for the identity, gifts, and calling of lay ecclesial ministers. *Co-Workers in the Vineyard of the Lord* encourages lay ministers to cultivate the "living union with Christ" that flows from baptism: "For lay ecclesial ministers, it is the ground of their ministry and the irreplaceable source of its authenticity and fruitfulness."[10] Many of the participants in this project have shown that their spirituality is indeed founded on

---

[10] United States Conference of Catholic Bishops, *Co-Workers,* 39.

the equality and dignity given to all who are baptized into Christ. The introductory rites of the Mass display this same spirituality of baptismal dignity, which can support lay ministers through difficult moments in ministry.

Three aspects of the introductory rites are particularly noteworthy. First, all who gather have access to the holy water in the font. It is not reserved only for use by the ordained. Thus, all the baptized have equal access to participation in the divine life of the Holy Trinity. *"All are family and all are welcome at the table . . . without judgment as beloved Children of God."* Second, baptism begins the communal journey of union with Christ, as evidenced in the procession following the cross of Jesus and Book of the Gospels. *"I found myself thinking that my life in ministry was 'a procession.' In that movement I am always accompanied by . . . Christ and others on the journey."* Third, all—assembly and clergy together—make the Sign of the Cross and the penitential act. Baptism saves but does not remove anyone from the sinfulness and suffering that are part of our human condition: *"No one is exempt; no one is unique –ordained, LEM, assembly—all are disciples together."* No one has reached perfection, and, by the grace of God, all can support one another on that journey.

Internal participation in these rites can foster in lay ministers a humble sense of their own God-given dignity, that of their co-workers in ministry, and all who have been baptized into Christ. In contrast to this spiritual perspective, some ministers have encountered co-workers who refuse to admit their own errors while berating and belittling their subordinates. Others experience parishioners who dismiss their authority because they *"are not Father."* A solid spirituality of baptismal dignity can uphold lay ecclesial ministers through such hurtful experiences by convincing them of their inner worth and identity. *"The more grounded I am in what I know to be true about my calling and dignity, the more likely I am to discern and follow a healthy path."* A balanced understanding of their own human imperfections can help them *"recognize complicity in the struggles of ministry, and pray for the courage to request and offer forgiveness."* Knowing that all of the baptized rely on others to nudge us along on the journey with Christ can encourage lay ministers to express their feelings and needs in respectful ways that may be fruitfully received by people who have wronged them.

A spirituality grounded in baptism invites lay ecclesial ministers to recognize the equality and dignity of all on the journey toward holiness. *"LEMs . . . have no power, except that which the Holy Spirit gives to their voice or actions."* The introductory rites of the Mass can help them find their voice by founding their ministry on a spirituality of baptismal dignity.

A Spirituality of Christian Discipleship

Co-Workers in the Vineyard recommends "Spiritual formation built on the word of God," and "based on the Liturgy . . . Celebration and study of the liturgical year will unfold 'the whole mystery of Christ' (SC 102) and deepen one's appreciation of God's ongoing presence in ordinary time and liturgical seasons."[11] By listening to the scriptures proclaimed in the Liturgy of the Word over the course of the liturgical year, lay ecclesial ministers allow Christ's spirit to penetrate and inform their ministries. As they do, they are formed in a spirituality of discipleship.

Several quotes from project participants affirm that following Christ through the liturgical year is ingrained in their ministries and spirituality :

- *As a LEM I am naturally well in tune with the rhythm of the liturgical year, my ministry in essence follows the flow of the liturgical year.*
- *Looking ahead and reflecting on the Sunday Readings is particularly powerful for beginning a new week.*
- *Psalms allow us to be in pain, and in that pain find God who is active and present in our lives . . . to face reality while remaining in . . . confident expectation.*
- *The psalms celebrate what God has done in the past and urge us to remember and not lose heart.*
- *I listen to seasonal liturgical music. In this way I can connect my experiences and challenges, joys and*

[11] Ibid., 39.

sadness, with feasts and seasons of the liturgical year.

In contrast, participants also named obstacles that the work of ministry poses to engaging fully in the Liturgy of the Word and the liturgical seasons:

- *I find myself so beleaguered with extra things to do as the parish celebrates Advent that I am left to wonder about my personal preparation for the coming of the Lord.*
- *One thing I most know about working in the parish: I had a permanent case of the bends! If Easter came early, sometimes we were starting Lent preparations before Christmas had happened.*
- *Sometimes I can't even hear the Word proclaimed because I'm reviewing the tempo and cues for the responsorial psalm in my head.*

It is possible to reframe these challenges as graced opportunities for lay ministers. First, like Jesus, those in ministry take spiritual nourishment from the very act of ministering to the community. Rehearsing the psalm and proclaiming it in the assembly allow the words to infuse and shape one's spirit to a profound extent. Second, also like Jesus, ministers are blessed with opportunities in the course of their work to listen to and pray with the word of God so that it can shape their decisions and ministries. Their "Advent" may not coincide chronologically with that of the community, but this may not be as significant as it seems at first glance. After all, the liturgical year itself does not follow a strict chronology: Advent prayers and scriptures already refer to the adult John the Baptist and the mystery of the incarnation, and we celebrate the martyrdom of St. Stephen on the day after the feast of the Nativity of the Lord! In these and in other aspects of ministry, lay ministers can find guidance in the ministry of Jesus, and follow his example of balancing work and prayer.

The Sunday homily should provide, as the General Instruction of the Roman Missal states, "the nurturing of the Christian life" (GIRM 65). While this is often the case, the gifts and passion for preaching do not always follow ordination. Lay preaching is explored elsewhere in this collection. From our brief reflection here, we can conclude that lay ecclesial ministers are in a position to draw profound connections between the Liturgy of the Word and the spirituality of discipleship. Those who offer their insights to homilists increase the likelihood that the homily at Mass will nurture the Christian life of discipleship in the community of faith.

A Spirituality of Paschal Mystery

Much has been said about the sacrifices that Catholic lay ecclesial ministers make in service of the Church. This group of ministers spoke of financing large tuition payments, accepting lower salaries than they otherwise might have received, spending long hours and many holy days away from their families. There are also intangible sacrifices. Some lay people are burdened by the knowledge that they will never be Catholic priests. Others experience humiliation at the hands of those who serve as pastors. Some deal with distrust from the communities they serve. Many have lost their jobs with the arrival of a new priest or bishop who may not share their vision of ministry.

The essay by Vivian Clausing in this collection beautifully unfolds the relationship between lay ecclesial ministry and the paschal mystery. It explores how a spirituality centered in the paschal mystery can give lay ministers hope and courage to endure the struggles of ministry. Here we will focus on two moments in the Eucharistic Prayer that the participants in this project pointed out as supporting this paschal spirituality: the invocation of the Holy Spirit and the institution narrative. Through the Eucharistic Prayer, the paschal mystery can shed light on the work of lay ministers and replenish their confidence in the transformative power of the Holy Spirit.

The prayer to the Holy Spirit over the gifts and the Church, called the epiclesis, engages those present in the mystery of the resurrection – the power of the Holy Spirit to bring life out of death, to make mere human gifts into the living Christ present here and now. This prayer invites those in ministries to offer their gifts and struggles to be transformed by the Holy Spirit into something new and holy for the life of the Church. One lay minister revealed his deep identification with the invocation of the Holy Spirit: *"the prayers of Epiclesis blessed and consecrated the people as they consecrated the elements of bread and wine. I'm not a liturgical scholar but I know and feel the transformation during these moments!"* The U.S. bishops affirm the spiritual value of such interior participation: "When lay ecclesial ministers cultivate a special devotion and complete openness to the Holy Spirit, the power of Pentecost will be alive in their hearts and at work through their ministry."[12] In fact, lay ministers find that they cannot survive long in ministry unless they cultivate hope in the transformative power of the Holy Spirit. The epiclesis nourishes that hope.

At the heart of the Eucharistic Prayer – and of the paschal mystery – is Jesus' self- offering out of love for the world. In the institution narrative, the Church recalls the words of Jesus through which he offered his life, suffering and death to God and summoned disciples to do the same. Lay ministers resonate with this call to imitate the loving sacrifice of Jesus and let it shape their identity and their ministry. *"I am trying to keep my Christ glasses on; using Jesus as the lens while growing and operating in my ministerial identity and direction in the midst of this angst. He stayed, he loved and sacrificed and extended himself up to his last breath. I want to speak from that position of strength and sacrifice."*

The summons to imitate Christ so central to the call to ministry finds its clearest expression in the institution narrative of the Eucharistic Prayer. One project participant described a liturgy during which these words opened her heart to re-envision her painful ministry situation:

> *Bringing my shock, disbelief and fear of the unknown into the Mass, I found myself paying particular attention to the prayer at consecration. "Take this, all of you, and eat of it, for this is my body, which will be given up for you."[13] I had a choice about how I responded to this situation. Perhaps I was really being called to give over my life, willingly as*

---

[12] Ibid., 52.

[13] "The Order of Mass," in *The Roman Missal,* Third Typical Edition, trans. International Commission on English in the Liturgy (New York: Catholic Book Publishing, 2011), 491.

> *Jesus did. Perhaps this was not so much a matter of others taking from me, as me giving up for them.*
>
> *The next part was even more startling. "This is the chalice of my blood, the blood of the new and eternal covenant, which will be poured out for you and for many for the forgiveness of sins. Do this in memory of me."[14] As I heard these words, I understood. . . . Following Jesus always leads to suffering and death. I felt a huge wave of relief. Although it felt like I had lost everything I cared about, I was doing exactly as God intended me to do. What was now death would eventually become new life. I just needed to have faith. I felt particularly close to Jesus, all of a sudden. I understood his ministry—and how I was to imitate it—in a way that I never had before.*

Co-Workers in the Vineyard of the Lord calls ecclesial ministers to embrace this spirituality, saying, "Paschal love, which always includes the cross, means that one is ready to sacrifice self so that others may experience God's abundant life, and so that all together, strengthened by hope, may hasten to the Resurrection."[15] When lay ecclesial ministers offer their ministries to God in the Eucharist, they do so in imitation of Christ, with the sure hope that the Holy Spirit will do something new, something that they may not have imagined and that will become a source of abundant life for them, their co-workers, and the community of faith. Such transformation almost always requires sacrifice. They may be called to walk away or stand firm, to exercise patience or act with courage, to listen with compassion or speak the truth. The Eucharistic Prayer has the power to sustain ministers in a spirituality of the paschal mystery as they seek to serve in imitation of Jesus.

A Sacramental Spirituality of Communion

Many participants in this project revealed a sacramental spirituality of communion that strengthens them in working together with other ecclesial ministers and with the entire community of faith. And the sacrament of Holy Communion celebrates the spirituality of communion that these lay ministers

---

[14] Ibid.
[15] United States Conference of Catholic Bishops, *Co-Workers*, 39-40.

claim -- a spirituality with both personal and communal dimensions.

As the US bishops note, Holy Communion brings lay ecclesial ministers into a "personal encounter and ongoing relationship with the Lord . . . the vital soul and source needed to bear lasting fruit."[16] This personal dimension of a spirituality of communion was described by one participant as desire for an increase in holiness through communion with God: *"The notion of holiness took hold of me. I began to delight in the thought of being one with God."* Another person also highlighted the connection between the sacrament of the Eucharist and personal communion with the Lord: *"When I celebrate the Eucharist there is often a moment when I feel the wine burn as it goes down my throat. Christ is always with me. There is both comfort and challenge in that knowledge. Knowing that Christ walks with me strengthens me for whatever lies ahead be that joy or sorrow."*

At the same time the Eucharist is profoundly communal. In the sacrament of the Eucharist the assembly enters into communion with both the Body of Christ and the Holy Trinity. In the Eucharist "Christ becomes present whole and entire, God and man."[17] Where Christ is "present whole and entire," the whole Church is present: The head cannot be severed from the members in the living, breathing Body of Christ. And where there is Christ, "God and man," there also is the entire Godhead, for the three are one. Jesus said, "As you, Father, are in me and I am in you, may they also be in us" (John 17.21). Participation in the Eucharist can thus be seen as communion with the Real Presence of all the members of the Body of Christ, living and deceased, united in the divine life of the Holy Trinity.

The communal dimension of the sacrament resonates with lay ministers' understanding of ministry. As one stated, *"we are not individual ministers--we are part of a community."* The Communion Rite can provide them with the spiritual and theological foundation to guide their faith communities in becoming a sacrament of communion. *"God breaks through at the moment of sacramental encounter, but God's grace continues*

---

[16] Ibid., 38.

[17] Pope Paul VI, *Mysterium Fidei* (Encyclical on the Holy Eucharist) (Vatican City: 1965), 39.

to be with us throughout our life, helping us to live the truth of the sacrament." All ministers assist the community in living out their trinitarian communion when they foster mutual sharing of love and work as equal, distinct persons. They build up communion in the Body of Christ when they enable believers to welcome everyone's gifts and heal wounds that prevent the healthy functioning of the whole Body of Christ.

This communal dimension may also show ministers a way beyond the common *"struggle between a 'Christologically' based presbyterate and a 'pneumatologically' based lay ministry. In reality, it is all one work, one mission, and we may be able to start to recognize that if we can recognize the entire Trinity in the Eucharist."* In 2001 then Pope John Paul II laid out a blueprint for facilitating this spirituality of communion. He urged all ecclesial ministers:

> to promote a spirituality of communion . . . to think of our brothers and sisters . . . as "those who are a part of me" [and] to see what is positive in others, to welcome it and prize it as a gift from God . . . to know how to "make room" for our brothers and sisters . . . and resist the selfish temptations which constantly beset us and provoke competition, careerism, distrust and jealousy. The new century will have to see us more than ever intent on valuing and developing the forums and structures which . . . serve to ensure and safeguard communion.[18]

These words of Saint John Paul II were meant to promote healthy relationships among ordained and lay ecclesial ministers--and this is no easy task. In the sacrament of Holy Communion all ecclesial ministers are invited to live as members of one another in the Body of Christ, united in the creative, saving, sanctifying work of the Holy Trinity. We do so when we open ourselves to one another's perspectives, gifts, and pain, and seek pathways of unity and peace: *"All are in need of mutual healing and understanding which leads to a renewed camaraderie that benefits and invigorates the wider church . . . let us pray for the*

---

[18] Pope John Paul II, *Nuevo Millennio Ineunte (*Apostolic Letter at the Close of the Great Jubilee of the Year 2000) (Vatican City: 2001) 43, 44.

church and all who labor in God's vineyard. May we all become true eucharistic people."

The Communion Rite beckons all ministers to center their spirituality in sacramental communion with the fullness of Christ. Such a spirituality compels them to join together in manifesting the differentiated unity and love present in the Holy Trinity and the Body of Christ. The "Emerging from the Vineyard" participants embrace that spirituality. The Communion Rite urges ministers to realize the Church as a sacrament of communion within their faith communities and among their co-workers in the vineyard.

A Spirituality of Loving Service

Every eucharistic liturgy closes with a dismissal – a sending forth to mission. The role of ministers in the life of the Church may be summed up as bringing the dismissal to fruition – that is, guiding the community in living out a spirituality of mission and service. This "spirituality of loving service"[19] is operative in those who were involved in this project.

Three quotes will suffice to illustrate their perspective:

- *Every Sunday we gather to celebrate Eucharist, but from that celebration we are to go and live Eucharist. The difficult thing is not so much the celebration of Eucharist, but the living of Eucharist.*
- *The call to lay ecclesial ministry is always about committed service to God and to God's People.*
- *Serving . . . is what we are sent to do.*

Co-Workers echoes this understanding: "In its broadest sense, ministry is to be understood as service *(diakonia)* and is the means for accomplishing mission in the communion of the Church."[20]

How might lay ecclesial ministers find support in the liturgy for sending the Church into mission and service? An example can be seen in the foot washing ritual of Holy Thursday. Several

[19] United States Conference of Catholic Bishops, *Co-Workers,* 39.
[20] Ibid., 20.

participants in the "Emerging from the Vineyard' project wrote about its power to inculcate a spirituality of service. John's gospel, as we know, does not include a narrative of Jesus breaking bread and inviting disciples to "do this in memory of me." In its place we find Jesus washing feet and inviting disciples to do as he has done. Thus, the washing of feet on Holy Thursday has the same meaning as the words of institution: Through the ritual of foot washing disciples are called to serve as Jesus served.

In one parish a lay minister expanded the ritual so that everyone had an opportunity to participate. He witnessed *"people smiling as they poured out the symbol of service upon each other's toes . . . an act of reconciliation . . . all who participated had [been] called forth by Christ . . . to serve each other, and they responded. Praise God!"* Thus celebrated, the foot washing ritualized the participation of the entire Christian community in Christ's ministry of service.

In some parishes, however, the rite is restricted only to those mentioned in the rubrics: "After the Homily, where a pastoral reason suggests it, the Washing of Feet follows. The men who have been chosen are led by the ministers to seats prepared in a suitable place. Then the Priest goes to each one, and, with the help of the ministers, pours water over each one's feet and then dries them."[21] When celebrated in this way, the foot washing can ritualize a spirituality that focuses narrowly on the distinct participation of the ordained in Christ's ministry. There is nothing inherently wrong with this focus, but it runs the risk of contradicting the rite's intended symbolic correlation with Christ's instruction to all disciples at the end of the Holy Thursday gospel pericope: "As I have done for you, you should also do" (John 13:15). When this is the case, or when the ritual is omitted entirely, an opportunity is lost for the liturgy to instill a spirituality of service in lay ministers and the entire faith community.

Thus, the liturgy can form – or de-form – the Christian community's sense of being sent into mission. Lay ministers have important roles to play in preparing liturgical celebrations that

---

[21] "Mass of the Lord's Supper," in *The Roman Missal,* Third Typical Edition, trans. International Commission on English in the Liturgy (New York: Catholic Book Publishing, 2011), 156.

foster a spirituality of service and in coordinating parish activities that send forth the faith community into the life of mission.

Implications for Lay Ecclesial Ministers

What does the eucharistic spirituality of lay ecclesial ministry that we have explored here imply for lay ministers and for the broader Church?

1. Nurture gratitude. Throughout the quotations in this essay one can sense an undercurrent of humble gratitude. These ministers recognize that their vocations and their successes in ministry are gifts from God to be offered back to God with, in the words of the Eucharist, thanks and praise. Thankfulness is like a taproot which is fed and watered by the Eucharist and out of which healthy ecclesial ministry flowers and bears succulent fruit.

2. Attend to the Sunday experience. We cannot overestimate the role that the liturgical renewal begun by the Second Vatican Council has played in fostering lay ecclesial ministry. The level and the quality of collaborative participation in Sunday liturgy affect both our vision of ministry and our understanding of the Church. Liturgical choices deserve careful attention, for they will have a profound influence on the future of lay ministry and the ministries of the people of God. At the same time, ministers who intentionally choose to enter into the Sunday Eucharist on a spiritual level, despite any internal and external obstacles in their way, will reap a rich harvest for themselves and the people they serve.

3. Cultivate pastoral presence. Lay ecclesial ministers find that their pastoral presence far supersedes any particular positions they may hold or tasks they perform. The Church's teaching on the presence of Christ in the assembly of the baptized supports this perspective. Lay ministers do well to broaden their gaze from a nearsighted focus on job descriptions and to-do lists to a vision of ministry as mediating incarnational presence in the communities they serve.

4. Facilitate the ministries of the baptized. Lay ecclesial ministers must learn early that their ministry is to facilitate the participation of all the baptized in the ministry of Jesus Christ. Liturgical principles and the Eucharist itself show us that the role of those in ministerial leadership is to model, encourage, and

guide the functioning of the Christian community, the Body of Christ. Lay ministers involve the community in the mission of Jesus by fostering the baptismal identity of the faithful, helping them connect their personal stories with the mysteries of our faith, providing opportunities for service, and acting as role models of full participation in the life, liturgies, and ministries of the Church.

5. Foster relationships among co-workers. Genuine collaboration among Catholic ecclesial ministers is called for by the spirit of the liturgy, the ministerial documents, and the nature of the Church. Collaboration—while often being more emotionally taxing and time-consuming than working alone—is fundamental to being "co-workers" in the vineyard of the Lord. It is also likely to bear more nutritious and abundant fruit in the life of the Church. Ministers further such collaboration when they engage in respectful dialogue, foster relationships, and commit themselves to working together with their colleagues in ministry.

6. Commit to seeking ongoing formation. Lay ecclesial ministers encounter many challenges from their life situations, their communities, and their colleagues in ministry. They must seek solid and ongoing spiritual formation in order to develop the inner authority and identity to overcome those varied hurdles. The Eucharist suggests that such formation be grounded in the dignity and functions of the baptized, nurture the life of Christian discipleship, and draw out the implications of the Church as a communion oriented toward mission.

The Eucharist offers lay ecclesial ministers both a sign and an instrument of a spirituality that serves the communion and mission of the Church. The Eucharist alone cannot provide all of the spiritual nourishment that ministers need. What it can do is to nurture a eucharistic spirituality of service and communion, reveal pathways of discipleship, open hearts to sacrifice and transformation, image collaborative participation in the ministry of Jesus Christ, and manifest the baptismal dignity and calling at the root of lay ecclesial ministry. Ministers who find their spiritual center in the Eucharist will find nourishment to collaborate in moving the Church toward greater realization of its true identity as a sacrament of communion for mission.

Questions for Reflection:

1. How does your experience of the Eucharist support or challenge you in your ministry?

2. What ideas from this essay would you share with others in ministry and why?

3. *Co-Workers in the Vineyard of the Lord* reminds us that ongoing formation is not a luxury but a permanent necessity for lay and ordained ecclesial ministers. What ongoing spiritual formation do you find in the liturgy? How does this essay encourage you to seek further formation for yourself and your colleagues in ministry?

Death into Life: A Spirituality of Lay Ecclesial Ministry

Vivian Clausing

Introduction

> *I have found myself wishing someone had told me that lay ecclesial ministry (LEM) would "be a roller-coaster ride." I entered into LEM full of joy and hope, never anticipating that I would have some dark and difficult days.*[1]

We don't often realize it, but the invitation to lay ministry is an invitation to both abundant life and to death. As lay people entrusted with church work,[2] we joyfully answer the call to serve as parish leaders, teachers, youth ministers, liturgical ministers, coordinators of social justice ministries, administrators, and support staff without much thought about how our service might end. In fact, within our ministerial and personal lives there are many endings, and with those endings, losses big and small.[3] What can we do with these "deaths," both in our secular lives and in ministry? As Catholics, we look to our faith, not only to make sense of what happens to us, but also to help us respond to the stress of our jobs and the inevitable transitions in our lives. Our lives in ministry, as in Christian life, are paschal mystery. Called to serve others as professionals in church, we become bread, broken for the lives of our communities. We both experience and

---

[1] Throughout, quotes from journal entries of lay ecclesial ministers involved in the "Emerging from the Vineyard" project will be integrated into the text. These quotes will be indicated by *use of italics*

[2] United States Conference of Catholic Bishops, *Co-Workers in the Vineyard of the Lord* (Washington, DC: United States Conference of Catholic Bishops, 2005).

[3] Death and loss can take many forms, and often our culture does not recognize losses except those associated with literal death. I have focused on losses associated with lay ecclesial ministry here, such as the losses associated with turnover in parishes and on campuses, as well as retirement, voluntary and involuntary. For a discussion about losses commonly encountered in life and resources for helping others through them, see Kenneth R. Mitchell and Herbert Anderson, *All Our Losses, All Our Griefs* (Louisville: John Knox Westminister Press, 1983).

make visible to others a cycle of birth, death, vigil, and resurrection that witnesses to our spirituality.

This essay is the fruit of many conversations with lay ecclesial ministers working in the vineyard of the Lord between 2010-2012. In sharing their stories, both in person and through an online forum, the participants often related experiences of marginalization, grief, and loss associated with ministry. Stories of conflicts, lost opportunities and periods of transition between ministries were most common; very rarely did lay ministers report that they felt secure and affirmed in their positions by the ecclesial structure that they served. While most would not give up their ministries for other pursuits, all struggled to make sense of their challenges and losses, particularly those associated with faith communities, because such communities strive to live out Gospel values and ideals.

But our Catholic faith offers much wisdom on how to live life in relationship with death. It is this ancient mystery that we Catholics understand as paschal mystery; over and over, we die in various ways, but having died with Christ, we rise again. This essay offers reflections about how we can die with intention. Our faith teaches that if we are following Jesus we die—to ourselves, to sin, and ultimately to the attachments that might keep us from fully embracing the life to which God has called us. In the process, we are formed, molded into the people that God wants us to be. In the process, we are called to enflesh the reality of Catholic lay ecclesial ministry in a way that bears witness to the Kingdom and the loving presence of God in our world.

Reflecting on our faith and on our stories, I have divided this essay into four parts that follow the liturgical sequence from Good Friday through Pentecost: (1) Death, (2) Vigil, (3) Resurrection, and (4) Pentecost. Quotations from lay ministers are noted in italics and have been de-identified to preserve confidentiality. I am grateful to my co-workers for the sharing of their experiences and the questions that they posed which have shaped this essay. The life experiences of these ministers, both in church and in the secular world, are a source of wisdom upon which others can draw.

I am indebted to theologian Ron Rolheiser for the notion of finding companionship during transitions through a deeper understanding of the paschal mystery as tied to our celebration of Easter.[4] However, I have departed from the model that Rolheiser outlines in his classic book, *The Holy Longing.* I spend time examining the notion of vigil, because in my experience, there is an important *liminal* space between the moment of death (Good Friday) and the awareness that new life has been given to us (Easter Sunday) that is important for lay ministers to name and reflect upon. In this age of Google, the Internet and email, we have lost the art of waiting. When death occurs, we naturally want the process to be over, and think that something is terribly wrong if we don't see the light at the tunnel. This essay challenges the reader to consider death as part of ministry and keep vigil—both individually and with others—as an intentional practice.

In addition, this essay suggests that Easter (Resurrection) is not the end of the process. Contrary to cultural expectations, resurrection is not healing and perfection, but acknowledging our woundedness and striving for deeper authenticity. During the period that follows death and the receipt of the fullness of new life (what Rolheiser calls "The Forty Days and Ascension" but what I call "Resurrection and Pentecost"), we learn to recognize and embrace the life that God has given us, and we accept new gifts and direction so that we can be sent forth again into the world. It is my hope that in hearing the experiences of their co-workers while reflecting upon the paschal mystery, the readers might draw strength from knowing that they are not alone, and that in fact, death is part of the gift of life that our good God gives to us.

Many Lives, Many Deaths

For lay ecclesial ministers working in the Church today, there are many ways to die. Some are extremely public. We resign from cherished staff positions after years of ministering in, and

---

[4] In relating their stories of how faith helped them to accept various "deaths," some lay ecclesial ministers pointed to a model laid out in Ron Rolheiser's *The Holy Longing* (New York: Doubleday 1999) 146-148. Here, Rolheiser describes the paschal mystery in five phrases: (1) Good Friday (death) (2) Easter Sunday (receiving new life), (3) The Forty Days (readjustment to the new and grieving the old), (4) Ascension (letting go of the old and letting it bless us), and (5) Pentecost (accepting the spirit of life you are given).

functioning as pillars of, our communities. Budgets are squeezed and our jobs are eliminated without warning. Influential parishioners disagree with us, and suddenly our ministries are limited or gone overnight. The lights in our hearts go out after we lose loved ones and our professional commitments prevent us from taking the time we need to grieve our own losses. Families leave our schools and programs, leaving us behind to mourn the loss of relationships and the chance for ongoing ministry. Beloved mentors retire, leaving us to work out new rules and ways of working with successors who might make radical changes without consulting us.

Other deaths are subtle, visible to us alone. We may discover that we don't have support for an idea that we thought crucial to good ministry. We might be asked to implement a program or idea without the opportunity to discuss it and collaborate with our co-workers. We might discover that being in our position means that we cannot speak freely unless we want to risk losing our job. We may see aspects of professional ministry that challenge our faith, or be asked to promote positions that we personally don't believe in. We may feel silenced, invisible in the shadow of another who does not know how to mentor us, or is unwilling to acknowledge our work and presence.

Sometimes, death is sudden and unexpected. Other times, death is long, drawn out, and seemingly never ending, hidden in the loss of privileges, lack of gratitude or exclusion from projects or committees. Death may occur during a confrontation away from our community but in front of our colleagues. Death may come behind a closed office door in a conversation with someone whose subsequent version of what was said differs markedly from our own.

And sometimes, we wake up one morning and realize that despite our best efforts, we are dying—that our ministry is draining us rather than feeding us—and that we cannot go on much longer. Perhaps we are the ones who seek change in order to survive. Or perhaps we choose to remain in our positions, hoping that new life will come to us in some unforeseen way.

Jesus, Us and Death

We cannot avoid death, but we can choose how to respond to it. For lay ecclesial ministers, death is part of ministry, just as Jesus' death on Good Friday, freely accepted, was part of Jesus' ministry. Accepting death and the pain, humiliation and vulnerability that accompany it is not something that we choose lightly. Nor was it a choice that Jesus made lightly. In the Garden of Gethsemane, Jesus prays, "Father, if you are willing, take this cup from me. But not my will, yours be done" (Luke 22:42). Through the Passion, Jesus models for us a radical love, one that calls us to give all for our communities, even those who persecute us. Through the passion, Jesus models how we can offer non-violence in the face of violence and forgiveness and blessing in the face of injustice.

Our American culture celebrates life[5], and as lay ministers, we live in the world. Much of our secular life urges us to seek power, status, and wealth. Most of us learn as children to hold fast to our possessions and to defend ourselves when threatened. Learning to die—to surrender, to release that which we most cherish—is a discipline that we must literally learn how to practice. For lay ministers, learning to surrender in ways large and small while trusting that "everything will be all right" is an ongoing spiritual discipline. One lay minister, a former advocate trained to defend others in the face of conflict, describes the process of learning to surrender in the following way when her volunteer ministry became caught in the paid staff's "office politics," resulting in its eventual elimination:

> *I learned that saying yes to death is very much like saying yes to life. It is in fact the same thing, but it does not look that way. Church teaches that we are to embrace death, yet every Church person I knew scrupulously avoided it. Somehow I was on unbroken ground as I continued to accept my lot, refusing to defend myself. It was hard to let others come in and take everything for themselves: my ideas, my dreams, my community, what I thought was my*

[5] See Ernest Becker, *The Denial of Death* (New York: The Free Press, 1973). Becker has written extensively on how, in order to cope with the idea of death, Americans in particular focus on life, and pretend that death does not happen.

future. But I learned that there is truth in the Scripture: "Whoever seeks to save his life will lose it. But he who loses his life for the sake of the Gospel will find it."

Victims or Witnesses?

As lay ecclesial ministers, the ways in which we die are very important. Because of our positions in ministry, others watch us closely. How do we ensure that our deaths are gifts to our communities and not self glorification on one hand or the perpetration of injustice on the other? What is the difference between offering one's life for the sake of the Gospel, and being "killed" senselessly?

Intention is everything. Death has a way of stripping away everything except our core selves. When we face death, we are tested and challenged both to live out of our authentic selves and to make decisions that feel crucial because death makes our situation feel so significant. In dying, we have the opportunity to see who we really are, and to return to God. How do we do this? By choosing good.

On Ash Wednesday, we are reminded that we came from dust and are returning to dust. With this humbling image in mind, we strive to turn away from sin and be faithful to the Gospel in all that we do. When we face death, turning from sin means having the strength to look at our situations honestly and seek the courage to make choices which are generative for those whom we serve. We acknowledge, with humility, that our desires may have to give way for the greater good of the community that we minister to. In order to do this, we must acknowledge that death is always looking back at us, but have the faith to believe that everything will be all right.

Reflecting on death, which makes us aware of how precious our lives are, we might ask ourselves some pointed questions. How well are we using the time that God has given us? Is our ministry continuing to bear fruit, or does the Spirit seem to be moving in a different direction? Are we in right relationship with our supervisor and co-workers, or has ministry become more about conflict than about ministering? Is there an injustice that should be addressed? What actions are realistic? What is beyond our control?

Most importantly we should ask, "What does love call for?" As Kingdom people, we are called to a love that is patient and kind, that does not seek its own way, and which rejoices not in wrongdoing but in the truth (1 Cor 13). The love that Jesus calls us to is revolutionary. It is beyond our cultural understanding of love as purely passion and emotion. Gospel love is about commitment, faithfulness, and fidelity. It is about serving, forgiving, and transforming. It is about loving others as God does.

Choosing Death, Choosing Love

To love as God does, we must know God intimately. As disciples and professionals serving Church, our lives must be rooted in prayer which strengthens our relationship with God, helping us to learn to depend on God as we seek to remain in community and to love with a radical love. In addition to our daily prayer and faithful Mass attendance, we should seek the advice of mentors, spiritual directors, and trusted wisdom figures in discerning our way.[6] Sometimes, choosing to leave a situation may be our best option. Other times, remaining for the sake of the community may be a commitment that we choose to make. Sometimes our very presence is an act of resistance, although it may look as if we are powerless. Whatever we choose to do, our actions should be sourced in love, and understood by others to be offered in the spirit of love and life.

Throughout our lives, as we choose to put our communities and the Gospel first, we will pay a price, but as long as we consciously choose to do so, we are witnesses, not victims. In the movie *Of Gods and Men,*[7] a community of Trappist monks living in Algeria during its civil war struggles to discern whether to stay and continue to minister or flee the war-torn country. Ultimately after much reflection and prayer, the community decides to remain despite the danger because witnessing to God's love is their vocation. They believe that their Christian values call them to love inclusively and to extend relationship even to their Muslim neighbors. This decision costs most of the community

[6] See *Co-Workers in the Vineyard of the Lord*, Part 2.B for standards of formation and suggested spiritual practices for lay ecclesial ministers.

[7] *Of Gods and Men*. Film. Directed by Xavier Beauvois. Australia: Sony Pictures Home Entertainment, 2011.

their lives, as they are taken hostage and executed by fundamentalist terrorists. So too, as a community of lay ecclesial ministers called into service to Church, we must discern how best to witness our vocation, a calling that at times calls for personal sacrifice.

Ron Rolheiser says it well when he points out that no one takes away that which is freely given for another:

> When is one a victim and when is one giving one's life for others? At the level of outward appearance, this can be indistinguishable. Outward action is not the criterion, inward freedom is. I am a victim when somebody takes my life. I am practicing selfless virtue when I freely give it.[8]

A mature spiritual person strives to become a cheerful giver rather than a bitter victim.[9] A mature spirituality leads us to speak our own truth as well as to honor the perspective of the other. Speaking our truth may mean pointing out circumstances that are uncomfortable, or unjust. But maturity leads us to use right speech, a respectful tone and to perhaps wait until initial outrage has passed before speaking. Only through prayer and discernment can we know when and how we might be called to love deeply by choosing to die in various ways. The paradox is that by doing so we ultimately experience freedom although we may not fully realize it for some time.

Vigil: "Reaching for God"

> *After my position in the parish was eliminated I learned to stare stubbornly ahead, and to hold onto my community, even if I did not feel like I was welcome there. I kept reminding myself that God is good and that I believe in Resurrection.*

---

[8] Ronald Rolheiser, "The Line Between Victims and Saints," *Daybreaks: Daily Reflections for Lent and Easter* (Liguori, MO: Liguori Publications, ed. Alicia von Stamwitz, 2005) 19.

[9] Ibid.

What Do We Mean by "Vigil"?

Between death and the fullness of new life is a period of waiting, of keeping vigil.[10] In the silence that follows our death, the impact of whatever has occurred sinks into our consciousness. Taken down from the cross but not yet resurrected, we wait in darkness for whatever is coming next. One lay ecclesial minister names this active waiting—a time in which we are attentive to what is going on in our lives as we try to make sense of where we now are. We have passed a point of no return. We are no longer the people we were before. We have departed from our familiar way of being and we face something that is entirely unexpected. We stand at a crossroads.

In order to become what God calls us to be, we must cross over this threshold space. The Holy Spirit is our guide, and Jesus our companion, but we choose to go with the process or to resist it. Pacing ourselves is important. Trying to move on before we have fully grieved might prevent us from taking in the lessons that we need to absorb so that we can apply wisdom in our future lives. Clinging to the past leaves us untouched, under-developed, at risk of repeating our experience all over again in the future. Moving between old and new is a journey and the process an archetypal human one. In ancient times, rituals of passage helped our ancestors to move effectively between stages in life.[11] So too, can our faith shepherd us from childhood to maturity, from grief to joy, from anger to open heartedness.

The space between death and new life can be a holy space, a time in which we draw nearer to the spiritual world. But liminal space is often not an easy place to be. Rolheiser says that crisis puts us into the Garden of Gethsemane where we are challenged, like Jesus, to accept God's will. We sweat blood in order to make

---

[10] William Bridges describes this place of waiting as the neutral zone. William Bridges, *The Way of Transition: Embracing Life's Most Difficult Moments* (Cambridge, MA: Da Capo Press, 2001) 3-6; 38-45.

[11] Bridges notes that we have fewer of these rituals available to us today and that we have lost some important truths about transitions. In particular we have forgotten that renewal comes to us through loss and giving up what we were before (Ibid., 42). Perhaps lay ministers should consider ways to ritualize "deaths" in order to help one another pass into new life.

peace with ourselves so that something new can take root in us.[12] Making peace may involve facing our own inadequacies. This can be challenging. The raw experience of death may cause us to focus on our regrets, rather than on what we did well in our past life. We may replay the experience of death over and over, trying to figure out how we might have avoided it. Even if we died for a good cause, there may be days afterwards in which we wish that we had not died at all.

Learning to Keep Vigil

As we slow down and face our demons, it is important to listen for God's voice in what may feel like chaos. Vigil bids us to turn to God, strengthening our relationship through prayer. Vigil is a time to listen closely and to move slowly. Hearing God can be extremely challenging when we are suffering, and we may need to exercise patience in order to discern. Vigil can be a time of profound grief as we face our losses. We might find ourselves attending to organizational details in life—cleaning out files, reorganizing work spaces, giving away things that we no longer need and struggling to make sense of our suffering. Perhaps the most difficult adjustments are those that come in our communities as changes in roles mean changes not only in how people interact with us, but in what we can do to express and live out our faith:

> *But my relationship with our school has changed. I feel uneasy entering the space. I used to be regularly called to help with Mass planning but have heard that invitation only once this year. Truth is, my heart is sad and broken and in some ways...reflect[s] the larger population of our community.*

Vigil can be a lonely time, a time when we feel isolated from old friends. The social expectations around our ministry may have changed and we may find ourselves on the margins, on the outside looking in: The old rules no longer apply and we struggle to know what to do, whom to talk to and what role we now play:

> *When I left my parish position, I knew that the probability that I would find a similar staff position when I was ready*

---

[12] *Daybreaks*, 36-37.

> *to return to ministry was slim. What I did not anticipate, however, was that I would find the door to ministry as a parish volunteer would almost literally be slammed in my face by parish leadership . . . These questions come to mind: We talk a lot about "empowering" others to do ministry. What do we do if we find ourselves dis-empowered? When the direction of a parish changes and we are willing to change with it, what do we do if we are shut out of the process?*

Vigil may be a time when it is challenging for us to remain in our church, and we struggle to participate in Mass, and even to pray. But God does not abandon us. Friends, spouses, and spiritual directors can keep vigil with us, holding space for our soul work, encouraging us to go on. Many of us find the time, previously filled with meetings and events, to develop a deeper prayer life. We might find comfort in silence, the practice of retreat, or the sacrament of reconciliation. One minister aptly points out that our liturgical calendar, with its celebration of life, death, and resurrection, helps to remind us of where we are:

> *I am able to find deep meaning for the deaths--life's little, and big disappointments by being fully connected to the feasts and seasons of the liturgical year. Taking time each day to pray morning and evening prayer certainly provides the language--the deep poetry of the church that offers a way to be one with Christ and our ancestors in faith who also struggled to find meaning. Ultimately it is the knowledge and experience of God's action and presence in my life that offers hope--the confident expectation that everything will be alright.*

Losing Life, Finding Hope

Learning to wait attentively and with hope is one of the most valuable skills that we can learn for ministry. We can learn to find hope in the small moments of our lives by cultivating an awareness of blessing. Years ago, a classmate described how she and her husband journeyed through the brain cancer that eventually took his life by starting each day with words that named the good in their lives. Sometimes these blessings were simple: the presence of beloved family members, the food that they shared, the irony of a situation that only they understood. This couple developed a ritual of blessing—gestures and daily words of gratitude that sustained them even when the husband lost his ability to speak. Developing the capacity to hope is a gift that living with death gives us. Similarly, one minister describes what she does to stay hopeful in the following way:

> *Years ago I was faced with a long illness. During this time I experienced a series of waitings. I looked to Dr. [Bernie] Segal [author and speaker] for inspiration. I remember someone asking him what he tells his patients to do in between office visits; he said, "live life." And so in all my many "illnesses" since that time, I have learned to live life. Day by day I give my attention to life-giving moments and opportunities. I seek out people who are life-giving and avoid those who pull me down. I [look] to my husband, children, teachers, mentors and friends for support. But in the end hope comes from past experience; if I let go, listen, and be attentive to the God who lives in and through me I will find my way at the crossroads.*

Theologian Michael Himes says that hope, like faith and love, is a virtue that lasts. Christian hope is sourced not in some idealized view of the world, but in our knowledge that we are intensely loved by God, a God who is always reaching for us.[13] This hope leads us to keep reaching for God. Himes uses the image of the miners trapped underground in Chile, who did not lose hope because they knew that the whole world was praying for them and that their rescuers were working to reach them. In the end, hope gives us a radical dependence on God that leads us to pray in order to persevere:

> *My faith tells me to pray, to be open to the Spirit, and to trust in God. My heart tells me that speaking the truth is not always easy, especially in a church that is so accustomed to circling the wagons when a crisis occurs. I may not experience what I would consider individual justice for me; there may yet be even more painful*

---

[13] Michael J. Himes, "Hope in a Wintery Season," lecture at Boston College (October 14, 2010), http://frontrow.bc.edu/program/himes1/ (accessed May 20, 2014).

experiences ahead, inflicting even deeper wounds. . . . I would summarize with what my faith tells me in this Scripture quote from James 1:2-4: "Consider it pure joy, my brothers, whenever you face trials of many kinds, because you know that the testing of your faith develops perseverance. Perseverance must finish its work so that you may be mature and complete, not lacking anything." [NIV translation]

Resurrection: "Peace be with You"

I do very much believe the continual conversion and transformation that is part of a Christian life is fueled by an ongoing cycle of dying to our old selves and rising to the new. In that sense we leave a trail of empty tombs behind. It's the gift of the paschal mystery.

Tomb/Womb

Like water trickling in between slabs of frozen granite, new life creeps in slowly, sometimes in such a subtle way that we do not realize that it is there. Over time, the sound of new life, like running water, begins to fill our consciousness and we feel we are moving forward. Gradually, we may feel refreshed and cleansed. We may realize one day that we are not rushing around the way that we used to, but that this new pace is wonderful and freeing for us. We may re-discover old interests and find that we delight in activities that we haven't had in our lives for years. We may find ourselves nourished by sitting in Mass without being in charge of anything. We may realize that feelings of frustration and anger that we harbored toward former co-workers have faded. We may realize that we are being invited to minister or volunteer in new ways. We may begin to feel excited about our lives again.

We may realize that we have left people and beloved places behind us. We are no longer present at key moments, nor do we have all the details of every situation. Others notice and comment about our absence. When we feel empty, the image of the empty tomb might serve as a reminder to us that in dying, we have been set free. Like Lazarus, we have been un-bound from that which has limited us in the past. Like Jesus, we now move freely in the world, returning to those whom we have loved, although unable to stay with them or relate with them as in the past. As we begin to embrace our new lives, we might take note of this freedom and know that we are on the right track.

Wounded Resurrection

At the same time, we may find that we are not completely healed. Often, our experience has marked us. Pain can resurface suddenly, surprising us with its intensity. We can think that we have forgiven the past at one moment, and then suddenly find ourselves passionately retelling our story to someone who had no idea that anything happened to us. But our faith offers wisdom to us. At the tomb, the risen Jesus reminds Mary, "Do not cling to me." Learning to treasure our births and new lives in the face of the temptation to look backwards is an important practice for lay ecclesial ministers to develop. This can be a challenge. Our identity may be sourced in the past, in the good work we did and the wonderful ministers that we were before we died. We may find ourselves repeating old patterns without realizing it. And yet, if we do not allow our new lives to transform us, we remain stuck in the darkness, unable to go on.

Our struggle to emerge from our tombs into new creations is part of the birthing process. Referencing Ronald Rolheiser, one minister says:

> *I have also learned that one of the most challenging parts of the paschal mystery cycle...is the Ascension; the letting go of the old and letting it bless you, the refusal to cling. In the midst of grieving my husband's loss, for example, I found myself fearing that if I "let go" that I would in some way diminish my memories of him... in the case of my challenges with ministry in my parish, perhaps it has been hard to let go as I hope against nearly impossible odds that things will change—that the death really didn't happen.*

When he appears to the disciples after Easter, Jesus does two very important things. He says, "Peace be with you," and he shows the disciples his wounds. In showing his wounds, Jesus reveals himself to those who are not sure of his identity. Our wounds become part of who we are; to deny their existence would be to lose our authenticity. But Jesus models for us our response when we confront those people and institutions which have wounded us. Instead of saying "Look what they did to me," we are challenged as disciples to remain in relationship and say, "Peace be with you."[14]

For us, resurrection is a dynamic process, one that unfolds over time. Remembering that we are still being molded and formed can help us to have patience with ourselves, as well as to continue to embrace our new life and growth. Knowing that we are called to be reborn over and over in our lives, we can be midwives for one another, encouraging our colleagues in lay ecclesial ministry to be people of peace and new life. Mindful that death is part of ministry, but that everything will be all right, we can choose to be healers in our church and world.

Pentecost: "Receive the Holy Spirit"

> *The movement...to Ascension and Pentecost often comes with the release of anger and the acknowledgement of ways the loss has blessed me. My restless heart becomes quiet and I find it within me to accept the new life offered to me and to move forward with plans to embrace it. The new life is not always the one I wanted or expected but I have learned to place my trust in God and accept his plans for me with a grateful heart. Never in my wildest imagination did I dream that I would be engaged in pastoral ministry in the later years of my life. That, however, was the new life offered to me by the Triune God after my husband's death. It is a life that has blessed me.*

Life after Death: A New Presence

The Easter of new life is not the end of our story. As Catholics we celebrate the fifty days after Easter culminating in Pentecost, during which time Jesus appears to his disciples and becomes present in the world in a new and different way. So too, after death and resurrection, we lay ministers become present in

---

[14] Roberto S. Goizueta, "Put Your Finger Here: Reconciliation and the Refusal to Cease Suffering," Keynote address at the 2006 Murnion Lecture for the Catholic Common Ground Initiative, Catholic Theological Union, available at http://catholiccommonground.org/2006-murnion-lecture (accessed May 20, 2014).

our communities and the wider world in different ways. Like the first disciples, we are transformed by the fire of Pentecost from people huddled in loss to evangelists sent on mission. We are formed into a new community, and in those new relationships, we find our strength and healing. As we connect with new people, we find the courage to become present once again in the world.

Jesus breathes on us, making order out of our chaos, urging us to receive the Holy Spirit. It takes courage and openness on our part to breathe in what is offered to us and to let it transform us. If we learn to accept the movement of the Spirit, we are blessed with new gifts, new perspectives and new places to share ourselves. One lay minister gives the following example of a new gift bestowed upon her by the Spirit:

> *I have feared and grieved the loss of passionate commitment that has come with age and experience. But now I am finding the courage to embrace the gift of wisdom that I have received.*

In learning to accept the Spirit, we may find that we have found our true identities, even as we have lost ourselves. We learn to value ourselves as children of God rather than coordinators of particular ministries, members of particular communities, or holders of certain positions within our families. We learn to walk with Jesus as disciples called to love and serve others wherever we are.

Sent Out in "New Skins"

Throughout our lives, we go forth again and again to proclaim the Good News, each time a little more changed. Mindful of death, we learn to cherish the smallest aspects of life, and to live more fully. Jesus indeed comes to us in order to give us life in abundance. This on-going transformation over our lifetimes keeps us moving and growing. For lay ministers, home life offers important perspective that we can take into ministry. Responding to a co-worker who was struggling to accept new identity after being called out of ministry to start a family, one lay minister advises:

> *It is difficult to put aside the course you have chosen and to set your feet firmly on another course—one that is not*

> *quite as well known or as comfortable as you have been used to in the past. It is about giving up a part of yourself. You will never be the same again. Even when you return to fulltime ministry, you will not be the same person. You will bring a whole new set of expectations and disappointments with you.*
>
> *It happens at every stage of life and it is never easy to transition through. Whether you are a newlywed, new mom, new widow—you are always a new something which implies there was something old there that is gone.*
>
> *As caregivers, we lose ourselves to find a new self--different from what we used to be but no less interesting to discover. Transition is never easy, learning to accept whatever tasks or directions is always a test of our ability to give up "our skins" and form a new skin.*

Over and over, we become new wine in new skins. When the life that we are living comes to an end, we have to say goodbye and bless those whom we leave behind. Each of our deaths prepares us more and more fully for life. As we walk with Jesus, we learn to open our arms wide, breathe in what sustains us, and remembering that we are present for only a short time, hold onto the present just a little less tightly.

Conclusion: "Waiting in Joyful Hope"

The cycle of life, death, resurrection and Pentecost bids us to take a long view of our lives as lay ecclesial ministers. The practice of our faith can lead us to develop a spirituality that can sustain us through the challenges and losses. The intentional practice of dying in ministry and life can teach us to surrender to God, to persevere in faith, to wait in hope, and to keep vigil with others. Although we can face significant suffering in our ministry, our faith reminds us that God is present and active in our lives and that good comes forth in the end.

Lay ecclesial ministry can help us to re-imagine the practice and symbols of our faith. Perhaps the cross is not so much the end as an ongoing vehicle of transformation, and an invitation to birth. As Ronald Rolheiser said once so eloquently, the cross takes everything that is difficult and undesirable and transforms it—and us—into that which is holy. As disciples we are called to take on the ugliness of the world—and perhaps even our workplace at times—and hold it until God transforms it into a new creation. The process of following our dreams, led by God, leads us to new places, and sometimes requires that we let go of the people we used to be. Following Jesus through the crosses of our ministry ultimately leads to life, although we may not see the fullness of this life for many years.

As lay ministers, we are professionals serving the Church, following Jesus and being drawn closer to God. Our call to holiness is lived out both in our secular lives and within the ecclesial structure. We are transformed and we transform those around us through our love, love that leads us to forgive, to heal, to bless and to be grateful. May we have the grace to always surrender to God with intention, and to continue our work in order to transform Church and the world.

Questions for Reflection:

1. What experiences of death and new life have you experienced in ministry or life? How did you react? Did your faith affect your reaction?

2. How might it affect your attitude toward ministry if you ministered with an awareness that death is always looking back at us?

3. The biggest question that this essay raised for me was whether we really can die mindfully. I have come to believe that our intentions do shape our actions and that there is a definite difference between giving one's "life" for others, and being killed senselessly. The writing group reacted very strongly to this notion, and asked me to clarify the difference between being a victim and self-giving. What do you think?

Section Four:

Communal Call and Authorization for Ministry

The Movement of Lay Ecclesial Ministry to the National Market: Young Adult Ministers' Perspective

Julie M. Billmeier

The rise of local farmers markets is something of a recent phenomenon in my area. "Buying local" has become a popular tag line for grocers, restaurants, and farmers. It is touted as being energy efficient, economical, and good for the community. For me, the image of "buying local" continually came to mind as I considered writing about lay ecclesial ministry, particularly as it connects with how ministers are authorized and recognized in their roles. Lay ecclesial ministers have often been recognized first in their own parish, their own "local market," for the gifts and talents that they bring forth to the community. The parish has provided a "market" for them to offer their gifts and served as a conduit for the parishioners to search for and find ways for their faith needs to be met. However, as markets grow and attract more people, and as products become more popular and distribution increases to a wider audience, the experiences of the people in the market change and sometimes a greater need for oversight and regulation comes into play. I believe the same has been true for the experience of lay ecclesial ministers.

My perspective in this essay comes as a young adult in lay ecclesial ministry. A 2010 survey by the Emerging Models of Pastoral Leadership Project estimated that only eighteen percent of lay ecclesial ministers (which the survey defined as paid, non-ordained parish ministry staff working at least twenty hours per week) were under the age of forty.[1] We are a minority in the world of lay ecclesial ministry, and many of our experiences have been different from the lay people who preceded us in this field. When young adult lay ecclesial ministers were surveyed for the Emerging Models of Pastoral Leadership project, two of the top four concerns were for better support/advocacy for lay ministry

---

[1] Mark M. Gray, Mary L. Gautier and Melissa A. Cidade, *The Changing Face of U.S. Catholic Parishes* (Washington, DC: National Association for Lay Ministry, 2011), 61.

and credentialing.[2] They see the need for better support for what they are doing, such as advocacy for lay ministry through official channels like vocations offices or commissioning ceremonies when lay ministers take on new roles.[3] This type of support would help with better recognition of lay ecclesial ministry on a national scale. Although the word "authorization" did not readily come up in conversations with young lay ecclesial ministers, attention to credentialing would help in being recognized for their professional competence when moving to a new place. However, the leap to a kind of standardized authorization process does not seem to be at the top of their minds.

Thus, this model of movement from a local market to a national market is done primarily to present a perspective on the experience of young lay ecclesial ministers today and to engage the question of authorization and certification as it relates to this new experience of young adults in ministry. Just as it is necessary for standards to be established in the marketplace, the Church must enact standards to ensure the appropriate use of those gifts to satisfy the needs in ministerial settings.

The Local Market

When it comes to lay ecclesial ministry, the local parish is the most natural "market" for laypeople to offer their gifts in service to the community, and the parishioners are the most natural "customer." (Of course, this analogy does not work perfectly as parishioners are not simply "customers," but really should be actively engaged participants in their community, but I will discuss this a bit later.) The parish setting allows lay ecclesial ministers to meet the ministerial needs of the people in the parish with the plentiful bounty of their gifts. The gifts in the community are sufficient for the needs, but the venue must be available and efficient for the gifts and needs properly to match one another. However, it is not as simple as matching gifts to needs.

---

[2] According to the survey, the other two top concerns of young adult lay ecclesial ministers were opportunities for spiritual development and financial support; Dean R. Hoge and Marti R. Jewell, *The Next Generation of Pastoral Leaders: What the Church Needs to Know* (Chicago, IL: Loyola Press, 2010), 107.

[3] Ibid.

Historically, many lay ecclesial ministers became ministers by responding to a need in their local parish. According to Edward Hahnenberg, in parishes today we find that "the many lay ecclesial ministers now working in the United States are the pastoral legacy of those first few parish volunteers and women religious who, in the mid-1960s, were hired by their pastors to bring some order to parish Confraternity of Christian Doctrine (CCD) programs."[4] A volunteer opportunity turned into a part-time or full-time job, which sometimes called for a certain level of training or education along the way.

Today, however, more and more young adults are entering undergraduate or graduate programs with the intention of becoming lay ministers, then beginning a nationwide search for job opportunities upon graduation. A report from a November 2010 gathering of young adult lay ecclesial ministers notes that "modern young adults . . . have often moved hundreds if not thousands of miles from home to attend college. And they continue this pattern by taking jobs that may lead them still further away from family and friends."[5] These young ministers are not sitting down with a pastor they have known for years, who knows their gifts and talents, and matching those with a need in a community. Instead they are being interviewed by a team of complete strangers to see if this new community is a good fit for them personally and spiritually. The young adult lay ecclesial ministers who gathered at the symposium in November 2010 recognized this shift, noting as one of their symposium's seven key insights that "pathways to ministry have changed, and today's young adults respond to God's call to ministry in new and different ways."[6]

So what are the resulting pressures within the local market of ministry as these new and different ways of entering the market develop?

---

[4] Edward P. Hahnenberg, "Theology of Lay Ecclesial Ministry: Future Trajectories," in *Lay Ecclesial Ministry: Pathways toward the Future*, ed. Zeni Fox (Lanham, MD: Rowman & Littlefield, 2010), 69.

[5] Jarzembowski, Paul E., ed. *The Next Generation of Pastoral Leaders: Their Chips Are All In* (Washington, DC: National Association for Lay Ministry, 2012), 56.

[6] Ibid., 5.

Oversight

Sometimes, local oversight of markets can shut down what appears to be a good connection between local producers and consumers. My city has closed down more than one market for a period of time while the food safety of the market was evaluated and new certification requirements were established. Generally, the need for oversight and regulation is in the best interest of the customers as it will protect them from the possibility of dangerous consumption of food that may not be handled and treated properly. However, sometimes the oversight is merely a power struggle between the people organizing the market and the regulators, sometimes driven by fear from competitors that their customers are being taken away by alternative offerings. Often when these markets are shut down, the farmers themselves express concerns that their freedom to offer their products is being removed unjustly. They argue that there is demand for their local product and they should be able to have a venue to supply these products to the consumers.

If lay people are going to be ministering to others in the name of the Church, some oversight is necessary to ensure that the ministry being offered meets the standards of the Church. Generally, this oversight is for the protection of those being served, protection of the people in the pews who rely on the ministers to guide them properly in the ways of the faith. Although the parish is the most natural "local market," the responsibility of oversight in a particular region falls to the bishop of the diocese. The US bishops, in *Co-Workers in the Vineyard of the Lord,* stress the importance of the role of the bishop in authorizing lay ecclesial ministers in his diocese. The bishop's authorization is the ultimate regulation for the "market" of ministry existing in his region and gives support to the work being done. "His authorization demonstrates to the community in which [the lay ecclesial ministers] serve that their work has his confidence and support" and also gives confidence to the people in the community that the ministry they receive is of good quality.[7] Even more locally, and more naturally in the "local

---

[7] United States Conference of Catholic Bishops, *Co-Workers in the Vineyard of the Lord: A Resource for Guiding the Development of Lay Ecclesial Ministry* (Washington, DC: United States Conference of Catholic Bishops, 2005), 55.

market," the pastor has responsibility for overseeing the ministries in his own parish. He operates under the oversight of the bishop, but he "has great latitude in organizing parish resources to meet the pastoral needs of the people."[8] *Co-Workers* recognizes the proper office for oversight responsibility to be with the bishop and his priests.

If you did an inquiry into all the dioceses in the United States, you would find great variety among the US bishops as to how they authorize lay ecclesial ministers. Some bishops leave this endorsement, or this authorization, to the simple act of hiring a lay person for a ministry position. Sometimes that responsibility is handed over to a pastor for parish personnel to hire parish staff at his own discretion; other times the responsibility is with one of the bishop's hired diocesan staff, or maybe he even takes it upon himself. Other dioceses, like the Archdiocese of Chicago, have an intimate involvement of their episcopal leader, currently Cardinal Francis George, in the authorization of lay ecclesial ministers who serve as pastoral associates through this program in his diocese. This archdiocese has an entire staff and program that trains and certifies lay ecclesial ministers for particular roles.[9] The pastoral associates who have completed the certification process are invited to participate in a Rite of Calling to Lay Ecclesial Ministry where they "commit to collaboration with the pastors of the Church and to leading Christ's people in love and fidelity."[10] The cardinal then writes a letter to commission the lay ecclesial minister to the parish of employment. Diocesan authorization at the level of the cardinal gives reassurance to those receiving the minister into their parish by stating a certain level of consistency and quality in training and formation can be expected by all who complete their certification program.

---

[8] Ibid.

[9] See Archdiocese of Chicago, Office for Lay Ecclesial Ministry, "Department of Personnel Services," accessed 5/29/2014, www.archchicago.org/departments/lay_ecclesial_ministry/lay_ministry.shtm.

[10] Archdiocese of Chicago, Office for Lay Ecclesial Ministry, "What Is Lay Ecclesial Ministry," accessed 5/29/2014, www.archchicago.org/departments/lay_ecclesial_ministry/what.shtm.

Power struggles

Similarly to how a need for regulation seems to increase after awareness and availability of a local product begin to spread to regional and then national recognition, it seems that as attention to lay ecclesial ministry increases some overseers find an increasing need to regulate and control what is happening under their purview. Occasionally, the responsibility for oversight is perceived (justifiably or not) as a power struggle between the overseer and those being overseen. When this happens, it is often seen as a roadblock to the connection between those ministering and those desiring the ministry. The struggle can be seen when a lay minister wants to do a Bible study written by one author, but the pastor thinks one written by another author is more appropriate for his congregation. Or perhaps all lay ecclesial ministers in the diocese are now being required to earn a master's degree or some other form of credentialing, even if they have been serving in their ministry role for many years. The power struggle could stem from a new requirement that all speakers coming in from outside the diocese must follow a rigorous approval process conducted by diocesan officials before the speaker can be invited. All of these examples manifest a pastor or bishop trying to ensure good quality ministry is happening under their purview, but can also be perceived by lay ministers as a way of tying their hands while they try to minister to the people in their community.

Fear of competition

Fear of competition in a marketplace is usually driven by inter-company competition. However, in our churches, sometimes the "competition" is within our own parishes. When roles and responsibilities are shared among many people at one parish, competition may occur over resources or responsibilities. Some priests, especially those who are pastors in a parish, may see lay ministers as infringing upon their responsibility at the parish. Some pastors lead by holding tightly to everything happening in their parish instead of letting ministries grow and flourish on their own through the gifts of the lay ministers. I had a conversation once with a newly ordained priest assigned to his first parish, a large suburban parish with over thirty employees. The priest commented to me that he did not know what his role and his ministry would be because everything seemed to be in control by the people on staff. I am not sure he saw these lay ecclesial ministers as "competition," but the existence of so many lay staff people at the parish caused a struggle for him and the identity of his priestly ministry.

Shutting down the market

Sometimes "the market" is so regulated that it becomes impossible for those with gifts to bring them forth. Some lay ecclesial ministers speak of experiences where their gifts have not been welcomed. They have been told that there is no match between their gifts and the needs of the parish. Not only is there no match at this current point, but as one "Emerging from the Vineyard" participant commented, *"not now, not in the future."*[11] These lay people come with gifts to share, master's degrees or diocesan certifications earned, and years of experience, yet the regulation is so tight that they are not even given a chance to offer their talents.

Different from a Market

The model of comparing lay ecclesial ministry to a local farmers market is of course not a perfect comparison. Our Church is not really one of a market and customer model. Parishioners are not meant to be shoppers of goods at a parish. Parishioners are meant to be full, active, conscious participants in the liturgical and communal life of their parish. This means not only receiving things, but giving as well. So the role of the minister is not only to provide ministry to the people in the pews, but also to engage them in ministry so they are learning to be disciples to one another as well.

The farmers market model also leaves out a particular influence that we believe exists in our Church, that of God. In the words of *Lumen Gentium*, we believe Jesus willed that the successors of the apostles, "the bishops, should be the shepherds

[11] Italicized phrases and sentences are from the participants in this "Emerging from the Vineyard" Project.

in his Church until the end of the world."[12] Our bishops are called and graced to lead our Church today and in the future. The Holy Spirit works through these men, and in necessary connection with the pope, guides them to lead the people of God. Although these men are *men*, human beings who can err, we also believe they are graced and gifted to lead our Church in the right direction. So their regulatory decisions are not solely based on the market or on a legal or political guideline as in the secular marketplace but are also based on guidance of the Holy Spirit and the vision of the Second Vatican Council. This same Spirit not only works through our bishops, but is calling forth the gifts of all the people of God. "The Holy Spirit empowers all with the various gifts and ministries for the building up of the Body of Christ" and this powerful movement of the Spirit in our Church makes our parishes and dioceses different than the power of the economic market that primarily controls the secular marketplace.[13]

So how do we balance the offering of gifts for the community, the freedom for the consumer and producer to meet and mutually offer and respond to needs, with the necessity for regulation, safety, and protection of the consumer? How do we encourage those who feel constrained and support their efforts to fulfill the demands of regulation? The steps that have been taken in dioceses to establish systems of support, such as lay ministry offices and continuing education opportunities, appear to be a good start. I have listened to lay ecclesial ministers in conference presentations who indicate that they feel supported to do their ministry. The "regulation" has led to communication and understanding within the diocese of the role of the lay ecclesial minister. However, what happens when that recognized lay ecclesial minister has to move from one parish to another or one diocese to another? What happens when that new parish or that new diocese does not understand the role that had been so clearly defined in the previous experience? What happens when someone from that "local market" decides to "go national?"

---

[12] *Lumen Gentium* in Austin Flannery, ed., *Vatican Council II Volume 1: The Conciliar and Post Conciliar Documents* (Northport, NY: Costello Publishing, 2004), 18.

[13] United States Conference of Catholic Bishops, *Co-Workers*, 7.

Going National

As food producers move from local markets to selling on a broader scale, they begin to investigate new outlets for their products. They turn to local grocers, regional grocery store chains, and eventually big national stores. Branching out gives them the opportunity to reach a wider audience, but this opportunity may come at a cost. The wider audience will begin to recognize the brand and accept the brand, but they will also demand a consistent, quality product. More attention and a wider audience will also require more strict regulations than the ones encountered at the local level. The expectation of consistent, quality products extends not only to the consumer, but to the regulators as well. The regulators will feel the need to have an approval process for the product to give confidence to the consumer. A move from local offerings to a national market causes a shift in the expectations and authorization of the offering.

Additional pressures become apparent with such a change in market strategy. Lay ecclesial ministry has grown in much the same way as a local food producer beginning to expand his or her market. It was not something declared by the magisterium of our Church, but rather was born out of a need in a parish, recognized by another parish, and spread as it was seen meeting needs in the community. The lay ecclesial minister today feels both the flexibility and the burden of being part of a ministry that is grass-roots and still growing. It has not yet reached the level of national brand recognition like a national grocery store chain such as Wal-Mart, but *Co-Workers in the Vineyard of the Lord* and focused research such as that done by the Emerging Models of Pastoral Leadership project have provided some amount of recognition and support at the national level.

The ministers themselves are experiencing some growing pains as a shift begins to happen from how lay people became ministers thirty and forty years ago to how they become ministers today. In particular, today's young lay ministers have a different experience of beginning a vocation to lay ecclesial ministry with a different perspective from older ministers on the idea of "local market" vs. "going national." Similarly to an expanding grocery store chain, these young adult lay ecclesial ministers are reaching out to a broader audience. They are looking beyond the people who already know their gifts and talents and are now asking a new community to recognize and accept what they have to offer. The opportunity to reach out to a wider audience provides these lay ecclesial ministers with more breadth of opportunities, a wider range of communities and spiritualities to encounter, and a broader list of ministry jobs and responsibilities to take upon themselves. The idea of young adult, as well as older adult, lay ecclesial ministers "taking their gifts national" not only raises the challenge of being recognized and authorized to serve in a broader range of parishes and dioceses, but is also a challenge to the minister to be well trained and formed to minister in a variety of cultural, economical, and spiritual situations.

Intentional branding

We, as lay ecclesial ministers, have encountered many barriers and roadblocks in our attempt to gain national recognition and support for our type of ministry. One difficulty is that people do not know what kind of product they are getting with the term "lay ecclesial ministry." The term does not evoke a clearly recognizable "brand." Priests, parishioners, and even bishops are confused as to what the term means. When one of the "Emerging from the Vineyard" participants was asked by his bishop, *"Who exactly comprises or fits under the title, lay ecclesial minister?"* he struggled with not having a ready answer. Another project participant shared an experience when professional confirmation coordinators were asked *"What is the Church's official name for those of us who are engaged in professional ministry?"* and none of the coordinators was able to provide an answer. The US bishops in *Co-Workers* describe the characteristics of lay ecclesial service (authorization, leadership, close mutual collaboration, preparation, and formation) and describe roles that a lay ecclesial minister might undertake, but do not give a solid definition of the term.[14] Hahnenberg uses some descriptions to help us create a definition of lay ecclesial ministry:

[14] United States Conference of Catholic Bishops, *Co-Workers*, 10-11.

- A vocational commitment of a fully initiated Catholic
- For a significant public ministry in the community
- That is recognized as such by the Church community and its leadership.[15]

Hahnenberg has since added a new dimension to his definition, that of serving "in the name of the Church." He explains that "lay ecclesial ministers are called into a new set of relationships, a new position within the ecclesial community: they minister in the name of the Church."[16] This service in the name of the Church as a lay person is what makes lay ecclesial ministry distinctly lay and distinctly ministry. The call to serve publicly as a lay person in the name of the Church is "[w]hat distinguishes the vocation to lay ecclesial ministry from the broader call to discipleship and the broader call to ministry."[17] Some of us serving as lay ecclesial ministers may be able to make sense of such descriptions. Yet even though there are many lay people serving in ecclesial ministry in our parishes and dioceses, a good understanding of the term "lay ecclesial ministry" is still not well established or widely accepted. However, I believe this key descriptor of "serving in the name of the Church" may help as we try more clearly to brand the lay ecclesial ministry "product."

Consistent oversight and regulation at the national level

As we, the lay ecclesial ministers, begin to look at how our ministry goes from local to national, we have to think how we personally see this change affecting us. What does it mean to our own ministry and how we do ministry? What does it mean for us to be authorized for ministry at a local level or a national level? Does it mean something different to someone who has been in ministry for thirty years than it does for a young adult just entering into ministry after completing his or her education?

---

[15] See Edward P. Hahnenberg, *Ministries: A Relational Approach* (New York, NY: The Crossroads Publishing Company, 2003), 131-150.

[16] Edward P. Hahnenberg, "Serving in the Name of the Church: The Call to Lay Ecclesial Ministry," in *In the Name of the Church: Vocation and Authorization of Lay Ecclesial Ministry*, ed. William J. Cahoy (Collegeville, MN: Liturgical Press, 2012), 47.

[17] Ibid., 51.

One new step that may help lay ecclesial ministers receive the credentialing they feel is important is the new national certification process for lay ecclesial ministers.[18] The Lay Ecclesial Ministers Certification website explains that certification is a "professional acknowledgement that you have met nationally recognized standards for competence in lay ministry."[19] It is available in the following specialized ministries:

- Director of Worship
- Parish Life Coordinator
- Pastoral Associate
- Director of Music Ministries
- Catechetical Leader
- Youth Ministry Leader
- Diocesan Youth Ministry Leader

Certification can be achieved through a process of submitting information about education, work experience, and references as well as a ministerial autobiography. The application will be reviewed by the partner organization for the particular specialization, then a national board, and finally the Alliance for the Certification of Lay Ministers Committee. It is important to note that this certification "is designed only to assess and acknowledge the competence of the lay ecclesial minister for a specific ministerial role" and is different from authorization.[20] *Co-Workers* reminds us that authorization is "the process by which properly prepared lay men and women are given responsibilities for ecclesial ministry by competent Church authority."[21] Certification is simply a tool that can be used when evaluating a candidate to be authorized for ecclesial ministry.

This new certification will give us an option to have a defined package for understanding the qualifications of lay ecclesial ministers. It will give bishops something definitive they could embrace if they choose to create a formal authorization program in their diocese. If done correctly, it may give us an answer to the

---

[18] See Alliance for the Certification of Lay Ecclesial Ministers, "Latest Updates," accessed 5/29/2014, www.lemcertification.org.

[19] Ibid., "What Is Certification?"accessed 5/29/2014, www.lemcertification.org/what.htm.

[20] Ibid.

[21] United States Conference of Catholic Bishops, *Co-Workers*, 54.

questions mentioned previously. It gives us something concrete to use when mentoring young adults contemplating this type of ministry. It gives us something that could be universally marketable and transferable if we are to move from one diocese to another. It gives us something to show parishioners that we are trained and competent to represent the Church in our ministry. Overall, it may be what we need to give us that "brand recognition" that is so important as we "go national" with our product of lay ecclesial ministry. It has its limitations, however, in that it is only offered for certain types of ministries, and for the frequently changing experiences of young adult lay ecclesial ministers, this could be a challenge. However, it does appear to be a good first step toward offering a national recognition of the competence of lay ministers.

Side Effects of Authorization

If we do say we want a standard form of authorization, then we are asking a bishop or priest to put his stamp of approval on our ministerial ability in a particular way. If we ask for standardized authorization, we may encounter a more standardized form of control over where we serve as ministers and how we serve. Deacons and priests certainly have the authorization to minister based on their ordination, but along with that authorization comes obedience to what their bishop asks them to do. If we receive the regionally or nationally recognized authorization, are we also prepared to serve as the bishop sees fit and forgo some choices when it comes to the location and the ministry we are called to engage? Or is there some other way that can be proposed? Is there something we can do nationally to receive not only certification, but also the authorization desired that can be recognized from diocese to diocese and parish to parish, while at the same time maintaining the unique character of the freedom that accompanies a calling to lay ecclesial ministry? The freedom that allows us to have families and consult our spouse on decisions instead of being required to move when reassigned by a bishop. The freedom to take a step away from ministry for a few years to raise a young family but return when the family life can be better balanced with our ministerial vocation. Can we have some sort of public recognition, public calling, and sending forth, that recognizes trained and formed lay ministers and presents them to the community for service in and for the Church, while still acknowledging that their typical calling to marriage and family will affect how and where they are sent forth?

This national response of a certification process or a request for some type of national authorization process will not be the final answer for defining lay ecclesial ministry. There are too many different roles, cultures, and needs that shape the type of ministry being done and how it varies from place to place and person to person. An ecclesial authority always needs personally to accept our certification and authorize us to do the ministry that we do. However, a national process offers a framework for giving confidence to our bishops as they try to find the best way to authorize our ministry. It could offer us a solid, concrete place to begin being able to explain who we are as ministers. It might be a good step forward in the effort of making our own little local product a great nationally recognized brand.

Questions for Reflection:

1. Reflect on your own experience of entering into lay ecclesial ministry. What did your path look like?

2. How have you seen or experienced this shift in the way lay ecclesial ministers come to their ministry?

3. In light of the current reality of young adults in lay ecclesial ministry, what changes need to be made (if any) to the way we approach authorization for lay ministers today?

Entering the Desert: Towards a Deeper Understanding of Ministry

Susan Yanos

For you were slain and with your
blood you purchased for God
those from every tribe and tongue,
people and nation.
You made them a kingdom and priests
for our God,
and they will reign on earth.
Revelation 5: 9b-10

In the informal conversations I have with many lay ecclesial ministers, a tension often exists between wanting to serve and receiving inadequate compensation not only for the hours spent in ministry, but the tuition dollars spent for the necessary training and credentials. All too often ministers succumb to burn-out, a term Henri Nouwen referred to as a "convenient psychological translation for a spiritual death." [1] Too frequently highly trained lay ministers will leave active ministry in a parish for other work that allows them to use more fully their skills while meeting their own families' financial needs. Or they leave Catholicism for another tradition which seems "friendlier" to women or to married individuals in ecclesial roles.

For me personally, this tension has appeared as an ongoing conflict over the locus of my own ministry. As a highly trained educator, I've wondered whether my ministry should be towards my Catholic community or the larger community. Should I offer my skills to nurture my fellow parishioners, to help them maintain their Catholic identity in the largely non-Catholic area where I live, to call them to become witnesses and evangelists to their neighbors? Or do I offer my skills in the secular climate of today's higher education, where students so desperately need a

---

[1] Henri Nouwen, *In the Name of Jesus: Reflections on Christian Leadership* (New York: Crossroads, 1989), 11.

teacher who is willing to allow the Christian perspective to enter the classroom once again? Unable to resolve this conflict, I frequently moved in and out of university teaching and parish work as a director of religious education. Both have been equally rewarding--and frustrating. Neither pays well. The settings of both are hierarchical in their own ways. Both can be demoralizing as I find myself sandwiched between those I serve, who do not automatically respect the position of teacher or lay minister, and the leadership above, who often relegates rather than cooperates in the work to be done.

So I continued this dance between academia and the parish, changing dance partners every seven to ten years or so, until I came to teach among Quakers.

Being with Quakers, or the Religious Society of Friends, has challenged me to face my own tendency to turn ministry into a career. I find that I have all too often witnessed in myself and others what Richard Rohr speaks of in *The Naked Now*: "When so many become professional church workers without going through spiritual transformation at any deep level, religious work becomes a career, and church becomes something one 'attends.'"[2] The Quakers' struggle to identify what it means to serve church and to serve as Church--not only now but throughout their history--has become for me the prophetic voice their founder George Fox wished to become to the clerical hierarchy of his day.

I do not want to dismiss the calls for just compensation, equitable working conditions, and acknowledgement of the validity of our vocation as lay ministers through our baptism. However, I find I can focus only upon my own journey in lay ministry, and that journey has led me to something of a desert, where the nights and days of reflection have revealed rather unsettling insights, especially about my own increasing dryness and bitterness. The questions proliferate: Is there a way through this bitter desert for me and the many other ministers I meet who are desperately in need of spiritual transformation? How can we adopt a realistic attitude towards the setting of our ministry so as not to succumb to "spiritual death"--either by being numbed by

---

[2] Richard Rohr, *The Naked Now* (New York: Crossroad, 2009), 37.

that setting or by being pulled into proliferating the conflicts and negative attitudes of it? In what ways are we contributing (unconsciously or consciously, willingly or unwillingly) to the sins of the institution? Are we stuck in a narrative of victimization, blaming others for our situation?

In the desert, potable water is so infrequent and unexpected that it is always welcome, no matter its source, and hospitality to friend and stranger alike is necessary for survival. While pondering these questions, I have received the grace of hospitality and nourishment from the writings of trusted Catholic friends, especially from the desert tradition, and from strangers who proved to be Friends.

Two Quaker themes became particularly useful to me for what they contribute to an understanding of Catholic lay ecclesial ministry: what it means to be "hidden in plain sight," serving from a place of ongoing spiritual transformation, and what happens when one becomes a "hireling minister," using success or accomplishment as a measure of the effectiveness of one's ministry. Becoming a hireling, I have come to see, is not about accepting a position as a hired and paid minister, but is about something else, about one's attitude in that position.

Hidden in Plain Sight

When I first began teaching at a Quaker institution, I wanted to include Quaker authors on my course reading lists, but found it surprisingly difficult to find them unless pointed in their direction by another Friend. Quakers purposefully do not announce their denominational affiliation and avoid "churchy" language, referring to their buildings as meetinghouses, their parishes as meetings, and Sunday as "First Day." How a Quaker lives is his or her testimony to the Spirit. Just as Mother Teresa of Calcutta advised her sisters not to attempt to convert the people they served to Jesus, not even to talk about Jesus, but to *be Jesus*, Quakers keep their religious identities hidden and work to align their words and deeds so that all can plainly see Christ through them.

Quakers have a strong social conscience as well, seeing their mission as being in and to the world. Their influence on peace and justice issues is far greater than their numbers would predict.

So my time with Friends has allowed me to explore how service to Church relates to service to the world. When Jesus said "Feed my lambs," was he referring only to those who had already embraced his message, or did his charge include an evangelical shepherding of the larger world flock? Are ecclesial ministers, whether lay or ordained, misguided in focusing their attention primarily upon church matters? Does the title "lay *ecclesial* ministry" distort in any way what Christian ministry should be because it brings to the foreground what should be hidden? When Paul writes that God's wisdom is mysterious and hidden and can be revealed to those who love God only through the Spirit (1 Cor 2:7-12), how do we rest within that wisdom, though seeming foolish to the world?

I found myself thrust deeper into the desert where I encountered the sayings of the fourth century *abbas* and *ammas*[3]: hermits or members of small monastic communities who fled the cities for a life of solitude and prayer in the arid wilderness. Theirs was the time when Christianity emerged from a persecuted to a state-sanctioned religion and was forged into a hierarchical institution. According to Thomas Merton, these men and women regarded the world as a shipwreck from which they had to swim for their lives, for "to let oneself drift along, passively accepting the tenets and values of what they knew as society, was purely and simply a disaster."[4] The fact that Christianity had become the accepted religion within the realm only strengthened their resolve.

One of the reasons they fled both the world and the institutional Church was they'd found that living in these places caused them to become divided. The divided life occurs when beliefs and values are separated from words and actions. On the individual, personal level, the divided life may appear in our refusal to invest our essential selves in our work, hiding behind titles and credentials, books and programs, checklists and

---

[3]*Abba* and *amma* were terms of respect used for these elders of the faith, *abba* meaning father and *amma,* mother. For their sayings, I recommend the translation by Benedicta Ward, *The Sayings of the Desert Fathers* (Trappist, KY: Cistercian Publications, 1975).

[4] Thomas Merton, *The Wisdom of the Desert* (New York: New Directions, 1960), 4.

committees. This not only diminishes the quality of our work but distances us from the very people we intend to serve. Or the divided life may appear when we hide our true identities for fear of being criticized or rejected, or our beliefs from those who disagree with us out of fear of conflict or from facing the realization that it is perhaps we who need to change. Or it might result when we choose to remain in settings or relationships that kill our spirits.[5] What the *abbas* and *ammas* realized is that to continue to live the divided life not only drowns the individual; it also contributes to the shipwreck of the community. Only when the individual can get a firm foothold on dry land can he or she extend a hand to help others.

So they sought that foothold in the driest places they knew. They sought to live the *un*divided life, and to do that, they had to go, paradoxically, into hiding.

Now as one lay ecclesial minister reminds me, being hidden is a complex metaphor, one that brings ambivalent, if not conflicted, feelings for women and other marginalized groups:

> *Hidden can mean dis-empowered, unimportant, voiceless. Recently, however, I read John Paul II's reflection on femininity in* Theology of the Body.[6] *He speaks of women as mystery, and mystery as holy. Carrying this image around . . . I have to admit that it resonates with me. There is something very sacred and special about hiddenness. The idea that a woman, or mystery opens only to those who are chosen and worthy is quite the opposite of voiceless and unimportance.*[7]

What is really important--what moves us profoundly--is often delicate, vulnerable, and beautiful, and it happens in secret. Human life begins in the secrecy of the womb. Intimacy and growth occur within the privacy of the family. Creativity buds

---

[5] For a fuller discussion, see Parker Palmer, *A Hidden Wholeness: The Journey Toward an Undivided Life* (San Francisco: Jossey-Bass, 2004).

[6] John Paul II, *Man and Woman He Created Them: A Theology of the Body* (Boston: Pauline Books and Media, 2006).

[7] Quotes from journal entries of lay ecclesial ministers involved in the "Emerging from the Vineyard" project will be indicated by *use of italics*.

forth in the solitude of the artist's studio. Ministry flows from the silence and vulnerability of prayer.

Cohesion, integration, harmony, unity: none can stand too much the public gaze which tends to hurry, harden, suffocate, and all too often standardize. Several great minds and spirits have lost their creative force through too early or too rapid an exposure to the public. Even Mark's Gospel seems to underscore this truth with its emphasis on the mystery of Jesus' identity. We may find it hard to grasp that the greatest part of God's work in our history could well remain completely unknown. If God is omnipotent, we reason, why isn't God's power more visible in this chaotic world? If my ministry is based on sound principles and practices, why isn't it more visibly changing people's lives? How can we counteract the world's values without going public with ours?

The truth is that the more lofty the spiritual ambition, the more dangerous the illusion we fall into. We must adopt another value system to buoy our ministry, one not based solely on tangible results, or we have carried the values of the shipwrecked world into our hiding place. The desert elders knew that such unwanted baggage led to failure, if not madness.

I wonder, then, if it is not a form of madness to divide Catholics into those who minister and those who do not because every Catholic, every Christian, is a minister through baptism and is called to teach, preach, provide individual pastoral care, organize, and celebrate according to his or her spiritual gifts. I wonder, too, if it isn't madness to divide ministry into various specialties within the helping professions because such a view can reduce a minister to a "handyman," to use the words of Nouwen, and ministry into "nothing more than another way to soften the many pains of daily life."[8] This is not to say that ministers should avoid the responsibility of cultivating the specialized skills needed for their ministries--that catechists should not be encouraged to learn theory and praxis, or pastoral associates counseling skills, for instance. However, the disorientation I felt when my Quaker students called me Susan, instead of the Dr. Yanos I had grown accustomed to, made me

---

[8] Henri Nouwen, *Creative Ministry* (Garden City, NY: Doubleday, 1971), xx.

realize that it was what my training and skills had wrought that mattered rather than my title and credentials.[9] *Who* I had become through my years of training and teaching taught students, ministered to students in ways I could only glimpse, and determined how open and receptive I was to being taught and ministered by them. Despite all the years since graduation, I had not yet realized fully who I had become and am still becoming.

Ministry is a way of life, not a mere occupation, whose vocation, as Nouwen says, "is to make it possible for man [and woman] not only to fully face his human situation but also to celebrate it in all its awesome reality."[10] Therefore, for me at least, it is madness to separate ministry to the church from ministry to the world, and to divide Catholics into lay ministers and lay ecclesial ministers.

And it is certainly madness to divide our essential selves from our ministry. If our ministry does not change us--perhaps more than it changes others--then we have failed.

Hireling Ministers

We are unfortunately all too familiar with the failures. We know, for instance, the abuses of the Church of England during the seventeenth century which led to George Fox's call for spiritual transformation: the selling of clerical positions, the complacency of the clergy around social issues so as not to anger their wealthy patrons, the poor preparation of ministers, etc. Fox's outrage at these practices expressed itself as a great abhorrence for paid ministers, an abhorrence still held by many Friends today who fully accept their denomination as a "kin-dom" where priests and prophets do not exist by title because each and everyone is called to serve as priests and prophets by God's presence within them. (Many Quakers resist the inequity and violence inherent in terms such as kingdom and king.) Although there are Quaker meetings that have ministers (known as "programmed meetings" vs. the traditional "unprogrammed meetings"), the historical Quaker church did not. As the Quaker

---

[9] As a way of living out the Quaker testimony of equality, they refer to all members by first name, not by title or rank. This practice extended to the seminary where I worked.

[10] Ibid., 92.

poet John Greenleaf Whittier wrote of Sunday (or First Day) worship in his beloved meetinghouse:

> There let me strive with each besetting sin,
> Recall my wandering fancies, and restrain
> The sore disquiet of a restless brain;
> And, as the path of duty is made plain,
> May grace be given that I may walk therein,
> Not like the hireling, for his selfish gain,
> With backward glances and reluctant tread,
> Making a merit of his coward dread . . .[11]

The irony is that Quakers did not eliminate the clergy, but eliminated the laity by lifting all the faithful to the level of clergy. And they did so by intentionally living out biblical passages such as Revelation 5: 9b-10.[12] All of their gatherings, whether a Meeting for Worship or a Meeting for Business, privilege each individual member in their process of prayerful silence, Spirit-led testimony out of the silence, community testing of discernment, and consensus. Although different members may assume various roles, no real distinction is made between individuals present, nor between purposes for the gathering.

While Catholic documents insist that the lay faithful share in the three-fold mission of Christ as priest, prophet, and king, a difference is noted between the common priesthood of the people and the ordained priesthood--an *essential* difference and not just one of degree. Yet most contemporary commentators call on the Church to resist the temptation to develop a new clericalism while trying to define the role of lay ecclesial ministry, or to relegate such ministers to a second class citizenship from clergy with a lesser call.[13]

---

[11] "First Day Thoughts," 1852, ll. 11-18. For on-line access, see The Project Gutenberg, *The Works of John Greenleaf Whittier*, Volume II (Ebook #9574), http://www.gutenberg.org/files/9574/9574-h/9574-h.htm#link2H_4_0083.

[12] ". . . for you were slain and with your blood you purchased for God those from every tribe and tongue, people and nation. You made them a kingdom and priests for our God, and they will reign on earth."

[13] See, for instance, the essays in *Together in God's Service: Toward a Theology of Ecclesial Lay Ministry* by the National Conference of Catholic Bishops (Washington, DC: United States Catholic Conference, 1998).

Today's abuses committed by the Church may be different from the seventeenth century, but they, too, require no less than a spiritual transformation. Even if we reject the egalitarian notions of ministry called for by Fox (for they have led Quakers into disunity and a loss of the Christian perspective in some meetings), we must re-examine our understanding of "a kingdom and priests" which reigns on earth now and not yet.[14]

The Quaker theology which developed around this notion of a minister-less congregation points to a deeply experiential understanding of Christian community which those of us engaged in ministry sometimes forget. Church as an institution springing from *commune*-ity, from communion, provides a different insight from church as hierarchical. In the words of James Hoffman, this insight is that the Church is "a matter of communion with God through Jesus Christ in the sacraments," and involves a building up of the faithful into the Body of Christ.[15] Every person is capable of achieving spiritual maturity, of incarnating Christ. However, because we are so prone to self-deception and sin, the faith community becomes the place where God's will can be truly known, where God's blessings can be shared, and where each can be supported and encouraged by others. God establishes relationships with individuals, but God's plan is carried out through the faith community. As ministers, our skills and talents are gifts from God which we are entrusted to steward for the building of the community, not just for building up ourselves. The Quaker Lloyd Lee Wilson writes, "A breakdown in either the direct stewardship of the individual or the indirect stewardship of the community for the gifts that have been bestowed will hinder God's plan, and eventually lead to the withdrawal of the gifts themselves."[16]

In this painful time of changing attitudes and roles, of insufficient numbers of priests, and declining attendance at Mass,

---

[14] Because God's Kingdom is *eternal*, we should not understand it solely as a future event or place. Rather it has already begun, is already present—but in seed form, as some of Jesus' parables describe, such as the parable of the mustard seed (Mt 13: 31-32) or of the yeast (Mt 13: 33).

[15] James Hoffman, "Ecclesial Lay Ministry in a Local Church," in ibid., 163.

[16] Lloyd Lee Wilson, *Essays on the Quaker Vision of Gospel Order* (Philadelphia: Quaker Press, 2001), 93.

lay ecclesial ministers have been called upon (either verbally or situationally) to preach, counsel, teach, spiritually direct, heal, administer, perform sacramentals, preside at funerals, and distribute communion in the absence of a priest. Although the community, including the institutional Church, can and does throw up obstacles to this extension of lay ministries, the greatest obstacle is often to be found in the ministers themselves: in their fear, anger, doubt, pride. If we do not want these gifts to be withdrawn, the relationship between the minister and the community is crucially important, both for the minister's spiritual maturity and for the community's. What I am about to say makes no distinction among ministers, applying to clergy and laity, those in paid ecclesial positions and those in volunteer community service, and all combinations in between.

When What's Hidden Becomes Plain

Three tasks, each shared by the individual and the community, await us in the identification and stewardship of spiritual gifts. I am indebted to Lloyd Lee Wilson for these tasks, although I have adapted them considerably. He drew them from his Quaker experience and history, as well as from his reading of Henri Nouwen.

1. Naming the spiritual gifts.

Surprisingly, this task, although a joint one, falls mainly on the community for three reasons: we cannot see ourselves clearly (e.g., Matt 7:3-5)[17]; the gifts often first appear in rudimentary or subtle forms; and we are easily confused by our own superficial desires, ambitions, and fears.

This third reason motivated some of the fourth century *abbas*, who also fled the community's call to ordination and ecclesial ministry when they fled to the desert. Although we might be tempted to judge their action as a refusal to assume their responsibilities to God and the Church, the *abbas* feared

[17] "Why do you notice the splinter in your brother's eye, but do not perceive the wooden beam in your own eye? How can you say to your brother, 'Let me remove that splinter from your eye,' while the wooden beam is in your eye? You hypocrite, remove the wooden beam from your eye first; then you will see clearly to remove the splinter from your brother's eye."

more their arrogance to claim through ordination a destiny that they knew required a lifetime of prayer and discipline to achieve. One story of Abba Theodore of Pherme illustrates this. Repeatedly the church elders brought Theodore back from the desert to the city, begging that he not abandon his role as a deacon. Abba Theodore replied:

> "Let me pray to God so that he may tell me for certain whether I ought to take my part in the liturgy." Then he prayed to God in this manner, "If it is your will that I should stand in this place, make me certain of it." Then appeared to him a column of fire, reaching from earth to heaven, and a voice said to him, "If you can become like this pillar, go, be a deacon." On hearing this he decided never to accept the office. When he went to church, the brethren bowed before him saying, "If you do not wish to be a deacon, at least hold the chalice." But he refused, saying, "If you do not leave me alone, I shall leave this place." So they left him in peace.[18]

A pillar of fire is a frequent symbol in the desert literature for the union of heaven and earth, which is what a spiritual pilgrim should desire to become. Theodore didn't yet feel he had become such a pillar. Although we may not now see ordination in quite this way, Theodore's story should give every minister pause, for it clearly suggests, as Rowan Williams writes, "that exercising a public role in the church's worship involves standing in the furnace of divine action that unites earth and heaven. If we can't see that this is a dangerous place, we have missed something essential."[19] Even if we can escape the more damaging temptations surrounding our desires for the power of ministry, we may still be ensnared by the partially veiled power games of our speech--the "giving and receiving of doubtfully truthful perspectives," including about spiritual matters, that can be so damaging to ourselves and others.[20]

---

[18] Ward, *Sayings of the Desert Fathers*, 77.

[19] Rowan Williams, *Where God Happens: Discovering Christ in One Another* (Boston: New Seeds, 2007), 74.

[20] Ibid., 76.

Therefore, the basis for the community's naming of an individual's gifts should not be so much the skills or ability visible, but the individual's ability to listen to God and speak what was heard in ways that the community can understand. To cite but one example, we instinctively know the difference between a musician who treats liturgies as performances and one who prays through music and inspires the congregation to do the same.

By naming the gift, the community claims it for itself, yet holds the individual accountable for it. The individual must then claim it for him or herself (see below). Of course, the community may or may not fulfill its role faithfully. In terms of lay ecclesial ministry, I have known faith communities who vigilantly named their members' gifts, but I have also known communities who would not name their members' gifts, or did so in such a way that they appeared undesirable, even harmful, to the individual and threatening to the group--at least to other leaders within the group. In my own case, my spiritual gifts were first named not by my faith community, but by outsiders with whom I worked, mainly by my students, leading to my confusion in deciding within which community I should exercise my gifts.

2. <u>Claiming and developing the spiritual gifts.</u>

The task of developing gifts should be shared by both the individual and community; but the task of claiming the gift--of accepting and stewarding it--is the individual's responsibility. Claiming our gifts may be linked to accepting a particular ministry, but it just as well may be that the ministry is but a stepping-stone to claiming what God bestows; or the ministry may prove a stumbling block, seeming too risky (whether the risk is real or imagined) or too comfortable to be given up when God leads. Wilson emphasizes that since gifts are given primarily for the community, at some future time the gifts may not be needed. This can be especially frustrating when much time and money have been spent acquiring training or the proper credentials to perform the work. Therefore, too closely identifying with a particular ministry is a danger on the spiritual journey, for it can encourage us to cling to what we have been doing or would like to do instead of opening ourselves to God's work within us and within the community. Rather ministers should root their identities in Christ.

Claiming the gift requires the individual to realize that he or she is exchanging some aspect of apparent independence for obedient and humble servanthood. What Jesus tells Peter could be said to all who serve the church: "'Amen, amen, I say to you, when you were younger, you used to dress yourself and go where you wanted; but when you grow old, you will stretch out your hands, and someone else will dress you and lead you where you do not want to go'" (John 21:18).

What never fails to amaze me as I read Scripture and church history is how God works wonders with sinners--no matter what their abilities, no matter what their style. For every charismatic leader like David, there is a reluctant Moses. For every Abraham or John XXIII who humbly heeds (eventually!) the Spirit, there is a Saul who usurps authority and commands his troops to failure. Yet each furthered God's plan in some way. I find it very reassuring to know that building the Kingdom is not up to individual efforts to achieve perfection. Ministers do not--I do not--have to be perfect.

Nevertheless, we do need to examine what leadership means since claiming our gifts often puts us in positions of leadership within our communities. Within ministry, leadership is itself a position of obedient and humble servanthood. Jesus' statement to Peter suggests not only Peter's actual death, but a transformation in Peter's way of serving God and community. When I think of other biblical models for leadership, the most powerful one for me is Moses. By studying Exodus, I have learned five things about leadership within the faith community.[21]

First, one is called to leadership, by the community or by the still small voice within. In the Old Testament, the prophets "test" the call, determining if it is truly from God and identifying the areas where they are weak so that God can strengthen. So accepting the call requires conversion and openness. Moses slowly, patiently underwent that conversion of heart in the years he spent shepherding in the desert until God called from the burning bush. Then God, in making Moses' arm leprous and restoring it to health (Exod 4:6-7), revealed to Moses that he, too,

[21] For a discussion of the Exodus story as a model for the spiritual journey, including the right use of authority, see Jamie Buckingham, *A Way Through the Wilderness* (Grand Rapids, MI: Baker, 1986).

was restored, reconciled with God after his sinful actions in Egypt. Faithful leaders must test the call and themselves before assuming leadership.

Second, this conversion is continual and ongoing. During the eighty years Moses spent in the desert--before and after God called him from the burning bush--he underwent conversion in three areas: he learned to channel his passion; he learned the right relationship of the leader to the led; and he learned the right relationship of the leader to God. Most readers feel great pity for Moses because he did not enter the Promised Land. My reading is that Moses is not being punished, but that in his old age, he is no longer able or willing to be open to conversion. He fell back on the old ways he knew would work when he tried to bring water from the rock a second time instead of the new ways God was guiding him toward.[22] If we look at the Israelites' situation from the most superficial level, this new land will require an agricultural people, not a band of nomads. On deeper levels, we know from the "rest of the story" as revealed through the other biblical books, God continues to call God's people into greater and deeper lived experiences of the covenant. Moses will not be able to make the changes necessary to guide the people into this new life. They need a new leader. To be an effective leader, a minister must always be open to God's call to conversion and change--continually reflecting upon the situation, what is needed, and what must be called forth from within--and not rely upon past successes and methods.

Third, leaders are empowered. Moses hedges at the burning bush not because he doubts God, but because he doubts himself. Eventually this doubt becomes so strong that it almost destroys him--which is how I read Exodus 4: 24-26.[23] It is not God who is trying to kill Moses, but his own self-doubt. By circumcising their

---

[22] Compare Exodus 17: 1-7, the first time Moses brought water from the rock, with Numbers 20:2-12. In the first instance, he strikes the rock as God commanded him. In the second, he strikes the rock twice, even though God commanded that this time he order the water to flow.

[23] "On the journey, at a place where they spent the night, the LORD came upon Moses and would have killed him. But Zipporah took a piece of flint and cut off her son's foreskin and, touching his person, she said, 'You are a spouse of blood to me.' Then God let Moses go. At that time she said, 'A spouse of blood,' in regard to the circumcision."

son then, Zipporah reminds Moses of God's covenant with him. He will succeed if he has faith. God has promised and will deliver.

But leadership also encumbers. Leaders can no longer be as they once were; they must be different; they must speak out; they must endure whatever befalls them because they have been given authority. Moses' life is never the same after the burning bush incident, but there is no turning back for him. To do so would bring more misery than Pharaoh or the desert ever delivered.

Fourth, leaders in turn empower those they lead. Most of us want a Great Benefactor who will make everything right. However, God shows us that we are a lot stronger, better, worthier than we thought. God wants us in union with God, participating in the divine--not inferior beings to be played with. Moses learns this lesson from both God and his father-in-law, and he comes to rely on his brother, Aaron. He acknowledges those with the skill to act as judges for the people. He allows others to take authority (even if it means destruction for them), letting God decide who are rightful leaders (Exod 18: 13-27; Num 11: 16-17). He continually teaches the Israelites to govern and sustain themselves as a community, despite their refusals to accept responsibility and authority for themselves. Leaders need patience and perseverance. The story of Korah and his followers, who understood God's presence amidst the people as reason to assert individual authority, is a sobering one for ministers. Their actions were deemed rebellious and resulted in their destruction (Num 16).

So finally, leaders are mediators for the people. As the Israelites' mediator, Moses had to teach them that their true complaint is never against the food or the journey or even against him. Their true complaint is their distrust of God. A leader helps the community discover not only their true purpose and value, but also their unwillingness to take the power which is rightfully theirs, their complaints, and the source of those complaints. But as Moses expresses in Exodus 32: 30-32, a leader is never separate from the group. Moses is one with the Israelites. If God destroys the people, Moses pleads that God destroy him, too. Unlike Korah, Moses begins to understand the nature of communal guilt and true dependence on God. Leaders must always remember that they have been granted authority in order to build community, never to build themselves. They are one with the community.

Quaker Parker Palmer writes that in his experience, "a community requires more leadership than a hierarchy does. A hierarchy has clear goals, a well-established division of labor, and a set of policies about how things are supposed to run; if the machine is well designed and well lubricated, it can almost run itself." But a community, especially one counter to the dominant culture as faith communities should be, is "a chaotic, emergent, and creative force field that needs constant tending."[24]

Therefore, Nouwen asserts that leadership means being led--not by the community itself, which is frequently unaware of what it truly needs, but by the Spirit speaking within and through the community. Allowing ourselves to be led is the only way to avoid the temptation to power, the temptation to kill the soul of a community by forcing it into a hierarchy. "We keep hearing from others," he writes, "as well as saying to ourselves, that having power--provided it is used in the service of God and your fellow human beings--is a good thing."[25] But power is a major cause of rupture for it offers an easy substitute for loving. "The long painful history of the Church is the history of people ever and again tempted to choose power over love, control over the cross, being a leader over being led."[26] Jesus' vision of ministry is the ability and willingness to be led with Peter to where we do not want to go.

3. <u>Exercising and receiving the fruit of our spiritual gifts.</u>

Both aspects of this task are the joint responsibility of the individual and community, with the emphasis on the community which provides continual guidance, affirmation, feedback, opportunities for growth, and help in discerning how and when the gifts should be exercised in new ways. A community is unfaithful when it refuses to receive the gifts. If not received, individuals often feel burdened by the ministry, sometimes to the

---

[24] Palmer, *A Hidden Wholeness*, 76.
[25] Nouwen, *In the Name of Jesus*, 58.
[26] Ibid., 60.

point of distorting it, and the community is thus unable to guide them toward faithful ministry.

Ministers, on the other hand, are unfaithful when they do not allow the community the opportunity to consent to receive their gifts. Perhaps it is because I have a teacher's heart, but I have always been troubled by ministers who complain that people will not come to their programs unless required to because, they say to me, their parishioners are too busy or ignorant or preoccupied or just unwilling to seek the knowledge and formation the ministers provide. I have no problem with requiring attendance--such as at meetings for parents of children receiving sacraments--and some people do indeed have their priorities wrong, but those we serve are not empty vessels needing to be filled by our knowledge and insights. Nor is it our ministry to fill them. God's Spirit is the fount of what they need.

We would be better prepared if we understood ministry as mutual--not the giving of something from a position of possession and power to someone who is in a position of emptiness and weakness, but as entering into a deep personal relationship. According to Nouwen, an insidious temptation is to view ministry as just another helping profession, enamored with efficiency, control, and most especially with being relevant, so that it "has no models to offer to those who want to be shepherds in the way Jesus was a shepherd."[27]

The temptation to be relevant is a great one. I am embarrassed to admit that I have succumbed to it, despite my awareness of its effects. I have been tempted to measure the success of my ministry by the numbers in attendance at my programs or the words of praise doled out by my community. Yet I know that the very person who glared at me for the entire six weeks of a program did indeed return every one of those weeks (to my dismay!) and then told me two years later that God had transformed her life by working through the words I'd said. And I know that even if attendance at Vacation Bible School was less than I'd hoped, especially given the praise parishioners had lavished on my efforts the previous year, one of the high school

---

[27] Ibid., 44.

volunteers eventually accepted the call to study for greater service to the Church.

Mutuality in ministry occurs not just between the individual minister and the community. It should also be witnessed in the joint efforts of all the ministers of the community, for the ultimate mutuality to which all ministry leads is that between Jesus and the community. Just as Jesus sent the disciples out in twos, when we share ministry with others, we make it easier for people to see that we don't come to them in our names, not even in the Church's name, but in Jesus' name.[28] "Coming in our names" is the tendency to decide for ourselves what should be the goals of our ministry--a sure recipe for failure. Since the root meaning of the verb *to minister* is to serve, true ministry is not goal-based. As Jesus came to serve rather than be served, we as ministers are to do the same in the way he did: through cultivating a relationship with God and with all those who come to us.

From Hireling to Shepherd

Through my work within the Church, especially through this "Emerging from the Vineyard" project, I have met many lay ministers. Our stories record not only the blessings of a life lived in service, but also the challenges of defining our ministries, of working through spiritual pain and exhaustion and doubt, of overcoming frustration and combating bitterness. We too often struggle with the temptation to become hireling ministers trapped in unhealthy ways of exercising our spiritual gifts within and to our faith communities--who may or may not name and receive our gifts. And we struggle to forgive and be forgiven as God's servants working within a sinful church. These desert experiences can remain dry and barren. However, if we choose to enter them as did the *abbas* and *ammas*, we may find unexpected springs of spiritual life within the sand and rocks.

We would do well on this journey to remember that the biblical image for mutuality is *covenant*. Yet the history of God's

---

[28] Quakers still to this day occasionally send two people as "traveling ministers" to other meetings or groups. For a Catholic's perspective and fuller discussion of what it means to come in Jesus' name as opposed to our names, see Nouwen's *In the Name of Jesus*.

people reveals our tendency to see our relationship with God as a contract, with an emphasis on expectations and outcomes, what I have come to understand as the "hireling" attitude. Ministers may have the same tendency to understand their work from a contractual basis. Even those who are not motivated by money and other tangible gains may still expect, if not their communities' gratitude, at least evidence of change within those to whom they minister--intellectual, emotional, moral, spiritual--or even evidence of change within themselves. I recall the evidence I hold dear: a glaring program participant who later affirms the minister, a teen volunteer who later studies for the priesthood. When such evidence is not visible, which it not always is, what then? Is it failure on the part of the individual minister, on the part of the community, or is it the mystery of God's work in the world?

If ministers do not want to become, as Nouwen describes, "spiritual prostitutes selling their love under the condition of change,"[29] they need reminding that God does not offer us a contract but a covenant. And it is a covenant of love.

In Jesus' parable of the Good Shepherd (John 10: 9-15), he contrasts his own love for those he came to save with the hireling who abandons the flock when threatened because one who ministers for hire does not see that he is one with his community, that their concerns are his concerns, and their life and salvation his. Unlike the hireling, the shepherd is willing to risk all for the community. To understand the kind of love Jesus proclaims in the parable--without denying a minister's need for healthy boundaries and priorities, rest, and a balanced personal life--requires a definition of love that is not based on any criterion of human success, not the feeling of goodwill towards another, not even the action of doing good to another. Merton is emphatic: "The fact is that good done to another as to an object is of little or no spiritual value."[30] Rather love is identifying spiritually with one's sister and brother. In some sense, we become the person we love, requiring a death of our own sense of self. Or Rowan Williams describes it as the active search for God's word within

---

[29] Nouwen, *Creative Ministry*, 56.

[30] Merton, *The Wisdom of the Desert*, 18.

others: that creative, life-giving element unique to each person and gift for the community.[31]

As ministers ministering with and from such love, we undergo a transformation that enables us to see that we are not "doing for" or "giving to" or "changing" someone else. What at first looks like a loving response just will not do. Rather we seek in the other what God is speaking to us and then speak from God's word within us to that reality in them. Such ministry is indeed a mystery hidden within plain sight.

Questions for Reflection:

1. Think of your relationship with your faith community in terms of the three tasks involved in identifying and stewarding spiritual gifts. How were your gifts named and by whom? How did you claim and develop them? How were the fruits of your gifts received by your community, and how did you allow them to consent to receive your gifts?

2. To be "hidden" can lead to a divided life and the loss of an essential part of yourself, or it can allow you to work towards a greater sense of integrity and a life of service in Jesus' name. What makes the difference, do you think? In what ways have you been hidden--and from whom?

3. When many first learn of the *abbas* and *ammas*, they find the desert traditions' spiritual practices too ascetical and the lifestyle too radical to imitate. Over time, however, they begin to see "fleeing to the desert" as a call to the contemplative life and transform their lives accordingly. How can we live contemplatively within a very active ministry? Is it even possible? Why or why not?

---

[31] Williams, *Where God Happens*, 83.

Conclusion

Maureen R. O'Brien

Any project must have established boundaries in order to reach completion. Yet for the participants in "Emerging from the Vineyard," the desire remains for the conversation to continue. On behalf of the authors, then, I will conclude by summarizing several prominent, common themes that they have identified in the present collection, as well as missing elements, as an impetus for further reflection and dialogue. I will then integrate these themes and elements with one another in light of my own observations.

Common Themes

1. Lay ecclesial ministry as a vital function of the Body of Christ and a sacrament of the Holy Spirit. The participants in "Emerging from the Vineyard," and many others, have taken to heart the opening words of Co-Workers: "God calls. We respond."[1] Steeped through their formation in the language of charism and gift discernment, they draw naturally upon it to describe God's insistent vocational summons, realized through finding their particular role among the interrelated parts of Christ's Body, the Church. In doing so, they have experienced their ministry as laypeople as a visible sign and symbol of the Spirit's work in the world. As one participant reflected in a journal entry:

> *. . . Lay Ministry isn't "Priesthood Lite," it actually is an entirely different animal. It is my life experience outside of the Church that helps me connect people to the Church. Because I have had to learn about and articulate the lived reality of my faith in meaningful ways for working mothers (me) and families (mine) I am accessible to people. . . . People know that I live a life similar to theirs, and so they talk to me. Being the hands and face of Christ is sacrament. It is as simple as that. No labels or*

---

[1] United States Conference of Catholic Bishops, *Co-Workers in the Vineyard of the Lord: A Resource for Guiding the Development of Lay Ecclesial Ministry* (Washington, DC: United States Conference of Catholic Bishops, 2005), 7.

> *hierarchies, just struggles to be like Christ and help others on that same journey.*[2]

2. Experiences of adversity and struggle in ministry, and the choice to speak out about these. The project provided many occasions for affirmation of the joy of one's calling, as well as lament for its inherent cost and pain. Suffering, especially in relation to the very ordained ministers with whom *Co-Workers* urges collaboration, sometimes led to expressions of frustration, anger, and depression. Blocks to sharing one's gifts resulted in deep-seated mourning.

Several essays in this collection have given voice to struggles that lay ecclesial ministers face in the "already and not yet" of the Reign of God in our Church and world. As witness to their accounts, I applaud the honesty of participants' reflections and wish to highlight how fully they embraced their desire to speak prophetically, yet respectfully, in relation to their ecclesial co-workers. An individual's journal entry expresses this collective desire:

> *In addition to serving the people we love by helping them experience God in ritual and service; we also feel a call to name the changes that we think the Holy Spirit is calling our Church toward. On the one hand our baptismal priesthood call makes us nurturers of our fellow believers. On the other hand our baptismal call to be prophets requires us to name truth and falsehood as we have discerned it.*
>
> *It is just one more both/and of the Catholic Church...*

3. The life-giving nature of sharing one's stories with others in the project. Again and again, participants affirmed the value of joining their "emerging" voices as a personal, professional, and spiritual benefit of the project. Several acknowledged that they had been able to survive deeply painful ministerial situations, in part, through the support of other participants. As one wrote in an online journal response to another:

---

[2] Throughout, quotes from journal entries of lay ecclesial ministers involved in the "Emerging from the Vineyard" project will be integrated into the text. These quotes will be indicated by *use of italics*.

> As always, thank you for sharing so honestly. Please write from this place because so many other [lay ecclesial ministers] are out there sharing your anguish without help or support. They are awaiting a hopeful word that others not only share their grief but that someone was willing to articulate what [it's] like to be there.

4. The essays' demonstration of how ministers' wisdom and capacity for love are ripened in the ministerial "vineyard" and in sustained theological reflection upon it. As one participant commented, *"Although I did not expect this project to help me process my experiences as much as it did, I am grateful that it helped me to gain perspective and move beyond where I was when this project began."* Another spoke strongly at the second colloquium about perceiving a "*sea change*" in the essayists' work between the first and second years. She believed that where the earlier writing had contained shades of negativity, tending to dwell on the ways that lay ecclesial ministers are constrained and disempowered, the later revisions had moved toward positive embrace of how they *can* minister, with passion and expertise, in the vineyard. Their voices came forth and were woven together with faith, hope, and love.

Missing Elements

The essays emerged organically rather than according to a set of predetermined topics. Those who contributed brought their particular interests and gifts so as to craft texts that expressed their lived realities as minister-writers who took seriously the critique and recommendations of fellow participants. And precisely as a finite group, limited in experiences and time, they acknowledge that many elements have not been treated, or treated adequately, in this collection. Prominent among these are:

1. Call and vocation. As implied under the first "common element," the authors have already journeyed far along their vocational path, and speak of "calling" naturally and without the need to define and explore its meaning in detail. They also recognize that other publications and formation programs deal

with these themes extensively, and commend the readers to further investigation.[3]

2. The role of gender in collaborative ministry. Lay women and lay men may face differing reactions to their ecclesial ministry from clergy and other laity. Further, the fact that most lay ecclesial ministers are female, while all clergy (bishops, priests and the growing numbers of permanent deacons) are male, can complicate collaborative efforts. The essayists acknowledge this dynamic and urge continuing dialogue about it.

3. Compensation and just wages for lay ecclesial ministers. While lay ecclesial ministers are fully aware that their profession will not make them wealthy, many experience financial difficulties for themselves and their families as they struggle to remain in ministry with low pay and inadequate benefits. As stated in *Co-Workers,* "The Church has a long history of speaking about the dignity of work and the proper recognition of people's service. . . . These issues can be particularly challenging when resources are limited."[4] As dioceses and parishes face severe monetary pressures, the needs of professional lay ecclesial ministers nevertheless cannot be ignored.

4. Culture, and ministering to cultures not one's own. Most of the essayists and project participants are racially and culturally homogenous—Caucasian and middle-class—and most minister in settings with people like themselves. While important strides are being made in addressing cultural diversity at the national level of the United States Church and related organizations,[5] most

---

[3] Many ministry formation programs devote extensive time to assisting laypeople in gift discernment and spiritual growth appropriate to following God's call. Edward P. Hahnenberg's *Awakening Vocation: A Theology of Christian Call* (Collegeville, MN: Liturgical Press, 2010) offers a sophisticated historical and theological treatment of vocation in Catholic and Protestant tradition. *Co-Workers*, while speaking of "vocation" for lay ecclesial ministers, acknowledges that the term and its underlying theology requires more extensive articulation (67).

[4] United States Conference of Catholic Bishops, *Co-Workers,* 63.

[5] See, for example, the process used in the 2007 and 2012 symposia held at Collegeville, Minnesota, on lay ecclesial ministry, where representatives of numerous dioceses, schools, and professional ministry groups formed commitments to further the growth of lay ecclesial ministry among multiple

employed lay ecclesial ministers reflect this homogeneity. Our collection does not address the vital issues of cultural sensitivity and the building of multicultural communities in today's United States Catholic Church. The essayists hope that others better equipped to do so can extend their work in these directions.

Avenues for Growth

As mentioned in the Introduction, the full body of journaling created by the project participants will be a source for ongoing research. In distilling the essayists' common themes and missing elements for this Conclusion, however, I glimpse two integrative paradigms that help to point the way toward future investigations:

1. "Common Themes" points to how lay ecclesial ministers work as "pastoral theologians" to create spaces for theological reflection.
2. "Missing Elements" shows how these ministers may wish to acknowledge their ecclesial position as both "marginal" and "central" so as to attend more fully to those omitted from their reflection.

Common Themes Paradigm: Lay Ecclesial Ministers as Pastoral Theologians

I have previously argued that ministers should claim a role as theologians.[6] Too often, we make a facile distinction between the "academic" or "theoretical" as constituting the work of

---

cultural populations (2011 Collegeville National Symposium on Lay Ecclesial Ministry, "Advancing Excellence in Lay Ecclesial Ministry," http://www.csbsju.edu/sot/events/collegevillle-national-symposium/2011-collegeville-national-symposium-on-lay-ecclesial-ministry [accessed June 2, 2014]). Recently approved standards of the Alliance for the Certification of Lay Ecclesial Ministers include numerous references to cultural understanding and intercultural competency for lay ecclesial ministers ("National Certification Standards for Lay Ecclesial Ministers (Standards)," http://www.lemcertification.org/standards.htm [accessed June 2, 2014]).

[6] See, for example, Maureen R. O'Brien, "A Study of Ministerial Identity and Theological Reflection among Lay Ecclesial Ministers," *International Journal of Practical Theology* 11/2 (2007): 212-233.

theologians, while ministers see themselves as "applying" theory or simply as concerned with the "practical" dimensions of life.

I believe, however, that the present essay collection offers an integration of these falsely construed poles. But what constitutes such an integrated model, and how is it enacted? The key lies in the style of *praxis*—action continually brought to reflection—utilized. Most lay ecclesial ministry formation programs make explicit use of theological reflection to help participants weave together descriptions of their ministerial experiences with the rich tradition of Christian faith, as well as with appropriate knowledge from other fields of study. Through prayerful reflection and open, supportive dialogue, new insights can be generated and brought back into ministry. The hoped-for "transformation of the world" that laity pursue, in the words of *Co-Workers*,[7] is given deeper creativity, energy, faithfulness, and effectiveness through such reflection. Learning a method for theological reflection and making it a habit in one's ministry—especially in conversation with others—will, I believe, confirm and develop ministers as pastoral theologians. Moreover, it will bridge the problematic gap between "practice" and "theory" for those laboring in the vineyards and those who observe them from the university or divinity school.

The essayists' list of "Common Themes" is the fruit of such sustained, integrative, and communal theological reflection. Essayists grew in their ability to name their ministry as vital to the Body of Christ, a sacrament of the Holy Spirit, a work of God's Kingdom, an experience of death and resurrection, an endeavor of love, and so on because they could hold up their experiences in a welcoming conversational space—whether face-to-face, or in cyberspace—in the light of faith and tradition, to find new angles of understanding. In previous research I have discussed images that ministers used to describe their reflection, such as peeling back the layers of an onion, or using a prism to see the rich

[7]"All of the baptized are called to work toward the transformation of the world. Most do this by working in the secular realm; some do this by working in the Church and focusing on the building of ecclesial communion, which has among its purposes the transformation of the world" (United States Conference of Catholic Bishops, *Co-Workers*, 8).

variety of colors emanating from a single ray of light.[8] Such peeling and turning, made into a communal activity through the work of writing teams, exposed new layers and revealed new angles for the essayists. Its habitual use by other lay ecclesial ministers is transforming the theological enterprise and all those who engage in it.[9]

Missing Elements Paradigm: Lay Ecclesial Ministers as Both "Marginal" and "Central"

It is natural to read the list of "Missing Elements" and interpret these in terms of the relative invisibility and tenuous status of lay ecclesial ministers within the Church. For example, while such ministers have themselves adopted the language of call and vocation for their ecclesial role, these descriptors remain, in the minds of many Catholics, primarily associated with the ordained and consecrated religious members of the Body of Christ. Furthermore, gender, pay scales, and culture or ethnicity may contribute to relative power or powerlessness within ecclesial structures.[10]

Such a reading shows the human tendency to focus on the areas in which *we* feel personally powerless and to give voice to this, often from the perspective of marginality or victimhood. One project participant, after being verbally abused by her pastor, compared the encounter to the vulnerability of African American domestic workers in relation to their white employers as depicted in the recent movie, "The Help": *"In some ways I couldn't help but think as lay ecclesial ministers, in many cases, we are 'the help.'"* A young adult minister felt marginalized because her youth inclined parishioners to discount her gifts for ministry. A middle-aged minister left the position he loved because a change in staff rendered his work unnecessary. An experienced, formed, and certified pastoral associate completed her training only to find a dearth of jobs awaiting her in the region that she and her family

[8] O'Brien, "A Study of Ministerial Identity and Theological Reflection among Lay Ecclesial Ministers," 228-229.

[9] See ibid. for brief case examples of how this occurs.

[10] And, of course, when such factors combine they produce what has been called "double" or "triple" marginalization. Consider, for example, the status of female, unpaid ministers of color within the Church relative to that of white, ordained males.

call home. Readers can undoubtedly add to this list of painful disruptions.

However, at the same time, project participants themselves often inhabit "centers" of relative leadership and status, even within the Church. They have had sufficient personal resources to pursue formation for lay ecclesial ministry; indeed, their very engagement in our project showed that they had adequate time, freedom, education, and self-confidence to say "yes" to it. Their race, culture, socioeconomic background, and family or community connections have helped to enable the pursuit of a long-term ministerial calling. They may even be appointed to a formal position of leadership in which, as one participant commented:

> *. . . [M]inisters in the field look to me as a leader. Sometimes, people defer to me in meetings. There are public events in which I speak, teach and help present policy. There are times when I represent Church.*

Thus, reflection on opportunities along with losses helps to frame engagement in lay ecclesial ministry as moving between "margins" and "centers." While realistic about the harms they have suffered and will yet suffer due to marginality, they can more fully draw upon their areas of influence—"centers"—to expand the circle of welcome within the Church.

In their journaling, it was evident that participants actively sought to understand and consciously work within, and between, the margins and centers of their everyday encounters. Yet, everyday demands of the institutions to which they are accountable—which, for many lay ecclesial ministers, may be large and suburban parishes—can result in an excessively insular focus. And regular reminders of one's multiple marginalizations as nonordained and perhaps female can result in bitterness. In such cases, lay ecclesial ministers are well reminded that other, more marginal people suffer and call out for their response. As one reflected after reading a book on the lives of the saints:

> *So I suppose one question that I find myself pondering is this: Why do we, as [lay ecclesial ministers] find it so surprising that we are attacked, marginalized, dis-possessed, restricted? And can we, like those ordinary*

> *people who went before us, find a way to continue, regardless? Can our faith help us work through our initial and very understandable reactions of anger, grief and despair? Can we find compassion in our hearts for others, especially those who are persecuting us?*

Quality formation for ministry is important in fostering such dispositions, as recounted by a second participant:

> *... But I found that I had become so different through my formation process that it didn't matter where I lived or worked when it came to who I thought I was at a basic level. I couldn't read the newspaper without hearing the overwhelming needs of the world, and adding those stories to my prayers. I couldn't join any group of people—parents, scout volunteers, school groups—without being aware of who was marginalized. When I interacted with extended family, I realized that I'd developed a deeper capacity for love and compassion (not easy!). Living in this way had become the norm, even before I found my current job. I wonder if [lay ecclesial ministry] is more a state of being than a question of what we get to do or where we are called to do it.*

A third came to a dynamic model of living the paradox and tension between margins and center:

> *If I were to draw a picture of my ideal pattern of relationship in the world of ecclesial ministry it would depict all in a circle pushing the needs of those at the margin to the center. We would live these words from* Co-Workers in the Vineyard - *"Holiness is nothing other than the gift of loving union with God and the sharing of this love in right relationship with others."*[11] *Power and control would be the last thing on anyone's mind.*

Missing elements from collections like this, I believe, can be usefully surfaced and incorporated when lay ecclesial ministers take seriously how their own burdens as disciples are not unique, but are borne in different and more challenging ways by their

---

[11] The quotation is from United States Conference of Catholic Bishops, *Co-Workers*, 19.

needy brothers and sisters. Without remaining silent about violations experienced in their attempts to live in ecclesial "right relationships," they are also called to recognize how their own exercise of relative power and influence can either damage or build up such relationships with others. The language of "margins" and "centers" can be helpful in such recognition.

A Continuing Rustling

Thus, in closing the collection the essayists are deeply aware that while offering their writing for lay ecclesial ministers and those who support them, they open new questions and invite new responses. With the US bishops in *Co-Workers,* they pledge to continue to work "together as a 'community of people united in Christ and guided by the holy Spirit in [our] pilgrimage toward the Father's kingdom, bearers of a message for all humanity.'"[12] At the same time, they are well aware of the unexpected twists and turns of this pilgrim Church's journey. As stated by the minister whose reflections opened this book, *"I remember that the history of the Church is still being written. It's likely we're not at the last chapter."*

In closing, then, a haiku by one of the participants expresses the restlessness, dynamism, and life-giving breath of the Holy Spirit that has touched this project and moves the entire Church forward:

Collaboration
Wild wind bending wheat heads low
Our spirits rustle

Amid the wheatfields and vineyards of this world, lay ecclesial ministers labor with co-workers and in the loving communion of the Trinity to bring forth rich harvests. As God's Spirit rustles their spirits—sometimes "wildly"—may they respond with energy and faithfulness.

---

[12] United States Conference of Catholic Bishops, *Co-Workers,* 67. The bishops are quoting here from *Gaudium et Spes,* 1.

GLOSSARY OF ABBREVIATIONS

AA — *Apostolicam Actuositatem:* Decree on the Apostolate of the Laity. (Second Vatican Council. *Vatican II: The Conciliar and Post Conciliar Documents*. Ed. Austin Flannery. Collegeville, MN: Liturgical Press, 1980)

CARA — The Center for Applied Research in the Apostolate, at Georgetown University

CCL — The Code of Canon Law

CCC — Catechism of the Catholic Church

CGTM — Called and Gifted for the Third Millenium. (United States Conference of Catholic Bishops. Washington, D.C.: USCCB Publishing, 1995)

CL — *Christifideles Laici:* The Lay Members of Christ's Faithful People (Post-Synodal Exhortation of John Paul II. Boston, MA: Daughters of St. Paul, 1988)

CVL — Co-Workers in the Vineyard of the Lord: A Resource for Guiding the Development of Lay Ecclesial Ministry. (United States Conference of Catholic Bishops. Washington, D.C.: USCCB Publishing, 2005)

DV — *Dei Verbum:* The Constitution on Divine Revelation (Second Vatican Council. *Vatican II: The Conciliar and Post Conciliar Documents*. Ed. Austin Flannery. Collegeville, MN: Liturgical Press, 1980)

GIRM — General Instruction of the Roman Missal, Third Typical Edition. (Translated by the International Commission on English in the Liturgy. New York: Catholic Book Publishing, 2011)

GS — *Gaudium et Spes:* The Pastoral Constitution on the Church in the Modern World. (Second Vatican Council. *Vatican II: The Conciliar and Post Conciliar Documents*. Ed. Austin Flannery. Collegeville, MN: Liturgical Press, 1980)

LEM — Lay Ecclesial Ministers / Ministry

LG *Lumen Gentium:* The Dogmatic Constitution on the Church. (Second Vatican Council. *Vatican II: The Conciliar and Post Conciliar Documents*. Ed. Austin Flannery. Collegeville, MN: Liturgical Press, 1980)

MF *Mysterium Fidei:* Encyclical on the Holy Eucharist. (Pope Paul VI. Vatican City, 1965)

NMI *Novo Millennio Ineunte.* (Pope John Paul II. *Origins* 30.31 (January 18, 2001): 489-508)

NIV The New International Version of The Bible

OCD The Official Catholic Directory. (New York: P. J. Kennedy, 2001)

RCIA Rite of Christian Initiation for Adults

RM The Roman Missal, Third Typical Edition. (Translated by the International Commission on English in the Liturgy. New York: Catholic Book Publishing, 2011)

SC (or CSL) *Sacrosanctum Concilium:* The Constitution on the Sacred Liturgy (Second Vatican Council. *Vatican II: The Conciliar and Post Conciliar Documents*. Ed. Austin Flannery. Collegeville, MN: Liturgical Press, 1980)

USCCB United States Conference of Catholic Bishops

YHWH God's most holy name as written in ancient Hebrew, which has no vowels

Contributors

Julie Billmeier, M.T.S., served as the Coordinator for Young Adult Ministry in the Diocese of Dallas. She taught for the University of Dallas Catholic Biblical School and other adult education classes and has presented at numerous workshops and conferences.

Rodney J. Bluml, M.A.T., M.Div., is a spiritual director and the Program Coordinator at Prairiewoods Eco-Spirituality Retreat Center in Hiawatha, Iowa. Previously, he served in parish ministry for seventeen years. He was a contributor to *Illuminating Ministry* (Liturgical Press, 2008) and writes a weekly e-worship aid with lectionary commentary (blumlwa@gmail.com to subscribe).

Vivian Clausing is a 2008 graduate of the Franciscan School of Theology in Berkeley with a Masters of Multicultural Ministry and a Masters of Theology. A former lawyer and convert to Catholicism, Vivian holds a J.D. from the University of California Los Angeles. For five years, she served as Associate Director of Youth Ministry for Archdiocese of San Francisco. Currently she does spiritual direction, ministers to the homeless in the Tenderloin neighborhood of San Francisco, and coordinates the Confirmation program for a suburban parish on the Peninsula.

Zeni V. Fox, Ph.D., is Professor of Pastoral Theology at Seton Hall University, South Orange, New Jersey. She is a nationally recognized leader in the development of lay ecclesial ministry through her extensive scholarship, lectures, and consultations. Her publications include *New Ecclesial Ministry: Lay Professionals Serving the Church* (Sheed and Ward, 2002) and the edited collection, *Lay Ecclesial Ministry: Pathways toward the Future* (Sheed and Ward, 2010).

Dan Frachey serves as Director of Christian Formation at the Church of St. Jude in Rochester, Illinois. He received his Master of Arts in Pastoral Studies and Certification in Spiritual Direction from the Aquinas Institute of Theology in St. Louis. Dan does spiritual direction and retreat ministry in the Springfield area and continues his ministerial formation with the Aquinas Institute's Apollos Program.

Kimberly Lymore is the Pastoral Associate at the Faith Community of St. Sabina in Chicago, a church known for its dynamic worship and social activism. She holds a Master of Divinity from Catholic Theological Union and a Doctor of Ministry from McCormick Theological Seminary.

Jerid Miller, M.T.S., serves as the Director of Lifelong Formation at St. Margaret Mary Catholic Community, in the Archdiocese of Louisville, Kentucky. His articles have appeared in *The Catholic Answer, Our Sunday Visitor Newsweekly* and *U.S. Catholic*. Jerid has worked in parish ministry for over a decade. He is a graduate of St. Meinrad School of Theology in Southern Indiana and is currently a student in the D.Min. program at the Oblate School of Theology, San Antonio.

Maureen R. O'Brien, Ph.D., is the director and researcher for the Emerging from the Vineyard project. She currently serves as Associate Professor of Theology and Director of Pastoral Ministry at Duquesne University in Pittsburgh, Pennsylvania. She has written, taught and spoken extensively on practical theology and ministry education, and has served as a lay ecclesial minister.

Clare Z. Poupard, M.R.E., is an approved lay ecclesial minister, certified Director of Religious Education and approved Adult Formation Director for the Archdiocese of Chicago. She has been published in a catechetical textbook series, contributed to catechetical websites, developed and led adult retreats for the Archdiocese of Chicago, teaches Archdiocesan Catechist Certification courses and currently serves as the Director of Family Spiritual Formation at a large suburban parish.

Linda Lee Ritzer, D.Min., is a Pastoral Associate in the Diocese of Pittsburgh, Pennsylvania, where she has served in parishes for twenty seven years. Ritzer is an appointed member of both the Diocesan Liturgical Commission of Pittsburgh and Advisory Board for the Diocesan Institute of Ministries. She also serves as a Master Catechist for the diocese.

Virginia Stillwell, M.A., M.Div., has been involved in lay ecclesial ministry since 1985. She currently serves as liturgist in a large suburban parish in Eagan, Minnesota. Previous publications include articles in *New Theology Review* and *CHURCH* magazine, scripture reflections for World Library Publications, and *Priestless Parishes: The Baptized Leading the Baptized* with Ave Maria Press.

Susan Yanos, M.A.P.T., Ph.D., has been a parish director of religious education, professor of writing and literature, and director of college writing programs, including the Ministry of Writing Program at Earlham School of Religion, Richmond, Indiana. She is a certified spiritual director and author of *Woman, You Are Free: A Spirituality for Women in Luke* (St. Anthony Messenger Press, 2001), as well as short stories, poetry, essays, and articles.

For Further Reading

Aland, Kurt. *Synopsis of the Four Gospels.* Rev. ed. Reading, UK: United Bible Societies, 1985.

Becker, Ernest. *The Denial of Death.* New York: The Free Press, 1973.

Bishops' Committee on Priestly Life and Ministry. *Fulfilled in Your Hearing: the Homily in the Sunday Assembly*. Washington, DC: United States Conference of Catholic Bishops, 1982.

Bridges, William. *The Way of Transition: Embracing Life's Most Difficult Moments*. Cambridge, MA: Da Capo Press, 2001.

Brown, Raymond E., Joseph Fitzmyer and Roland Murphy, eds. *The New Jerome Biblical Commentary.* Upper Saddle River, NJ: Prentice Hall, 1990.

Cahalan, Kathleen A. *Introducing the Practice of Ministry.* Collegeville, MN: Liturgical Press, 2010.

Cahoy, William,ed. *In the Name of the Church: Vocation and Authorization of Lay Ecclesial Ministry.* Collegeville, MN: Liturgical Press, 2012.

Craddock, Fred. *As One without Authority*. Rev. ed. St. Louis: Chalice Press, 2001.

DeLeers, Stephen, *Written Text Becomes Living Word: The Vision and Practice of Sunday Preaching*. Collegeville, MN: Liturgical Press, 2004.

Dulles, Avery. *Models of the Church.* Expanded ed. Colorado Springs, CO: Image, 2002.

Fitzmyer, Joseph A., SJ. *The Interpretation of Scripture: In Defense of the Historical-Critical Method.* Mahwah, NJ: Paulist Press, 2008.

Fox, Zeni, ed. *Lay Ecclesial Ministry: Pathways toward the Future.* Lanham, MD: Sheed and Ward, 2010.

Gray, Mark M., Mary L. Gautier and Melissa A. Cidade. *The Changing Face of U.S. Catholic Parishes*. Washington, DC: National Association for Lay Ministry, 2011.

Hahnenberg, Edward P. *Awakening Vocation: A Theology of Christian Call.* Collegeville, MN: Liturgical Press, 2010.

Hahnenberg, Edward P. *Ministries: A Relational Approach*. New York: Crossroads, 2003.

Hall, Thelma. *Too Deep for Words: Rediscovering Lectio Divina.* New York: Paulist Press, 1988.

Hayes, James E. "Ongoing Formation of Preachers within a Diocese: A Collaborative Model." Presented to the faculty of the Aquinas Institute of Theology, Saint Louis, MO, in partial fulfillment of the requirements for the degree of Doctor of Ministry in Preaching, 2004.

Hoff, Marie D. *Happy the People: When Love Becomes Justice*. Liguori, MO: Liguori Publications, 2013.

Hoge, Dean R., Marti R. Jewell and Joseph W. Estabrook. *The Next Generation of Pastoral Leaders: What the Church Needs to Know.* Chicago: Loyola Press, 2010.

Hudock, Barry. *Faith Meets World*. Liguori, MO: Liguori Publications, 2013.

John Paul II. "*Novo Millennio Ineunte*," in *Origins* 30.31 (January 18, 2001): 489-508.

Klimoski, Vic, ed. *Illuminating Ministry: A Journal.* Collegeville, MN: Liturgical Press, 2010.

Kwatera, Michael, OSB. *Come to the Feast: Liturgical Theology of, by, and for Everybody.* Collegeville, MN: Liturgical Press, 2005.

Lakeland, Paul. *Catholicism at the Crossroads: How the Laity Can Save the Church.* New York: Continuum, 2007.

Lakeland, Paul. *The Liberation of the Laity*. New York: Bloomsbury Academic, 2004.

Lowney, Chris. *Pope Francis: Why He Leads the Way He Leads*. Chicago: Loyola Press, 2013.

Lumen Gentium in Austin Flannery, ed. *Vatican Council II Volume 1: The Conciliar and Post Conciliar Documents*. Northport, NY: Costello Publishing, 2004.

McBrien, Richard P. *Catholicism: New Study Edition.* New York: HarperOne, 1994.

McClory, Robert. *Radical Disciple: Father Pfleger, St. Sabina Church, and the Fight for Social Justice.* Chicago, IL: Lawrence Hill Books, 2010.

Mitchell, Kenneth R. and Herbert Anderson. *All Our Losses, All Our Griefs*. Louisville: John Knox Westminster Press, 1983.

National Conference of Catholic Bishops. *Together in God's Service: Toward a Theology of Ecclesial Lay Ministry*. Washington, DC: United States Catholic Conference, 1998.

Nouwen, Henri. *Creative Ministry*. Garden City, NY: Doubleday, 1971.

Nouwen, Henri. *In the Name of Jesus: Reflections on Christian Leadership*. New York: Crossroads, 1989.

Old, Hughes Oliphant. *The Reading and Preaching of the Scriptures in the Worship of the Christian Church.* 5 vols. Grand Rapids, MI: Wm. B. Eerdmans Publishing, 1998-2004.

Osborne, Kenan. *Ministry: Lay Ministry in the Roman Catholic Church: Its History and Theology.* Maryknoll, NY: Orbis, 2006.

Osborne, Kenan. *Orders and Ministry.* Maryknoll, NY: Orbis, 2006.

Ostdiek, Gilbert, OFM. *Mystagogy of the Eucharist: A Pastoral Resource.* Collegeville, MN: Liturgical Press, 2014.

Palmer, Parker. *A Hidden Wholeness: The Journey Toward an Undivided Life*. San Francisco: Jossey-Bass, 2004.

Parachini, Patricia A. A *Guide for Lay Preachers*. Chicago: Liturgy Training Publication, 2000.

Rolheiser, Ronald. *The Holy Longing: The Search for a Christian Spirituality*. New York: Doubleday, 1999.

Sofield, Loughlan, ST, and Carroll Juliano, SHCJ. *Collaboration: Uniting Our Gifts in Ministry*. Notre Dame, IN: Ave Maria Press, 2000.

Stone, Douglas, Bruce Patton and Sheila Heen. *Difficult Conversations.* London: Penguin Books, 1999.

Tisdale, Leonora Tubbs. *Preaching as Local Theology and Folk Art.* Minneapolis, MN: Fortress Press, 1997.

United States Conference of Catholic Bishops. *Co-Workers in the Vineyard of the Lord*. Washington, DC: United States Conference of Catholic Bishops, 2005.

United States Conference of Catholic Bishops. "Two Feet of Love in Action." Washington, DC: United States Conference of Catholic Bishops. http://www.usccb.org/beliefs-and-teachings/what-we-believe/catholic-social-teaching/two-feet-of-love-in-action.cfm (accessed 3 March 2014).

United States Conference of Catholic Bishops. "Complementary Norm for Canon 766." Washington, DC: United States Conference of Catholic Bishops, 2001. http://usccb.org/beliefs-and-teachings/what-we-believe/canon-law/complementary-norms/canon-766-lay-preaching.cfm (accessed 24 August 2012).

Wood, Susan. K., ed. *Ordering the Baptismal Priesthood: Theologies of Lay and Ordained Ministry.* Collegeville, MN: Liturgical Press, 2003.

Zannoni, Arthur E. *Tell Me Your Story: The Parables of Jesus.* Chicago: Liturgy Training Publications, 1989.

CPSIA information can be obtained at www.ICGtesting.com
Printed in the USA
LVOW12s0406140714

394033LV00004B/548/P